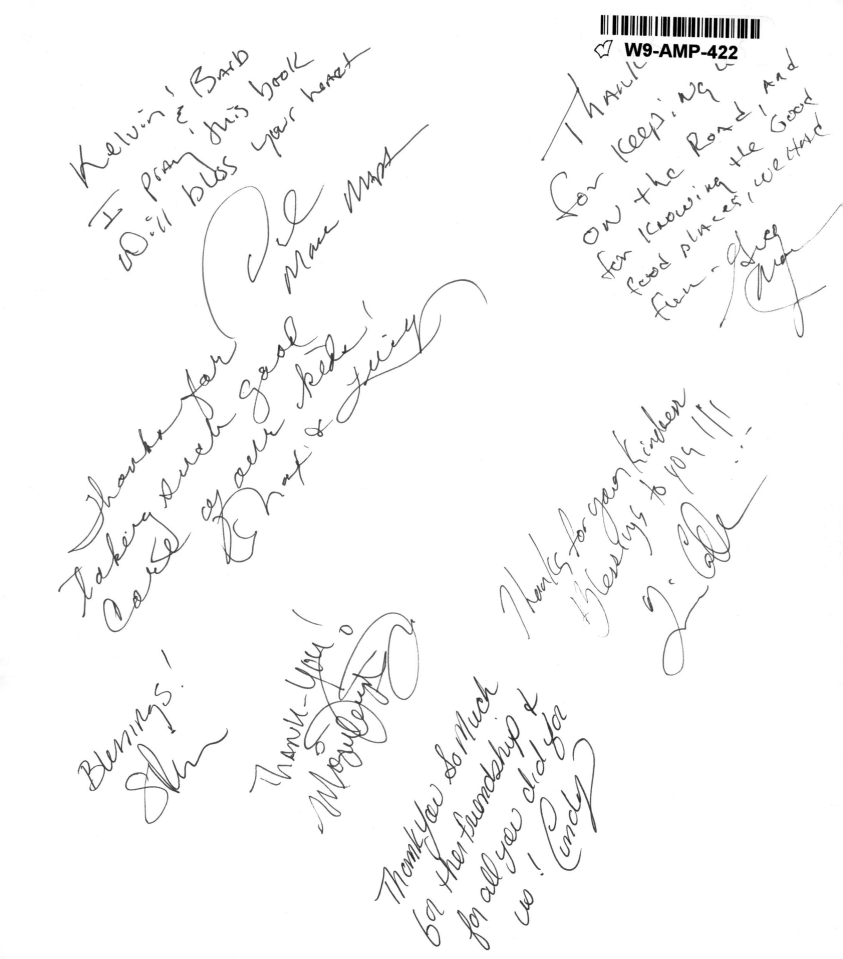

Kelvin & Barb
I pray this book
Will bless your heart
Mark Myers

Thanks for
taking such good
care of our kids!
Ghat & Juicy

Thanks
for keeping us
on the Road! And
for knowing the good
Food places! we Hard
From Greg

Thanks for your kindness
Blessings to you !!!

Blessings!

Thank you !

Thanks for your Kindness
Blessings to you !!!

Thank you so Much
for the friendship &
for all you did for
us ! Cindy

THE HERITAGE SINGERS STORY

Beyond Our
Dreams

by Max & Lucy Mace

with

Joanne Velting Mullin

Credits:

Editing: Nicole Batten, Bettesue Constanzo

Cover Photo: Michael Easley, Vital Excess

Layout and Design: Mark Bond

Typeset: Calluna 10/14

PRINTED IN USA

by Color Press, Inc., Walla Walla, WA

First Printing, May, 2010

max@heritagesingers.com

heritagesingers.com

PO Box 1358 Placerville, CA 95667

TABLE OF CONTENTS

SECTION I
A Musical Journey

SECTION II
A Bus-shaped Life

SECTION III
At the Crossroads

Dedication

Dedicated to Jerry Brass and Cecil Coffee

In 1971, when the Heritage Singers were trying to get started, you believed in us enough to contact churches in the region, encouraging them to invite us to perform for their congregations. Thank you for paving the way for the Heritage Singers at the time when we needed it the most.

With Special Thanks to Greg and Val

You have been with us through it all and have sacrificed many things to dedicate your lives to the Heritage ministry. You had other opportunities to do other things with your lives, but you chose to stay with us and help us continue God's work. Both of you have become so important to this ministry. We thank you from the bottom of our hearts, and we thank the Lord for blessing us with such talented and dedicated children. We love you and your families very much.

PREFACE

A NOTE FROM MAX AND LUCY

When we first launched the Heritage Singers ministry, we knew very little about what we were getting into, and no matter how much we learn along the way, we will always be in awe of the number of people's lives touched by the Heritage Singers. We continue to be overwhelmed by the many hurting people we come into contact with as we minister. There are a lot of people, even among Christians, who are exhausted and discouraged.

That's why we do what we do, and that's why we wrote this book. People who are weighed down with the concerns of this life need to have their eyes drawn upward to the God who loves them. And, sometimes it takes a song or a personal testimony to get that message across.

We have always believed that we are God's voice to those without hope. Our purpose is to let you know you're not alone. When you're ready to give up, God will be there to help you. We know because we've been there. God always gives you more than you could ever dream.

Our story is not about doing anything on our own. God made an impossible dream become a reality beyond our dreams. We want to share with you how God worked through us and provided for us. Many people have sacrificed to help keep this ministry going over the years, and we are grateful to each one. There are too many names to mention, but we want each of them to know that we will never forget their contributions to this ministry. They are as much a part of this ministry as we are.

Whenever we get discouraged, all we have to do is look back at how far the Lord has brought us through the years, and the words to the song "To God be the Glory for the things He has done" comes to our minds! Looking back gives us strength for the future. I can't believe that we're still here after all these years, and we will continue as long as God provides a way.

We pray that as you read our story, you will be caught up in the vision God has given for this ministry—for reaching people with His life-changing power. We hope our story will encourage you to trust in the wisdom and power of God to lead the way in your life.

Yours in His Service,
Max and Lucy

Forward

A note from Joanne Velting Mullin

During parts of 1975 through 1977 I traveled and sang with the Heritage Singers. I was 20 years old when I became part of something that would change my entire life.

It was a dream come true to be on stage and travel with the Heritage Singers. From their first album in 1971 I had idolized them - memorizing their songs and attending as many of their concerts as I could. The whole experience of being a Heritage Singer was much greater and more meaningful than I ever dreamed it would be.

My research for this book took me many places, and it was a joy and a blessing to be reunited with many of my old friends and to make even more new friends. I had the opportunity to get to know a lot of Heritage Singers and supporters I would not have known otherwise. My direct access to Max and Lucy was a wonderful side benefit of working on this project.

The Heritage story evolved over a period of more than 39 years. The biggest challenge for Max and Lucy and I was the editing process. The task of deciding what events are most important and what can be cut out without hurting the story was really hard to do. I relied on Max and Lucy to inform and guide these decisions. It is, ultimately, their story, not mine.

Another challenge was the gap in my knowledge of what Heritage has been doing for the past 30 years. Max and Lucy, along with many of the current and former singers helped bring me back into the ever on-going Heritage story. We did our best to get all of the facts straight, but if we missed something, we hope the readers will forgive us. Different perspectives make the Heritage story very interesting. Every person I spoke with about their Heritage experience had a slightly different take on things.

The real story of the Heritage ministry lies somewhere in the mix - in the careful blending of all of the stories. It is similar to Max's ability to work with different combinations of singers - with very different voices - and maintain his signature Heritage Sound year after year. We all have our own voice, but when added to the mix, the one true story emerges.

Writing this book with Max and Lucy was a wonderful experience. I am very happy with the way it turned out and I hope you will enjoy it. As you read, imagine that we are all sitting around the living room fireplace at the Heritage ranch. You will hear voices from every Heritage generation telling stories of miracles and healing; stories of conflict and reconciliation; stories of what day-to-day life as a Heritage Singer was really like.

You will also hear from many people who were touched by the Heritage ministry. They will tell you how God worked through Heritage and changed their lives. It is an incredible story of how God took Max and Lucy's dream and made it a reality. I hope it inspires you to follow your dreams. I know it inspired me to follow mine.

"It's more than the singing..."
—Max

"Happiness comes from someone who dreams,
and has the commitment to follow through."
—Lucy

Section 1

A Musical Journey

CHAPTER ONE

The Impossible Dream

With God, all things are possible.
— Matthew 19:26

MAX RACED HIS TWO BROTHERS—RONNIE AND JERRY—ACROSS THE BIG YARD, HIS BLONDE HAIR FLYING back from his tanned, freckled face. The boys all entered the house together in a whirlwind, arguing about who had actually gotten there first. It was dinner time and the boys' stomachs rumbled with hunger, probably from all the work they had done on the farm that day. Man, could they eat!

Ever since he could remember, Max and his two brothers had worked on their dad's cattle ranch in Eagle, Idaho. The ranch had been homesteaded more than 140 years earlier by their great-grandfather. But being a farmer wasn't Max's dream. He wanted to play sports, preferably fast-pitch softball. He was a good spray-hitter, fast on the ball and could easily steal bases. And, when Max wasn't playing sports, he was listening to music. Max loved music so much that he fastened a transistor radio to the tractor so he could listen while he worked. Max even had a radio in the barn to listen to while he milked the cows.

Max loved tight harmonies. He especially liked music groups such as the Anita Kerr Singers, the Ray Conniff Singers, the Johnny Mann Singers, the McGuire Sisters, Rosemary Clooney,

Perry Como, Patty Page, the Andrews Sisters, the Ames Brothers, Andy Williams and the Modernairs. And of course, the Mills Brothers and the Ink Spots!

Max did eventually play on his town's fast-pitch softball team, which was part of the ASA (Amateur Softball Association). His team won the Idaho State Championship two years in a row. They went on to the Regional Championship and came within one game of going to the World Softball Tournament—a loss Max remembers to this day.

Music was always a part of Max's close-knit family. Max remembers sitting around the Philco radio after supper and listening to music with his family. They all loved to sing along with it. Every week the family attended the Little Country Church in

Eagle and sang together—Whitey, Dorothy and all three boys. The boys even formed the "Mace Trio."

Max's family did more than sing together. They went bowling on Saturday nights and ate out at a local Chinese restaurant. They went to jalopy races and motorcycle hill climbs. They went boating together and had picnics in the park. And every Wednesday night the whole family attended prayer meeting.

Max often spent time at his grandparent's house. He would lay on the couch listening to a ball game on the radio while his grandma rocked in her rocking-chair and read her Bible and his grandpa played solitaire. Once in a while his grandpa would pull out his harmonica and play old cowboy songs like "Sweet Betsy from Pike."

Max and his brothers enjoyed a Christian education—something very important to their parents. Their school was a just a little room off of the church. If they had 12 students, it was a good year!

Max remembers his teacher, Mrs. Lovejoy, working with him to put a song together for amateur hour. She was a talented piano player who used to play for silent movies before becoming a teacher. At the time Max felt embarrassed about all the attention Mrs. Lovejoy gave him. Max remembers her telling him, "God has a plan for your life. I think God has something for you in music." Even though he was more interested in sports at the time, Max never forgot those words.

One day Max was sitting on the tractor, looking up at the vast, blue Idaho sky, listening to his radio. He began wondering what was out there for him. What was God planning for his life? Just then, a jet plane flew overhead. As his eyes followed the plane across the sky, Max found himself saying, "Someday, I'm going to be on that plane. Someday that's going to be me up

Max's father, Whitey and mother, Dorothy with older brothers Jerry and Ronnie

there." And then he prayed, "God, if there's any way you can use me out there somewhere, please use me."

There were many times that Max got into trouble with his dad for staying in the house listening to music when he was supposed to be out on the tractor. Milking cows and farming just wasn't for him. Max knew it—and his dad knew it.

After Max graduated from Gem State Academy, he decided to leave the farm and attend Walla Walla College in Washington State. It was a blow to his dad, who really needed Max's help on the farm. He looked at Max and said, "Well, Son, you're on your own." Max knew that was his dad's way of telling him he wasn't going to be able to provide any financial support. So Max immediately looked for a job in the Walla Walla area.

Naturally, Max looked for a job where he could also play softball. He took a job working nights at a saw-mill. One rainy night he was pushing logs from the pond and thought to himself, 'What are you doing here, Max?' "I was so miserable," explains Max, "So, I quit."

Max was then approached by Lloyd Hoffman, the manager of the College Place Merchants softball team. He offered Max a job in the bakery if he would play on his team. Max took the job, and it wasn't long before a certain young lady caught his eye.

"There was a young lady who kept walking by the bakery, and I wanted to meet her," Max reflects. "A mutual friend finally introduced us. Her name was Lucy Hatley. She had just finished her junior year in academy. We started spending time together. She watched me play softball and attended concerts with me (where I sang in a male quartet).

Max continues, "That was the summer of 1956. I was still trying to find my way. I took some college classes in the fall, but I soon decided that college wasn't for me. I knew I had some good qualities and felt that I had a good chance of making it without my degree. I was anxious to go out and do something."

On January 5, 1958, Max and Lucy married. They then moved back to Max's home state, Idaho, where he worked in construction and at the Meadow Gold Dairy. He also worked at a glass company, and then as a deputy assessor for Ada County. During this time he was involved with a male quartet. He was also the assistant director of a barbershop chorus in Boise called the Chord Busters. Before long Max and Lucy had two children, Gregory and Valerie.

Max on the cattle ranch in Eagle

Max still felt something was missing. He explains, "I had a wonderful wife and two beautiful children, but I was still searching for what I wanted to do with my life. I wasn't really happy doing what I was doing."

About this time Max's brother, Jerry, called from his home in Portland, Oregon. He worked for United Medical Laboratories, which wanted to start a professional softball team. He asked Max if he would be interested in trying out. Max says, "They wanted to create one of the best softball teams in Portland, which sounded pretty good to me. I went to Portland and tried out. They not only hired me to play softball, but offered me a job in the endocrinology department at the company. So, Lucy and I moved our children to Portland."

Max still wanted to do something in music though, so he started a singing group for United Medical Laboratories. Known as the Rose City Singers, the group performed a variety of patriotic and folk songs, combined with some religious music. Max says, "I really loved the newer sounding gospel music I was hearing from people like Ralph Carmichael, Otis Skilling and Thurlow Spur. It inspired me to add gospel music to our group's repertoire."

The Rose City Singers began traveling all over Washington, Oregon and Idaho doing concerts at colleges to promote the medical laboratory and to recruit future employees. They were also flown around the United States and Canada to do secular concerts at other Christian colleges. On the weekends they did some religious concerts in churches. Although the group was paid for their secular concerts, they were not paid for their religious concerts— even when it was for the same audience. Often, the churches wouldn't even allow them to take up a free-will love offering. There seemed to be a reluctance to pay for anything religious, regardless of the expenses it took to put on a concert and travel.

The Rose City Singers quickly became popular, especially throughout the Northwest. They even performed at the Junior Miss California Pageant and at the International Convention for Attorneys. "The more we performed, the more we enjoyed singing the gospel songs," says Max. "I really wanted to focus on the religious music and perform in churches. I talked to some business leaders who were Christians and told them that I wanted to go out on the road full time with a religious singing group. I asked them for their help in getting started. They all said, 'Good luck, but we can't help you.' I was so discouraged."

By the end of the fourth year with the Rose City Singers, Max decided—after much prayer—that he was going to take the group on the road full-time. Max says, "I wanted to do it full-time, even if it was only for a year or two. The more I thought about it, the more I wanted to do it. Then Thurlow Spurr came to town."

Naturally, Max jumped at the chance to go to a Thurlow Spurr concert. He had always loved Spurr's sound—tight vocal harmonies, smooth melodies and rich chords. As he sat in that concert soaking in the sounds, Max was inspired. "The music was so professional. Spurr had six to eight singers and a full back-up band. I'd never heard anything so moving and so well done. I also realized at that moment that this was what I wanted to do. I could envision myself doing it—putting together those harmonies and working with the voices to get that sound. Maybe not the back-up band—the audiences I was familiar with wouldn't be ready for that—but I could do the vocals. I knew that this was what I wanted to do, and I was certain that I could do it."

"Max came home from the concert all excited," says Lucy. "When he told me what he wanted to do, I was shocked! We both had good jobs, a house, a car and two kids in church school. Where on earth was the money going to come from? I just looked at Max and said, 'You want to do WHAT?!' I could see that he was serious though, so after a minute I said, 'Max, if you really believe God is calling you to do this, I'm behind you.'"

Mace brothers, Ronnie, Max and Jerry

Max began immediately lining people up for a full-time singing group. He asked people he knew or had sang with in the past—including some of the Rose City Singers. "I asked them if they would be willing to quit their jobs and go on the road with a group that would be totally self-supporting. Some could, but some couldn't. Lucy's brother played bass for a group from Canada called the Waymark Singers. Gerry and Rita Leiske were the leaders and had a great sound. Lucy and I met with Gerry and Rita and asked them if they'd like to join us. They said 'Yes!'"

A management team was formed that consisted of Max, Gerry Leiske and Les Barreth. Les acted as the business manager and was in charge of raising funds to help the group get started. The plan was to go on the road full time in a few months—giving them time to raise money, learn their songs, print marketing materials, buy performance clothes and book some concerts. They also needed to find transportation and choose a name for themselves.

Max and Lucy, Jerry and Rita Leiske, and Les and Lil Barreth were joined by Judy and Bryan Lee, Bev Smick, Dick Siebenlist, Bob Silverman, Tom and Pam Buller, Gerald Allen, and Bruce and Darlene Twing, as well as five of the singers' children (all under the age of ten). "We started meeting every other weekend to put together our music," remembers Max. "We alternated between Portland and Vancouver, Canada, because some of the singers lived there. Soon a little community church a block from our house let us practice in their facility. This saved us a lot of travel time and expense."

The first concert was booked for June 4, 1971, in Yakima, Washington. This gave the group four months to get ready. During this time, Max asked each of the singers to come up with five suggestions for names for the group, and they would vote on the name. Gerry Leiske was the one who came up with the name "Heritage Singers."

Three months before they planned to go on the road, Max and Lucy met with the president of United Medical Laboratories, which employed them both. They told him they felt God was calling them to go on the road full-time. Max and Lucy gave their three months notice. The president didn't say much, but it was apparent he wasn't happy. A few weeks later the president called Max back into his office and said, "Are you really sure you want to leave a secure job? Your wife works here too, you know. And you have two kids in church school. Are you sure about this? You know the church isn't going to support you in this." But Max was confident that he was doing the right thing. "I really feel God is calling me to do this—to share Jesus through music," replied Max.

A few days later the president again called Max into his office. This time he was more adamant. "You'll never make it out there," he said. "Max, you don't even read music! There is no way you're ever going to make this work." Max went home that evening and told Lucy, "He's going to fire me." Lucy suggested that he just lay low for a while.

In the meantime, Max made plans to fly down to visit Pacific Press in Mountain View, California. Max thought the Heritage Singers could be under the umbrella of Pacific Press and travel around the United States on its behalf. "We could do concerts to promote their record label, Chapel Records," Max thought. "We could even do joint concerts with other Chapel artists, which would result in more album sales and increased visibility for them. It would be a good thing for both parties."

The night before Max was to leave for California his boss called him at home. It was almost 9:00 p.m. when the phone rang. Max recognized the voice on the line as that of the president of the laboratory. "Max, I need you to come down to the office. We need to talk." Max agreed to come in. As soon as he hung up the phone, Max looked at Lucy and said, "This time he's going to fire me." Lucy replied, "Whatever you do, don't quit! Let him fire you, so you can get unemployment." Max entered the office and sat down to hear what the president had to say. "Well, Max, we're going to have to part ways. You've lost your loyalty. I'm going to have to let you go." Just like that, it was over. Stunned, Max went home to pack his bag for his flight to California. Max tried to put his job loss behind him. He knew he needed to focus on his upcoming meeting at Pacific Press.

The next day the Pacific Press' board members listened patiently to Max's pitch about how the Heritage Singers could help promote Chapel Records. Max says. "At the end they all left the room for a while. When they came back, they stated, 'We're sorry, Max, but there is no way we can do this. It's just too costly. It just won't work.'" Max left the meeting totally devastated. Not only was he not going to get any financial assistance, he wasn't going to get any organizational backing either.

Over-whelming disappointment and disbelief flooded through him as he felt the door close behind him. Was his dream really all that outrageous? Devastated and confused, he began to question the idea himself. Was he so caught up in his own dream that he was on some ill-fated ego trip? What was he doing taking people away from their families and jobs and going on the road without any source of income? Maybe traveling full time and hoping to live on whatever they could get from freewill offerings, donations and record sales was a crazy idea. How would they even afford to record albums? How would they travel from place to place? It was such a huge undertaking. Was he being foolish? Some of the singers had children who would have to be uprooted and taken on the road. How would they keep up with school? Maybe he shouldn't even be thinking about doing such a thing.

The Bible says, "People may make plans in their minds, but only the Lord can make them come true. You may believe you are doing right, but the Lord will judge your reasons" (Proverbs 16:1–2, NCV). That's what Max was struggling with. He was wondering whether his motivations were pure. The text goes on to say, "Depend on the Lord in whatever you do, and your plans will succeed" (verse 3). So that is what Max did—he turned his questions, fears and self-doubt over to God.

"The day I was turned down by Pacific Press was my darkest day," Max admits. "To top it off, I had just been fired! When I called Lucy to tell her the bad news, she said, "You won't believe what's happening here at work. Mr. Michael is firing every one of the singers who were planning to go on the road with you. They

Max and Lucy's wedding, January 5, 1958

had given him three months notice of their plans, but they've been fired on the spot. He's telling each one of them that they've lost their loyalty."

Max went home to try to figure out what to do. Here they were—three months before their first scheduled concert—all of them suddenly without jobs and no source of income. Just when Max thought things couldn't get worse, Lucy was called into the president's office. She was the main switchboard operator and receptionist for the entire company. She was the only person who knew how to set up an overseas conference call—among other things. Losing Lucy was really going to hurt the company. The president had put off firing Lucy for as long as he could. He really didn't want to do it; she was not going to be easy to replace.

When he gave her the bad news, she just looked at the president and said, "Haven't I done a good job?" "Yes, you've done a wonderful job," he replied, "in fact, you're the best switchboard operator we've ever had." "Then why are you firing me?" asked Lucy. The president struggled to come up with a good reason, until finally he replied, "I'm firing you because, well...uh... you're married to Max!"

Max remembers the sudden panic they felt. "We were far

Max, third baseman for the Portland Pacers

from being ready to go on the road. All of our financial support had been abruptly cut off. We had no savings. We didn't know very many songs yet. And, we had no transportation. What we did have was a bunch of people without jobs all looking to me for their next move. We spent a lot of time on our knees."

To Max's surprise, an investigation was conducted by the Industrial Relations Division of the Labor Department to see just what Mr. Michael, the president of the laboratory, considered "disloyal" behavior, and whether or not he had been justified in firing any of them. The Labor Department found that none of them had been disloyal in any way; in fact, they were star employees. So, the laboratory was forced to pay them all unemployment.

Getting fired turned into a real blessing. Now they had lots of time to prepare to go on the road. Max says, "We had so much to do—songs to learn, marketing materials to print, performance clothing to obtain and a sound system to assemble. Having time to do all that was really what we needed. Satan tried very hard to discourage us, but as things began falling into place, we realized that God was providing for our needs. That's when we knew God was in it. We realized it wasn't just our grandiose plan. God was behind us and that assurance gave us the confidence to keep going."

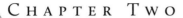

CHAPTER TWO

Leaps of Faith

Faith is the substance of things hoped for, the evidence of things not seen.
— Hebrews 11:1

Tʜᴇ ᴇᴀʀʟʏ ᴅᴀʏs ᴏꜰ ᴛʜᴇ Hᴇʀɪᴛᴀɢᴇ ᴍɪɴɪsᴛʀʏ ᴡᴇʀᴇ ᴠᴇʀʏ ᴇᴍᴏᴛɪᴏɴᴀʟ. Tʜᴇʏ ᴏꜰᴛᴇɴ ᴅɪᴅɴ'ᴛ ᴋɴᴏᴡ ᴡʜᴇʀᴇ their next dollar was coming from. Everything was a leap of faith. Everyone made sacrifices.

Early on, God began working miracles for the Heritage Singers. Lucy remembered trying to find matching outfits for the singers to wear at their concerts and not having much money to do it with. She found inexpensive red and white skirts for the girls to wear, and then a very generous lady made a second set of dresses for the girls at her own expense. Lucy was able to purchase navy blue suits for the men in Canada—the exchange rate made them less expensive there.

In order to book concerts, Lucy began sending letters to the churches where the Rose City Singers had performed—telling them about the newly formed Heritage Singers. Max asked others for help, many of which offered him no encouragement. Two individuals who believed in Max's dream were Jerry Brass and

Cecil Coffee. "These two men really believed in what we were doing," Max said. "They stuck their necks out and wrote letters to churches throughout the Northwest, encouraging pastors to invite us to their churches. They said, 'These are good people. We know them. We've seen them in concert. If you invite them into your church you'll be blessed.' We couldn't have made it without their help. They gave us the courage to keep going. Jerry Brass also offered the use of his office while we were on the road. His secretary followed up on the letters we had sent out to churches and continued booking additional concerts for us."

Another individual who was a big encouragement to Max was Earl Johnson, who worked at Pacific Press. "We'd talk on the phone a lot. He helped me through some tough times. He was always very supportive of what I was trying to do, and he was always there for me," Max remembered.

There were others that encouraged Max, including Richard Lange, Elder Lampson and Mike Carter. Richard worked in the same office with Max and encouraged Max to pursue his dreams. Elder Lampson, from the Union office, often invited Max into his office. There they knelt together and prayed for the Heritage Singers. "He was such a Godly man," reflected Max. "He really encouraged me to follow my dreams. We often prayed for the Lord's guidance." Mike Carter, a recording engineer Max had worked with on the Rose City Singers' recordings, knew a man who owned a printing company and suggested Max go talk to him. "I shared my dream with this man," Max said. "He was so enthused that he offered to print our posters and flyers at no cost! That encouraged me to keep going. My own Dad had told me he didn't think the church would support me, and here a complete stranger believed in me. It meant a lot to me."

Max Torkelson, Earl Amanson, Ron Wisby and Ralph Martin also believed in Max. It was because of their help and encouragement that the Heritage Singers began receiving invitations from churches. Slowly, but surely, the calendar was filling up.

One of Max's biggest thrills during those early days was putting the "Heritage sound" together. He knew the sound he wanted—smooth, lush, rich chords and tight harmonies. Before

Original Heritage Singers: Dick Siebenlist, Tom Buller, Lucy Mace, Brian Lee, Rita Leiske, Judy Lee, Bruce Twing, Bev Smick, Max Mace, and Jerry Leiske

Max and engineer, Mike Carter, mixing our fist album "Come Along With The Heritage Singers"

going on the road, the group performed several "practice" concerts at churches throughout the Portland area.

Eric Haaplo was in the audience at one of the first "practice" concerts. "What a sound!" he remembered. "I soaked in that beautiful blend of human voices with harmonies swelling like the gentle California surf—carrying words of hope and inspiration! I sat in the audience drinking in the whole experience. It was an evening that would change my life." Max soon asked Eric to play guitar with the group.

Eric remembered Max and Jerry discussing the feasibility of their group being able to make it financially—singing full time without any other source of income. "The timing seemed right," Eric said. "Christian music was beginning to blossom into something more contemporary and relevant. The music was more current and the harmonies were rich and intricate. There was a new freedom in musical expression—a new way for God's message to be brought to the world. From the simple, heartfelt folk-gospel of the youth, to the more urban, harmonically rich sounds of Carmichael, Skilling and others, to the exuberance of Southern gospel groups like the Imperials, all the way to the excitement of contemporary Black gospel and the warm, sweet sounds of the Gaither Trio, Heritage had a wonderful smorgasbord of music styles to choose from. It was an exciting time to start a group like this."

The Heritage Singers needed albums to sell at their

upcoming concerts, so they recorded two albums: *Hymns We Remember* and *Come Along With the Heritage Singers*. "Just to walk into a recording studio with the Heritage Singers was incredible," Eric said. "We recorded, sang, talked, laughed, prayed and got to know each other. When Max asked me to come with them on the road, I didn't need much convincing. These were people I felt I had to be with."

It wasn't easy to record those early albums. The group stood around in a circle in the recording studio, sharing microphones, and recording the vocals along with the instrumentation of the live band. If one musician or singer made a mistake, they had to start all over. There were some very long recording sessions because of all the retakes the singers had to do.

With the date of the Heritage Singers first concert quickly approaching, Max still didn't know what they were going to do for transportation. Bryan and Judy had sold their car. Max and Lucy's car engine had blown up and they couldn't afford to repair it. The other singers didn't have reliable cars either. But, God had a plan. "We needed a way to get to our concerts," Max recalled. "What we were hoping for was a bus, but we didn't know how we were going to afford that! Bob Hoag, a friend of mine, told me he had recently bought a retired bus from the Greyhound Bus Company. He said that if you wrote a letter to them about how a bus could help further a worthy cause, they'd give you a good price on a retired bus. So, we wrote a letter. Weeks went by and we still didn't hear anything. We continued to pray about it, but still did not get a response."

The week before the first concert, the group got together

Max during our first recording session

Guitarist Erik Haapalo

and once more prayed about the situation. "Lord, we know You are behind us, and we thank You for leading this far," they prayed, "but we don't know how You want us to go to all of these concerts. We had hoped for a bus, but we'll go however You want us to go." No sooner had they said, "Amen," than the telephone rang. Max still shakes his head in disbelief when he tells this story. "The phone call was from the Greyhound Bus Company. They told us that they had a lot of buses they were getting rid of and that we needed to come to San Francisco right away to select one. It's unbelievable, I know, but that's what really happened."

Jerry Leiske and Bruce Twing both had the driver's license required to drive a bus—and they knew more about buses than anyone else in the group. They flew to San Francisco to choose a bus. Their plan was to drive the newly acquired bus back to Portland to meet up with the rest of the group in time for the first concert.

When they arrived at the Greyhound depot and saw all of the buses, they felt overwhelmed. How in the world would they choose the right one? They could pick one that looked good from the outside, but how would it run? Most of the buses looked really bad. They had certainly seen better days. Not knowing where to begin, Jerry and Bruce began looking around. Suddenly, they heard a voice and were startled to see a man had approached them. "What are you looking for?" the man asked. "We're trying to find a bus with a reliable engine that would be good for road trips for our Christian music group, but honestly, we don't know what to look for," Jerry and Bruce explained. The man smiled and replied, "Well, I know a lot about buses. I'll help you."

They looked at several buses. One of them was especially ugly. The Greyhound logo had been sanded off. The interior was stained yellow and reeked with the stench of many years of cigarette smoke. However, after a little more checking, Jerry and Bruce saw that the mileage was lower than many of the others. The man who was helping them stated, "This is the bus you should have. The engine has just been rebuilt, and it is mechanically sound." Jerry and Bruce looked at him skeptically. This was the ugliest bus on the lot! "Are you sure?" they asked him. "Yes, believe me. I know buses, and this is the one you should have," he assured them.

Jerry and Bruce parked the bus and went inside the office to fill out the paperwork. They found out that the bus had been inspected, but the low mileage posed a problem. Technically, the rebuilt engine didn't have enough miles on it to qualify as a retired bus. It wasn't supposed to be available to sell to them. However, after some negotiation, the Greyhound representative agreed to sell the bus to them for $4,000—but they would have to pay for new tires. The total came to around $6,200.

"You've really made a good choice," the Greyhound representative said as the papers were signed. "How did you happen to choose this particular bus?" "Well, there was a gentleman helping us," answered Jerry, "He said he knew a lot about buses." The Greyhound representative got a very strange look on his face. "Nobody is allowed on this lot except our security guards, and none of them are here today." He paused and leaned back in his chair, taking them in skeptically. "No one could've possibly been out there, other than the two of you." Mystified, he sent someone out to the lot to look for the man, but no one was found. The man had disappeared.

Max and Lucy are convinced that God sent a special messenger to help Jerry and Bruce that day. "We think it was an angel. There's no other explanation. It was just another example of how God provided for us."

Because there was not enough time for Bruce and Jerry to get back to Portland to pick up the group and get to the first concert, Max and Lucy decided to rent a bus. Lucy called a bus rental company and got a quote for what it would cost to get from Portland to Yakima. They had just enough money to pay for that trip. On June 4, 1971, the Heritage Singers gave their first concert in Yakima, Washington.

Unfortunately, Max soon learned that Bruce and Jerry would not be able to meet them in Yakima after all; they would have to meet them a day later in Wenatchee. This meant additional costs to rent the bus longer. Lucy said, "When we left our home in Portland and climbed onto that rented bus with our suitcases—not knowing when we'd be returning, if ever—it was a big step of faith. We didn't even know how we were going to pay for the extra rental fee and diesel costs to get from Yakima to Wenatchee. Just as we were about to leave, I felt impressed to check the mailbox one last time. I was totally humbled and amazed to find a letter with a check in it for $300, which turned out to be the exact amount we needed for the extra expense! It brought us such peace. We rode to our first concert with the assurance that God was once more meeting our needs."

When Jerry and Bruce finally arrived in Wenatchee, they drove the "new" Heritage bus (actually, a 1956 Scenicruiser) into the driveway of Dennis and Marley Peete's house—a home where some of the singers were staying. There were shouts of joy at the sight of the bus. "We were so excited!" Lucy recalled. "We had our own bus! Oh, it was ugly, but it was ours! We scrubbed it and scrubbed it. We cleaned the linoleum floor and shampooed

Our first bus, "Old Blue"

the seats and the walls—even the ceilings—trying to get rid of the tobacco stains and the stale smell. The outside of the bus looked pretty bad too. The greyhounds were faded and just about sanded off. We looked into how much it would cost to have it painted, but it was more than we could afford."

Max shared the miraculous story of how they found the bus with the camp meeting audience that weekend. He also mentioned that the bus would have to be painted. At the end of camp meeting, a man named Jimmy Wagner gave Max a check for the exact amount they needed. "The weird thing was I had never mentioned what the cost was going to be, and the man had no way of knowing what we had been quoted either. He just made the check out for exactly the right amount," remembered Max. "To this day it is still unbelievable."

The original Heritage Singers in 1971.

That was the beginning of the Heritage Singers' journey. "We stepped out completely in faith," Max said. "But you know what?

God never once failed to clearly show us the way we should go."

Judy Lee remembered those early days well. She said, "We didn't realize how much we were going forward into the unknown. It was a time of testing, a time of excitement and a time of life-long friendships. We didn't know what it would turn into or how it would change our lives. If we would have known what we were in for, we might not have done it."

Within three months of the Heritage Singers first concert, they had repaid all their loans and were operating in the black. They even had a bus with their name on it. Their concerts were booked and people loved their sound. Everyday God provided for the group's needs. It astonished Max again and again to see God working to open doors for their new ministry. "We had no idea our prayers would be answered so directly," Max said. "It was our encouragement to keep going. How could we quit now?"

CHAPTER THREE

A Ministry is Born

THE HERITAGE SINGERS MINISTRY TOOK OFF QUICKLY. AFTER THEIR FIRST CONCERT IN YAKIMA, THE GROUP toured California, Idaho, Montana, Oregon, Washington, and parts of Western Canada, performing at ten camp meetings within the first three months. Traveling on the bus and singing night after night was a big adjustment for everyone.

Greg and Val were quite young when Max and Lucy took them on the road. "We left right after the end of the school year," Greg remembered. "I was ten years old, in the fifth grade, I think. We knew we were going to get on a bus and tour around, which sounded like fun."

Val was nine years old. "I left my favorite things behind—my two dogs," she said. "That 40-foot bus became everything to me, my security, my home, and my school-room. It was a very unique life."

There were other children who toured on the bus as well. Bruce and Darlene Twing

Val and Greg

had a three-year-old daughter, Denise, and Jerry and Rita Lieske had two children, a five-year-old boy named Kim and a six-year-old girl named Jackie (who sang with the Heritage Singers a dozen years later). The closet in the back of the bus became a makeshift playroom for the children.

Touring on the bus was particularly challenging for Lucy. She not only sang full-time, but was also responsible for keeping the group's records and homeschooling Greg and Val. "I was school teacher, singer, mother, bookkeeper, and, in my spare time, I'd try to sleep!" Lucy laughed. "The kids grew little science projects, until winter came and froze all of their tomato plants. We eventually hired one of our singers, Prudy Matthews, to tutor the kids. They did everything they would have done in a regular classroom and they got to see the world."

Val was homeschooled on the bus from the fourth through ninth grade. She then went to Pacific Union College Preparatory School her sophomore year. Greg attended school in Portland so he could continue to be on the basketball team where he was voted most valuable player for his age category. "The hardest thing I've ever done is leave Greg behind," Lucy stated. "I remember an interviewer asking me about Greg. I just started crying. I couldn't stand it anymore. So, we brought him back on the road with us. The children always had the option of going to boarding school, but they preferred this life. They both received their high school diplomas and went on to attend Pacific Union College."

Singing five concerts a week and doing camp meetings and crusades required a large repertoire of music. Whenever they could find the time, which was often while on the bus traveling to the next concert, the group practiced and learned new songs. New albums also needed to be recorded every few months, just to keep the material fresh.

New albums also meant photo-shoots to create an appealing album cover. One of the most memorable photo-shoots was for *The King Is Coming* album. "The group wanted to do something really special for the cover," said Max, "so we decided to do the photo-shoot along the Oregon Coast with the bus on the beach. It was a picture perfect day," remembered Max. "All of us were in our freshly cleaned and pressed performance clothes. We drove the bus out to Cannon Beach on the Oregon Coast and waited for the tide to go out. We tried to make sure we stayed on the firm, wet sand, but in the process of trying to angle the bus in front of a large rock, the back tires slipped into the dry, soft sand. We were stuck. The harder we tried to get the bus out, the worse things got. The weight of the sound system, which was in the bottom of the bus, was no help either.

"Well, the tide began to come in. We knew we needed help, so we called a wrecker. A small tow truck showed up, but it wasn't big enough to pull out the bus. While we waited for another tow truck to come, we unloaded the sound system onto the sand. People who were on the beach came running to our aid. Some drove their pickups out, loaded our equipment, and drove it to higher ground. As we watched our sound equipment disappearing, we hoped we'd see it again.

"Meanwhile, the water was rising. We only had a short time to get the bus out of there. When the big tow truck arrived, the driver hooked onto the bus. However, he forgot to close the door and it caught on the tow truck cable. This caused one of the hinges to break. As the tow truck pulled the bus to safety, the bus door was just dangling there." Max laughed as he remembered that day. "To top it off, Judy Lee broke off the heel of her shoe trying to get across a muddy place," he said. "Jerry laughed at her, and she got so mad at him. Then, on the way home, our bus driver was driving too fast, and Jerry asked him to slow down. He got mad at us and slowed down to a snail's pace. He drove the whole way home that way, just to aggravate us."

As the Heritage Singers continued to travel, they saw evidence of God's blessing. "People were coming to Jesus," Max said, "and that's what was important." Of course, there were some people who were skeptical of Heritage's music style. "The majority of the people liked us," Max pointed out. "But, some didn't know what to think of us. What we were doing was so new. Some people said we were a breath of fresh air and others thought we were too contemporary. They weren't used to such a happy sound or live instruments—especially guitars. Some people would walk into a church, take one look at our guitars sitting in their stands, and decide they weren't going to like us," Max remembered. "We couldn't let that discourage us. We had two choices - we could either move past it or fail. We chose to keep on singing."

Those who didn't like the music made things difficult for Max. Since he was always sensitive to his audiences, Max bent over backwards to try to please people. If he thought a song selection for a concert should be adjusted on the spot, he would do it. "Our desire from the beginning was to work with church organizations, to work with the pastors and their youth programs," Max pointed out. "Still, some churches wouldn't touch us." As more people heard the music and word spread, people began to flock to the Heritage Singers concerts. Max said, "I hope that today people aren't so quick to judge groups that come to their churches. We should never pre-judge anyone. God uses all kinds of messengers to deliver His messages."

Because some churches weren't sure whether the Heritage Singers' music was appropriate for their worship services, the Pacific Union Committee decided to vote on whether to allow the group into their churches or not. The states that were included in this vote were Arizona, California, Hawaii, Nevada, and Utah. Pastor Miller Brocket, who was on the committee, stood up in the meetings and fought for Max and said, "I've been to their concerts. I've seen people coming down the aisle and giving their hearts to Jesus. These kids are doing great things." When the votes were counted, the Heritage Singers had won by only one vote! "If they had voted against us, we would have had to quit," Max said. "There was no way we could have made it without being able to sing in all of those churches. I'm so grateful to Miller Brocket for standing up for us. I know God sent him to us."

The highlight of that first summer was when the Heritage Singers were invited to sing at the Soquel camp meeting. "It was so hot that day," Max remembered. "The place was packed and the auditorium didn't have air conditioning—or if it did it wasn't working. We were very nervous too. We were still trying to get people to accept us. We got up there and sang, and by the time

Miller Brockett, our dear friend

we were done, we were dripping wet—just sweating like crazy. When we walked outside, a man followed us out. He came up to me, reached out to shake my hand, and said, 'Max, I'm Elder Blacker. I'm the Pacific Union president. I just want you to know that I believe in what you're doing, and I will support you.' Then he reached into his pocket and pulled out a $10 bill. The money wasn't important; it was his support, his endorsement of us, that meant so much."

The endorsement of the Pacific Union president helped the Heritage Singers get into more churches. Despite this, there were still some pastors who told Max they "wouldn't bring the Heritage Singers into their church if they were the last group on earth." Max's response to them was, "Well, maybe one day we'll be neighbors in Heaven." Max didn't let it discourage him. He knew there were others who would welcome the group. With the support of those who weren't afraid to try something new, the group made it through their first summer.

After only three months of being on the road, the Canadian singers in the group had difficulty renewing their visas. This meant that Rita and Jerry Leiske, Les and Lil Barreth, Bryan and Judy Lee, Eric Haapalo, and Gerald Allen all had to return to Canada. It was a blow to lose so many key people—almost half of the group! Max was faced with recruiting new singers and training them. It was very important to maintain the consistent "Heritage sound" for which the group had become known. But, by then, lots of young people had heard the Heritage Singers perform and were eager to join.

Living on a bus and traveling full time wasn't easy. It required patience and understanding. The group lived in close quarters and had a hectic schedule. They traveled all over the United States, taking only two weeks off for Christmas and two weeks for music camp in August to learn new music. In the mornings they'd have worship together, and then work for most of the day learning how to handle a microphone, and how to put expression in not only their voices, but also in their faces while they were singing. One of the hardest things for some of the people was learning how to blend together as one voice.

"People living that close together all the time—it's ripe for problems," said former singer Bill Truby. "Naturally, we had a lot of interpersonal problems. We were doing God's work after all. Satan was tempting us, causing us to attack each other. Some concerts probably weren't as inspired or as blessed as they could have been because of the strife going on within the group. It's not good, but it happened."

Log cabin where the Heritage girls stayed

Lucy explained, "Everybody on that bus was human. They all had their own things to deal with, and then they had each other to deal with too. Unless you spend time with the Lord every single day, personally and with the entire group, there's just absolutely no way you could make it. Whenever things got tense, that's when we would get together and pray about it and work it all out."

In the early days, there was a lot of bus travel. Bill remembered, "Sometimes, we'd travel for eight hours to get to the next concert. We'd arrive exhausted, but quickly be revived by the warm hospitality and great food so generously provided for us by our hosts. Then, after the concert, we went home with the various people who had volunteered to house one or two of us singers for the night. Other than the food provided by these kind people, we ate our meals in restaurants. Once a week we stopped at a laundromat and did our laundry."

This lifestyle was especially hard on Lucy. Pulling her kids out of school and feeling responsible for all 19 people on the bus was really difficult for her. "And, we didn't even have a place to go home to," she remembered. "We'd go back to our business manager John and Lillian Musgrave's house and sleep on a fold-out sofa. I'm a homebody. Not having a home was very hard for me. Also, we didn't have anything to base anything on. This had never been done before. When I got discouraged, Max would try to encourage me and when Max got discouraged, I'd try to encourage him. Never having any time alone was also hard for me. We were around people all of the time." Max said, in looking back, he realizes, "the only way the singers could have been content with this lifestyle was through the grace of God."

During the early years, the Heritage Singers did not have a place to call home. Up to this point they had been using their business manager's garage in Sacramento for their office. Max knew that they needed a place for offices and their annual music camp. Then he heard about a 103-acre parcel of land in Placerville, California. It was more than they needed, but the land encompassed beautiful trees and was on top of a mountain, away from the traffic and noise. It seemed like the perfect spot for their ministry to call home. The property had been for sale for 20 years, but each time a prospective buyer would come to look at the land the owner would ask what they planned to do with the property. If they answered we want to cut the trees down, he told them, "It's not for sale."

When Max told the landowner about the group and its ministry, the man offered to sell it for $20,000 down. It was a fantastic price, but Max and Lucy knew they didn't have that much money. However, they thought they might be able to come up with $10,000. The owner took their offer and sold it to them for $10,000 down and $800 an acre.

At first the group lived in the two log cabins that were on the property and put tents up for music camp. Eventually, a nine-bedroom lodge was built with an office complex, an apartment for John and Lillian Musgrave at one end, and an apartment on the other end for Max and Lucy. Jim Craddock was the builder. He and his family loved the Heritage Singers and worked very hard to make a special place for the singers to come home to. The home and office complex soon became known as "the Ranch" because the property had once been a working cattle ranch.

Lucy recalled those early days when the group lived in the log cabins, "The boys' cabin didn't have hot water. I'll never forget the sounds of the boys screaming each morning as they took cold showers! We used a wood stove to cook our food on and a picnic table outside to eat our meals at. Mike Madonna was our cook. There was this beautiful old apple tree in the yard that gave us the best apples I've ever tasted! They made the best apple pie and apple crisp. I remember a nice German lady who brought us loads of fresh produce from her garden. She had a very bountiful crop of zucchini that year. Mike was very creative in putting together all kinds of meals that included—or disguised—zucchini."

Lee Newman remembered living in the cabins too. He said, "It was the best of times and the worst of times! The guys had to sleep in an old cabin that wasn't much bigger than a chicken coop, while the girls stayed in the larger cabin. It was wonderful though. I can still remember when Chuck Fulmore came down from Idaho and we all gathered around the piano while he played and sang one of his new songs for us."

Lee joined the Heritage Singers family in 1973. At first he didn't have any interest in joining them. Lee confessed, "I had lost interest in religion. It had become a collection of do's and don'ts to me. I was looking for happiness outside of the church." Lee was in medical school at the time and some of his college friends were in the Heritage Singers. "Max was looking for a bass singer, and my Heritage friends had told him about me. When I found out they were going to have a concert near where I lived, I decided to go, just to see my friends. I really had no desire to join Heritage."

After the concert, Lee began talking with his friend Larry Matthews who was in Heritage at the time. "I saw in him a genuine happiness that I had never seen before," Lee said. "I wanted to be that happy! Larry told me he had found a friend in Jesus and it had made all the difference in his life." Max wasn't able to talk with Lee that night, so Lee went to the Heritage concert the next night. "I thought about what Larry had said. God was working on me. At the end of the concert Max formed an impromptu quartet, which served as my audition. Max asked me to join the group that night, and I surprised myself by saying 'yes' on the spot!"

Lee made arrangements for a one-year leave of absence from medical school and started singing with the Heritage practice tapes. "I had just finished the first part of the National Medical Board exams," he recalled. "It was grueling. I was also getting acquainted with my new best friend. Suddenly I noticed I was having difficulty swallowing." Lee scheduled an x-ray to have it checked out. The night before the x-ray he did a little of his own research. He had all the symptoms of esophagus cancer—usually a fatal condition. "I was devastated!" Lee said. "I hit rock-bottom. It was at that point that I completely gave what was left of my life to Christ. The next morning on the way to the hospital I was singing with the Heritage practice tapes. As I began to sing, 'My Faith Still Holds Onto the Christ of Calvary,' I broke down. I began sobbing so hard that I couldn't drive anymore. I pulled over to the side of the freeway and sat there for a few minutes until I could drive again."

Lee's x-rays showed a completely normal esophagus. His symptoms disappeared. "I still don't know if the swallowing difficulty was due to a cancer or just a bad case of stress," Lee said. "But either way, I experienced a miraculous healing! I knew then that being in Heritage was what God wanted for me."

Lee wasn't the only one that God led to join the group. Bill Truby was also in college when he heard about the Heritage Singers. A friend of Bill's told him that the group needed a guitar player and a tenor, so Bill decide to check into it. "I was always up for an adventure," Bill remarked, "so I borrowed my dad's station wagon and drove up to Portland, almost on a lark. It was an overnighter. We drove all day, auditioned, stayed overnight, got a few hours of sleep, and drove home. I can still remember Max asking me if I wanted to join the group. I told him I would have to talk to my parents. If they would let me, I would do it. I was 20 years old, but I had no belief that my parents would let me. I prayed about it, then, I went home and explained it to my parents. Mom and Dad had never heard of the Heritage Singers, and I didn't know much about them either. Well, Mom cried, but said I could do it. I packed my stuff and went right to Portland.

Bobby Silverman doing what he loved most

"We went to Big Lake Youth Camp to learn all of our songs. I remember that John Musgrave, the business manager for Heritage, came onto the bus and expressed to everyone the excitement of what was going to happen. It was all a little overwhelming for me. None of it really made any sense. I had no clue as to what I was getting into. I just knew I enjoyed making music with everyone. Max kept asking me to sing 'There's Something About That Name.' That was sort of my signature song."

Terry and Perry Mace and Tricia Cawdry joined Heritage at the same time. Trish later left to attend Pacific Union College. After she graduated, Trish and Terry got married and went back on the road with Heritage. Imagine just getting married and instead of going off on your honeymoon, you head for Placerville, California, to join the Heritage Singers, who are rehearsing for a new season. That's exactly what Terry and Trish Mace did!

Terry Mace remembered the group operating out of John Musgrave's home in Sacramento and rehearsing at the academy in Sacramento. "In those days the singers were paid $150 a month," Terry said. "Out of that we had to pay for things like dry cleaning and food, when it wasn't provided to us. I remember

someone once gave us 50 coupons for free hamburgers and fries at a fast food place, so we ate there twice a day! We'd do anything we could to conserve!"

"We were like family," continued Terry. "It was the Maces—Max, Lucy, Greg, Val, Perry, Trish, and I, plus the Truby brothers—Bill and Tim—Pete McLeod, Deb Walker, Lee Newman, and Bobby Silverman. Of course, just like a real family, people got on each other's nerves. When you're traveling together all the time, you eventually see everyone's flaws. Some of the singers had pretty unique ways too. I remember one guy who kept his clothes in a pile by his feet on the floor, all wadded up against the side of the bus. We said he invented the perma-wrinkle process for clothes. We gave him a nickname; in fact, we ended up nicknaming everyone in the group, some of which are still being used to this day!"

When Lee Newman was growing up, he had always wanted a nickname. "When I joined Heritage, Terry tried out several nicknames on me like Leeman, Noodle, and Peduncus. Finally, Noot stuck. Now, to this day, my close friends still call me Noot!"

One of the most beloved people who traveled with the group was Bob Silverman. He played the piano for the Heritage Singers for more than a decade. "Many people thought he was a musical genius," Terry Mace explained. "He could play any song, in any style, in any key. He could also make every song sound alike if he wanted to, or completely change it. Whatever Max heard in his head, he communicated to Bobby, and Bobby got it."

"He was also quite hard on himself," said Terry. "After each concert he'd make sure Max was happy with his performance. We weren't very polished in the early days, but Bobby gave us musical flair. Bobby's talents didn't end there. His mind was like a computer. He could memorize lists of phone numbers. He knew the call letters and location of every radio station in the United States. He knew all of the telephone area codes and postal ZIP Codes for the entire country. He was also a math genius. Bobby could tell you things like what day any given date fell on. He was always surprising us with his knowledge of details."

"Bobby's special talents set him apart," smiled Terry. "And his prayers—well, they were epic. Bobby made sure the Lord knew exactly where we were on the map that day, giving God all of the geographic details. We had to make sure we had plenty of time when Bobby said a prayer! Bobby also liked routines. He wanted to do the same thing every day and wasn't comfortable with unexpected changes, but the life of a Heritage Singer was all about constant change and surprises. It was a challenge for all of us. We had to learn to go with the flow because anything could happen."

Ginny and Rudy Yost with their daughter Alanna and her favorite stuffed dog

"Bobby liked certain clothes we wore at concerts," remembered Terry. "Because we performed so often, we had three or four different outfits we'd rotate. Bobby liked what he called the 'full blue' outfit.

Alanna recording "Something Happened to Daddy"

Whenever Max would look at Lucy and ask what we were going to wear that night, Bobby would always say, 'Let's wear full blue.' Sometimes after a big Saturday night concert, we'd all go out to dinner and Max would pick up the tab. Well, Bobby knew the value of a dollar, and often would say, 'You know, Max, I'm really not all that hungry. Can I just have the money instead?' This became a favorite comment at group dinners for years."

Terry and Greg Mace took a lot of photographs that they developed themselves in their hotel room on their days off. Terry said, "We tried to get really ugly pictures of everybody in the group. I'd try to get them at their worst angles. I think I took a whole roll of Bobby. By this time, Bobby had already recorded two solo albums. I told him we could use some of the new shots for his next album cover. He loved it."

Pete McLeod remembered Bobby's reaction to being teased. "He is such a unique guy," Pete explained. "When Terry Mace played a trick on him, he wouldn't even get angry. He'd just say, 'Terry, I guess this is what you call good, clean fun!'"

In 1973 Rudy and Ginny Yost came into the Heritage family, along their little girl Alanna, who was just getting ready to start kindergarten. They were living in Sacramento at the time and knew Max and Lucy. Rudy had been thinking about making a change in their lives, so he and Ginny prayed for guidance. Rudy decided that if Max asked him to join Heritage, he would know it was God's will. That is exactly what happened. During dinner one night, Max asked them if they would like to come on the road with the Heritage Singers. Rudy left his job as a pharmaceutical sales representative and sold their home. They then moved onto the bus with the other singers. "It was a drastic lifestyle change," Rudy said, "but there were many blessings ahead."

"Our first tour took us across the United States," Ginny remembered. "While in Miami, Florida, Max introduced us to a song, 'Something's Happened to Daddy.' Rudy and Alanna sang that song at almost every concert from that point on. It touched so many hearts! What a blessing it was for Alanna to be involved with Heritage at such a young age!"

At the end of a concert in Mt. Shasta, California, Rudy invited individuals in the audience to search their hearts and rededicate their lives to the Lord. As people began coming forward to pray privately with the singers, he noticed that nearly the entire audience was coming up. "The Holy Spirit was so evident every night we sang," Rudy recalled. "We also felt the presence of God's watchful care over us each day as we traveled long distances on the bus."

"I'll never forget having Thanksgiving Dinner in our motel rooms," Ginny laughed. "We were in Atlanta, Georgia, and we actually fixed a wonderful dinner in our rooms. We did blow a fuse here and there, but it turned out surprisingly well, considering we didn't have a kitchenette. The restaurant next door to our motel even provided free pies for us!"

"One time Lucy and I went shopping on our day off," Ginny remembered. "We took the city bus to a shopping area and headed back to our motel a little late. The bus route stopped quite a distance from our motel, and it was a very scary neighborhood for us 'country girls' to be walking through alone. We prayed all the way back to our motel!"

Alanna remembered what it was like to be a kid on the Heritage bus. "I was only allowed to bring one case of Barbies on the bus. But, I did have my favorite stuffed dog that always sat in my seat. I especially loved swinging down the bus aisle on the arms of the seats. I also remember watching Gerry sleep with her eyes open—and her catching me once! I celebrated several birthdays on that bus."

Val and Greg celebrated many of their birthdays on the bus too. Lucy said, "We had a nice party for Val on her 16th birthday. Her present was a bicycle. We attached it to the front of the bus, where we thought it would be fine. The next day Pete was driving the bus and rear-ended someone. That was the end of Val's bike!

For another one of Val's birthdays we got her a camera she had been wanting. We ordered it and had it shipped to the church where we were scheduled to sing on her birthday. The package arrived at the church in plenty of time, but two days before we arrived, someone broke into the church and stole her camera!

"Greg had most of his birthdays in foreign countries. He's had candles in doughnuts, muffins, and pies since a traditional birthday cake was not always available. No one can say that my kids didn't have memorable birthdays!"

As the Heritage ministry grew, so did the office staff. This enabled the group to begin publishing a monthly newsletter that was mailed to supporters and friends. The first newsletter was published in 1974. It was through these newsletters that much of the Heritage Singers' experience was documented.

Each year the Heritage Singers' ministry expanded, bringing new opportunities to share God's message. The group began getting invitations to perform at youth congresses, evangelistic crusades, and Weeks of Prayer at Christian high schools. They were even invited on the *It's Your World* program, hosted by Art Linkletter.

Lee Newman remembered one Week of Prayer the group did for a Christian high school. "There were a lot of bad things going on in that school—drugs, drinking, gambling, prostitution, even Satan worship," he said. "We arrived on a Sunday night. 'Old Blue' broke down as we were coming into town. The bus just wouldn't start, so we all got out and pushed it through town to the campus. The next morning we were singing and smiling like we always did. The students looked at us and said, 'You're phonies! We know that you were up half the night pushing your bus through town, and now, here you are all bright and cheery. We know that you're faking it. It's all just an act!' But that week we ate with them, talked with them, played sports with them, and went to classes with them. By the end of the week, the students had completely turned around. They knew it wasn't an act. They knew that a life with Christ could give them joy, even in the worst of circumstances."

One of the first crusades the Heritage Singers performed at was a month long crusade in Walla Walla, Washington. Their job was to provide all of the music during the event, as well as participate in the visitation program. They went out each day in teams of two to visit and pray with people in their homes. Rudy Yost remembered one young man they visited, "His wife had divorced him and he had the responsibility of raising their eight-year-old son. He told us he had been away from Jesus for many years, but attending the crusade series got him to think about changing his life.

"Apparently, he felt guilty for the way he had treated his former wife, and he began praying she would get in touch with him as he didn't know where she was living. Before the crusade was over, his ex-wife called him. They had a long talk and he asked her to forgive him. When she said she would, it was like a big weight lifted off his shoulders. On the last night of the crusade he dedicated his life to God," said Rudy. "It is experiences like that that really give us a blessing. We are just so thankful that Jesus is able to use us in some small way."

During that same crusade, a local Saab dealership loaned the Heritage Singers a fleet of orange cars. The singers used the cars for their visitations each day, as well as for getting around town. Terry Mace said, "For that month-long crusade, orange Saabs were all over Walla Walla. We got a lot of attention!"

Another highlight of the Heritage Singers early years was being invited to perform at the Christian Booksellers Convention. They were part of the opening "Gospel Sing," performing beside other groups like the Hawaiians, Evie Tornquist, Henry and Hazel Slaughter, Dino, and the Imperials. During an autograph party, the group gave away a thousand copies of its newly recorded album *Let's Just Praise the Lord.* Terry remembered, "It

Terry Mace

was such a joy to be a part of a convention where there were representatives from every state in the nation and many foreign countries, all with the goal of praising the Lord."

Another memorable occasion was being invited to Lake Havasu, Arizona, to sing at the dedication of the newly reassembled London Bridge. The singers even got to walk across the bridge!

Soon after, the Heritage Singers began producing television programs. Terry recalled, "We taped approximately 20 half-hour programs. We lived in the South Pasadena Sheraton Hotel for a month while we worked on them, performing local concerts in the evenings. Somewhere in the middle of all of that, we found time to go to Disneyland. Someone had given us free passes, so we went to Disneyland whenever we could. We probably went ten or twelve times, and to this day I still love to go there!"

About the same time the television series was being taped, a film producer in Hollywood put together a film project in Hawaii for Heritage. The project encompassed all of the Hawaiian Islands. Some of the most scenic spots had been scouted out for the production. Terry said he would never forget the day the group was filming on the rocks on Oahu, outside of Waikiki. "We were all dressed up—the guys in their suits and the girls in light-colored chiffon dresses. The ocean was in the background. The breeze was gently blowing the chiffon dresses. The girls had spent a lot of time getting ready. Their hair and faces were perfect. It was just a beautiful shot. Well, that day the waves were bigger than usual, and just as we were in the middle of shooting, this big wave came along and totally washed over us. In one second, we went from being picture-perfect to being drowned rats! Max quickly looked over at us, and without missing a beat, mouthed 'Keep singing! Just keep singing!' So there we were, totally dripping wet, lip-synching away like nothing unusual was happening!"

Max began introducing a more professional edge to the group's sound. They hadn't yet used lighting or choreography. Max took the group to Thousand Oaks, California, where the *Faith for Today* television programs were produced. "These people were experts on what looked good on stage and on television," Terry said. "They taught us how to have stage presence and how to use production elements like lighting and sound."

Greg and Terry were responsible for the sound system, so they went out and bought some new equipment, like dimmer switches. It was pretty primitive at first, although they eventually were able to build a professional sound system—complete with equalization and stage monitors—with the help of a sound-system expert in Hollywood.

"We were never able to get the stage monitors quite right," explained Terry, "We had to keep adjusting the volume levels and relying on Max's signals to us from stage. He'd point his finger up or down until we got it right. Because this could be a little distracting during a concert, we decided to create a system where Max wore a belt with doorbell buttons on it. All he had to do was push the right button and a light would come on, letting the sound man know whether to turn the stage monitor volume up or down. It was a flawless system, except for one thing—Max couldn't find the buttons on his belt. So, we tried foot switches, but Max had difficulty finding the switch while he was singing. We ended up scrapping all our ideas and going back to just using hand signals."

As the Heritage Singers ministry expanded and their popularity grew, Max found himself having to choose between many wonderful opportunities. The group just could not keep up with the demand for their concerts. It seemed that God was opening doors faster than the singers could walk through them.

A local Saab dealer loaned seven cars to the singers during a crusade in Walla Walla, Washington

CHAPTER FOUR

Growing Together

IN 1974 THE HERITAGE SINGERS WERE ASKED TO PERFORM AT THE WORLD'S FAIR IN SPOKANE, WASHINGTON. They also received an invitation to provide the music for a new television series, *Come Alive,* which was hosted by speaker Roy Naden from Australia. Because the group was in so much demand, Max felt God was telling him to expand the ministry. He decided to form a second group and split up the bookings geographically between the two groups. The original group would be known as Heritage Singers USA and would tour primarily on the West Coast. The new group would be called Heritage II and would tour the East Coast and Midwest. Max invited Rick Lange to direct the new group. Rick had performed with Max when they were both part of the Rose City Singers.

As an evangelist's son, Rick grew up singing. "From about nine years old on, I sang in a quartet, night after night, at the crusades my dad was involved with," he explained. "I then joined the Texas Adventist Youth Association under the leadership of John Thurber, and we did up to six concerts a day!

"When my parents moved to

Pam and Rick Lange

Portland, Oregon, my dad went to work at the medical laboratory that sponsored the Rose City Singers. I became part of the singing group, under the direction of Max Mace. When Max began expanding into religious outreach and formed the Heritage Singers, I remember my dad encouraging him. My dad told him, 'Just follow your dream, Max.'

Although I couldn't be a part of the new group at that time since I was going to college, my wife, Pam, and I joined Heritage later when Max needed a leader for a second group, Heritage II."

In the fall of 1974, Heritage II met for the first time at the Heritage ranch in Placerville. Duane Hamilton remembered that first music camp. "We gathered at the ranch for a month and learned enough material to record two albums. We also spent the month soaking up the Heritage experience. Although we had attended some of the group's concerts before, we were not prepared for the wall of sound that came from them. It was impressive. Max's group had about 16 singers—a small choir. After music camp, we headed to Glendale, California to record our new albums. I remember being impressed when I found out we were recording at the same studio, and with the same engineer, as Barry White's hit 'Love's Theme.'"

After some touring in Southern California, Heritage II left for a month-long crusade in Littleton, Colorado. Since the group was new, they had a repertoire of only 20 songs. They needed approximately 100 songs for the crusade. "In the mornings we'd get together and listen to Heritage albums," Rick said, "learning three or four new songs each day. In the afternoons we would participate in home visitations and then come back to perform the songs we had learned earlier that day. Then we'd do it all over again the next day. By the time the crusade was over we could perform a large number of songs in concert, giving us a variety of material we could comfortably draw from for our concerts."

Heritage II spent the remainder of their first season touring the Eastern and Midwestern States, and even recorded a third

front: Pete, Gerry, Carol, Jim, Perry, Val
back: Lucy, Max, Jeff, Debbie, Dick, Terry

album before the year was finished. Under Rick's direction, the group was able to develop its own identity while maintaining the much-loved "Heritage" sound. "The early days in Heritage II were not easy," Rick said. "As a new Heritage group we were not well known, and there was some question as to whether the group could hold its own financially." Thankfully, Heritage II albums began selling well and concerts filled up. New music and singers gave Heritage II a contemporary edge, making them particularly popular with the young people.

Joanne Velting Mullin remembered being a freshman at Andrews University in Berrien Springs, Michigan and memorizing the Heritage albums. "I'd put the LPs on the spindle, and using a candle for a microphone, I'd sing along until I knew the songs by heart. I learned all of the Heritage music, and especially enjoyed the music of Heritage II.

"Whenever I was asked to sing for church, I'd always choose a Heritage Singers song. I patterned everything I did musically after them. I collected as much sheet music as I could, and whenever a new album came out, I'd buy it. The music was fresh and contemporary, and it spoke to me. I loved their sound. I envisioned myself on stage, singing with them.

"Eventually Heritage put a concert on at Andrews University. This was my chance to audition. After their concert, I joined the 30 others who had come to do the same thing. Later, I sent a tape to Max. Within a few weeks Max called. 'We like the sound of your voice,' he said, 'and we think you'd blend in with our group, except for one problem. You have a noticeable lisp, and

I'm afraid it would show up in our recordings. I'm sorry, but it's not going to work out.'

"Well, I wasn't going to get this close and not make it into the Heritage Singers," recalled Joanne. "Somehow I persuaded Max to give me time to do some speech therapy and then send in another tape. That summer I found myself going to speech therapy with second graders at an elementary school near my home. I sat in little chairs, learning how to pronounce letters, as if I was learning a foreign language. It felt so awkward. I was using unfamiliar combinations of muscles. The exercises I had to do at home were met with much skepticism on the part of my family. 'You sound funny,' my sister would say. Or, 'You sounded better before.' But I was very determined.

"After hours of practice and many awkward attempts, I finally got the courage to make a second audition tape for Max. This time he liked it and invited me to join the group for music camp at the ranch. I was thrilled! I was to be in Heritage II, the group that toured the eastern half of the United States. Even though I wasn't going to be in Max's group, I was still going to be a Heritage Singer! I packed up my Ford Pinto and drove from Michigan to California all by myself in 30 hours.

"In the days that followed, I soaked up everything Max taught us about blending and harmonizing, and about putting a smile into our voices. I began to feel more comfortable and started connecting with the other singers. I got it. I could do this. It felt good to just let it happen and to blend in with the other voices and disappear into that velvety blanket of sound. It made chills run up my spine!

"In a matter of days Max transformed us. We went from a group of strangers trying to prove ourselves worthy of being

Heritage II front: Mark, Sue, Rhonda, Louie, middle: Barbie, Duane, Doug, Pam, back: Frank John, Carole Lynn, Rick, Omera, Reger

Heritage Singers to a circle of friends blending our voices in perfect unison. We sang as one voice.

"Our crash course in how to be a Heritage Singer also forced us to put aside our personal importance. As individual singers, we may have been an elite few, but within the group context, we were equals, just like one instrument in an orchestra is equal to the next. This was tough for some of the singers who were soloists by nature. It felt almost like they were being asked to become invisible. They had to learn to give up the need to be heard and acknowledged. Success in Heritage meant making your voice so transparent that it imperceptibly overlapped with the person next to you to sound like one single voice. If you stuck out, you weren't doing it right.

"As Max worked with us on style and technique, Rick helped us polish up the Heritage II material. Before long, we had learned enough songs to start sounding and feeling like Heritage Singers."

"Even though Max was faced with this situation every time new singers came into the group," said Joanne, "he handled each new combination of singers with fresh energy and enthusiasm. He never knew what he was going to have to deal with. It didn't matter that concerts were scheduled to begin within days, or that an album needed to be recorded as soon as possible, Max always had a great deal of patience. He inspired in us the desire to do our best.

"And Lucy," recalled Joanne, "she had enough energy to keep all of us going. She put our performance wardrobe together and stocked the albums, tapes, and sheet music. She also figured out where everyone was going to sleep, fixed and served meals, and cleaned up after everybody. Under her supervision, the Heritage Singer support team was organized and prepared for another touring season."

"The early days on the road with Heritage II were a lot of fun," said Joanne. "We acted like high school kids on a class trip, playing silly tricks on each other and exploring the different places we traveled to. It was a big adventure. I remember piling into our old Continental Trailways bus and heading to Medford, Oregon for our first evangelistic crusade experience. We were there for two or three weeks, performing every night at the meetings and visiting people during the day. We also had to keep learning new material.

"As during all crusades, we lived in a motel and were given a small daily allowance for food. Our evening meal was usually a potluck dinner provided by the local church members. The rest of the day was up to us. Our food allowance at that time was three dollars per day. Even then, it didn't go very far. We could eat maybe one meal at a fast food restaurant for that amount. So being the ingenious and thrifty kids that we were, we pooled our money and bought groceries to prepare meals in our motel rooms. Some of us had hot plates for cooking up macaroni and cheese or hot cereal. Most of us relied on bread, peanut butter, and applesauce. We created a refrigerator of sorts by draping a blanket over the in-room air conditioner unit and turning it on full blast. That's how we kept our milk and fruit fresh. We even boiled water in an electric teapot so we could cook our vegetarian hotdogs.

"Crusades were a great time for us to get to know each other better and to rehearse a lot of music every day. We also got to know the local people pretty well, even borrowing their cars while we were there. Of course, some of these cars were well past their prime. One car of mine had a hole in the floor, right in the front seat. You could see the road going by under your feet," laughed Joanne. "Another one of our cars didn't have a

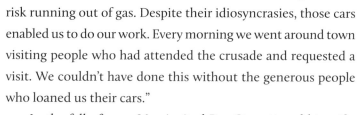
Buz and Kathy Starrett

working gas gauge. So, whoever used it had to fill it up first—or risk running out of gas. Despite their idiosyncrasies, those cars enabled us to do our work. Every morning we went around town visiting people who had attended the crusade and requested a visit. We couldn't have done this without the generous people who loaned us their cars."

In the fall of 1975, Max invited Buz Starrett and his wife, Kathy, to take over the musical direction of Heritage II. Rick and his wife, Pam, returned to California where they wrote several children's songs and developed the Heritage Bear program for kids. Buz remembered, "I not only inherited Rick's singers, I also got his performance suits. I have a smaller build, so alterations had to be made. I ended up with two suits, and the only thing that fit me was my dress boots."

The early days weren't easy and tested their fortitude. "I remember doing a crusade in Columbus, Georgia," said Buz. "There were no motels to speak of in that town, so we ended up renting some apartments. They must have been old military housing, because they felt like barracks. Anyway, at night the cockroaches would come out, and they were huge. Whenever we turned on a light we could hear them scurrying to hide. One night Kathy and I were about ready to fall asleep when we heard a loud 'boingggg!' A spring from our mattress had popped up through the sheet!"

In addition to the sometimes less than ideal living conditions, Buz was faced with the challenge of finding the group's unique sound. As the musical director he struggled with building on the established Heritage sound while developing his own take on it.

The adjustment to Buz's style was hard for some of the singers. They weren't used to working from printed music. Many of them couldn't even read music. Joanne said, "It was so different from what we were used to. It wasn't standing in a circle, listening to each other, and blending as one voice, as Max had taught us. The feeling of the songs, the sweetness of the harmonies, the seamless blending of our voices and the integrity of our concerts all seemed to get lost in the process. It didn't feel like Heritage anymore."

"Here we were, kind of thrown together," Buz said. "We were learning how to blend our voices, as well as our lives and personalities. It was not easy for any of us." Finally, the group had a heart-to-heart meeting to try to settle the differences and establish areas of authority. Joanne recalled, "It was the lowest point of the season. This wasn't in the brochure and this wasn't the Heritage Singer adventure we had joined up for. It was so uncomfortable to be in the midst of all of that emotion and conflict. There were many differences of opinion among us, but everything was laid out on the table and painfully confronted." Some good did come out of the meeting because they all prayed together. Joanne said, "We rededicated our ministry and asked God to work through us despite our differences. In this way, it became a time of spiritual renewal. Somehow, in baring our souls and facing painful issues, we began to heal."

The dynamics of the two Heritage groups were quite unique unto themselves. Each group was a part of the Heritage ministry, but in a very different way. Accommodating for those differences and blending the ministries into one was challenging at times. Joanne said, "We needed to realize that each of us had our own unique gifts and to allow for differences. We were not meant to be homogeneous, just harmonious. In the meantime, we all had to ride on that bus together for hours every day and keep getting on stage and putting our energy into our nightly concerts. When our relationships faltered, music became the glue that held us together. Singing allowed us to connect on an equal level and encourage each others' gifts."

In spite of the conflicts, Heritage II had a successful season, developing its own following, especially in the South and the East. They even began receiving invitations to return to some of the places they had been to the previous season. Buz remembered one church they went back to several times, "It was a Baptist church in Gainesville, Georgia. The people really liked us there. One night after a concert a man was talking to Ken Smith, and he said, 'You're talking to the next president of the United States!' We didn't recognize him at the time, but it was Jimmy Carter, who would indeed become our next president."

Another church Buz remembered well was an active charismatic congregation in Texas. The Heritage Singers had never witnessed people speaking in tongues and being "healed" before. "This particular church met in a beautiful auditorium, and their service was professionally produced," Buz recalled. "They had a band, a great sound system, and lights. It was quite a place, and we were looking forward to singing there. But, we didn't realize that this was a charismatic church. Before we came out on stage, their band started playing some very contemporary, very rousing music, and it just kept getting bigger and louder. It was as if they were working the audience into an emotional frenzy. Then, suddenly, the music got really soft and eerie."

People from the audience started coming to the front. Three or four men would gather around someone who had come forward as the pastor placed his hand on their forehead. The person would then just fall over backwards into the arms of the other men. This happened several times. During all of this, individuals throughout the audience would burst into unintelligible languages and look like they were having a seizure. It was a scary thing to watch. All of the Heritage Singers felt pretty nervous, and wondered if they should even be there.

"We prayed about it, and decided to proceed with the concert," Buz said, "but we changed our program and only sang very quiet songs, mostly hymns. We got through it okay, but when we were getting ready to leave, a lady from the audience came up to our bass player and bus driver, Doug Botimer, and said, 'I've been told that your group is going to be in a very bad accident.'" Naturally, her comment didn't do much for Doug's confidence or the group's peace of mind. Fortunately, she was wrong about the accident, but the group never forgot the unsettling experience."

"We were getting quite an education out there on the road," said Joanne. "Being exposed to such a variety of people and worship styles helped us realize that God's children are everywhere and worship in many different ways. As the concerts rolled by, our little group became more mature, emotionally and spiritually. We learned how to be more patient and tolerant. We learned that it really helps to pray about things and trust God to lead us through difficult situations. At the same time, our overall sound gradually evolved into something more complex—with richer harmonies, and at times, even soulful. It seemed that Heritage II was coming into its own."

"We had some phenomenal talent in Heritage II," said Lucy. "One distinguishing feature of Heritage II was it had African-American singers in the group. Reger Smith, Duane Hamilton, and Rhonda Green Ramzy were all in the first Heritage II. Omera Dawson and Lynn Davis were also in the group for a while. Gerald Smith joined the second season. It was extraordinary because there were still so many churches with segregated congregations."

Reger Smith added, "Having Black singers in Heritage, though not always well-received, ended up opening a lot of new opportunities for the group. We were able to get into venues we wouldn't otherwise have been invited to."

Heritage II was invited to perform in African-American churches in New York City and Chicago—places the Heritage Singers had never been. Buz told of one concert they gave in New York City. It was a large church. They must have done a good job promoting the concert because the church was packed an hour before the event. By the time the concert was to begin, people were crowded into the aisles and up into the choir loft, even out the doors and into the street. Children were crawling up onto the stage. Some people were even climbing up on top of things or jumping up and down behind the crowd, just so they could see. The confusion escalated into a dangerous situation.

"It became frightening," Buz remembered, "because the people were yelling and were trying to get inside, and we couldn't calm them down. Duane Hamilton got up and tried to reason with them, even promising that we'd do a second concert for those who couldn't get into the church. The aisles were so packed that people couldn't have gotten out if they wanted to. Adding to the confusion, the church was built directly over a subway. So every time the subway went through, the whole church rumbled and shook. Between the subway and the people who were shouting, we couldn't hear a thing coming out of our monitors. I think we sang only three songs and then had to stop. We apologized to the people and told them the only way they were going to get to hear us that day was to buy an album. We sold albums for three hours until we were completely sold out! We emptied our bus!"

Not all of the East Coast churches welcomed Heritage II. There were a few Caucasian congregations that made things difficult. Buz remembered a crusade that Heritage II participated with in Columbus, Georgia, shortly after he and Kathy joined the group. He said, "We had arranged to use one of the local churches to rehearse. Back in those days, they had one church for Caucasian people and another one for African-Americans. We were supposed to practice in the church for Caucasians. I'll never forget this. There was an elder in the church who was there to meet us, and he actually refused to let our African-American singers into his church! We had to practice somewhere else. It blew my mind that this sort of thing still went on."

"I remember another time when we were somewhere in Texas," shared Buz. "Our concert was planned for a Saturday night, but we had a couple of days off prior to that. Some of the singers went to get their haircut at a local barbershop and saw one of our promotional posters in the window. The men in the barbershop told our guys they had heard that the Ku Klux Klan was planning to burn the church down because of the African-American kids in the group. We prayed about what to do and discussed it with the concert organizers, and ended up canceling the concert. These are the kinds of things we faced in those days."

Lucy recalled a time when the group performed at a church in Southern California. They were unable to find a home for one of the African-American singers to stay in. "All of the other singers had been signed up for by the church members, but no one wanted to take this singer home with them. The pastor said so right in front of her. Very upset, and rightfully so, she ran out of the church. Max and I had to go looking for her. When we found her, we asked our hosts for the evening if we could take her home with us. We were amazed and appalled that this kind of racism and prejudice still existed in the United States, especially among Christians," said Lucy.

Daily study and prayer helped the group face these and many other challenges. Each morning when they got on the bus, they spent an hour in quiet time. "We would ride down the road in total silence just reading, studying, and spending time in prayer. It was an especially good way to start off our day," said Joanne.

"The spiritual experience of traveling on the road and singing together as a group each evening is something we'll always remember," said Buz. "Once we arrived at our destination and had everything set up for the concert, we would spend about 30 minutes of worship time together. That was always a highlight. It was time to get in-tune for what we were trying to present. It was not just a concert. We were doing something that was making a spiritual impact and making a difference in people's lives, including our own."

"We appreciated Buz and Kathy," said Joanne. "They were the kindest, most loving people you could ever meet. They obviously cared about each one of us like we were their own kids. They truly loved the Lord, and it was clear that they were sincere and had the best of intentions. None of us could have known what we were getting into. We all just wanted to do the right thing, but disagreed about what that was. At the end of the season, we were all asked whether we wanted to stay in Heritage II for the next season. That's when I decided to leave Heritage, and Tammy Taylor was hired to fill my spot."

"I wanted to be a Heritage Singer from the moment I heard my first concert as a teenager," Tammy recalled. "I never thought it would be a reality for me. One night the Heritage Singers' New Creation group came to Little Rock and my friends encouraged me to audition. Not long after that I was asked to join the group and was overjoyed!

"With God's help, Buz and Kathy put together a group of the most cohesive people you can imagine. We were a happy family. Throughout our tour I cannot think of one discord among any of us. We just meshed well. Even when we were exhausted, we always held each other up. I'll always be grateful to Buz and Kathy, who were caring and compassionate leaders," said Tammy.

Buz and Kathy Starrett decided to change the name of the group to "New Creation," signifying the uniqueness of the group, as well as laying the groundwork for recording an album. During the summer break, Buz and Max traveled to London, England, to record the orchestration for the new album. Buz remembered the excitement he felt at getting to work with Toby Foster, Paul Stillwell, and of course, Dave Williamson, who arranged the scores and conducted the sessions. "I've always enjoyed hearing the orchestration on the *This is the Time I Must Sing* album. And other than running through the airport to catch our plane, carrying heavy spools of freshly recorded tape, Max and I had a really good time."

Duane remembered coming back to the Heritage Ranch in the fall and learning the new parts for the album. "These new arrangements were different than anything Heritage had done vocally in the past," he said. "We were very proud of our sound and excited about the upcoming tour." It was also the only time Buz and Kathy spent at the ranch. Buz said, "The two groups each had their own individual rehearsals, as well as time to get together for worship and meals. I remember praying together in a large circle, and I remember singing. It was a very special time."

While at the ranch Buz also discussed his ideas with Max for what he wanted to do musically. "It was during that conversation that I realized that I couldn't go too far off the Heritage path, because we really were just a second group of Heritage Singers," remembered Buz. "At one point, Max looked at me and said, 'Buz, you really need to do your own thing.' He was very nice about it. He was just being honest with me. I didn't really give it much thought at the time. But in looking back, I can see that the conversation was the beginning, in some sense, of the change that was coming. It wasn't anything I had been thinking about, but I did feel that God was leading."

After practicing for a month, New Creation started its tour with a crusade in Denver. They recorded the vocals for their album in the daytime and worked the crusade in the evenings. Duane recalled, "The experience of recording the New Creation album took our music to a new level. I felt I could finally enjoy the group from a musical standpoint. The vocal arrangements were interesting and more complex. We also worked on staging and choreography, making our concerts visually interesting as well. Things were going well, and I felt the promise of the first two years was coming to fruition."

Behind the scenes, however, there was an underlying insecurity regarding the future of the group. Buz had been hearing things that implied financial difficulties in the Heritage organization and sensed that some changes were being considered. He felt that the group's future role in the Heritage organization was uncertain. He believed that if Max was forced to cut expenses, there would be a good chance that New Creation could be taken off the road.

Max and Lucy always wanted the two groups to be unified as one ministry. It was not Max's way to have a ministry pulling in opposite directions. "There's only one Heritage," he always said. Heritage had always been about wholeness and harmony, about working together with one purpose. Max would have preferred to reconcile whatever differences there were between the two groups.

About this time, New Creation had a crusade in Lincoln, Nebraska. While there, some Lincoln-based investors approached Buz and offered to provide financial backing if he'd split off from Heritage and start a new group. The group would be based in Lincoln and would work as part of an evangelistic team. This would enable him to keep doing the musical evangelism that he loved, with the added benefits of having more creative control and more financial security. From Buz's perspective, it seemed like God was opening a door.

Buz prayed about it, and he talked to the singers about it. By then, it was going in only one direction. They voted unanimously in favor of Buz accepting the new opportunity. From the singers' perspective, they really didn't have anything to lose. Already feeling separate from the Heritage organization, they no doubt considered the change to be a welcome adventure. Some of them had never even been to the Heritage ranch. To them, Max was a distant concept. They felt loyal to Buz, their day-to-day leader.

To someone who wasn't there, it seems absurd that Max was not brought into this decision, this little change in plans that would have a huge impact on the Heritage ministry. Buz didn't just walk away from Heritage. He also took the group with him. It also left Max wondering how to get his bus back. And, although this was a great disappointment to Max, he wished Buz well. He never wanted to hold someone back from doing what they felt God was leading them to do.

In the summer of 1977, New Creation became "Harvest Celebration," moving its headquarters to Lincoln, Nebraska, under Buz's leadership. Not all of the singers stayed with Buz. Duane decided to join Heritage USA at Max's invitation. Duane said, "After having been through the previous season of seeing New Creation finally reach its musical potential, I could not face starting over again. So I accepted Max's invitation."

Over the years the Heritage ministry has been through many hard times. "I've learned that it always leads to something better," explained Max. "Sometimes we have to confront our situation and choose a new direction. We have to admit our faults and ask for God's healing. But we're not alone. God suffers with us. He gives us new opportunities to turn our losses and disappointments into something good."

During the three years that Heritage II/New Creation had been operating, Max was able to expand Heritage USA outside of the United States. Invitations to tour other countries were coming in, along with offers of financial sponsorship for the trips. Duane and Joanne both joined Heritage USA just in time to be included in the group's first trip to Central America and Brazil.

Prior to leaving for Brazil, Heritage did a series of five concerts with the gospel singer Doug Oldham. The series began on the West Coast, and upon the group's return from Brazil, continued on the East Coast. Sharing a concert with Doug Oldham exposed the group to a whole new concert experience. The concerts were professionally promoted and tickets were sold. The venues they played were large civic auditoriums with professional lighting and stage managers. Joanne remembered, "We were energized by the experience and enjoyed spending time with Doug and his group, some of whom were part of the original Heritage Singers group. It was all very exciting."

The months that followed were a transitional time for

Heritage and Heritage II meet in Denver, Colorado

Heritage. Max decided he needed to lighten up his travel schedule by focusing on concerts in the West and only traveling on weekends. This new group would be under his direction and would be known simply as The Heritage Singers. The full-time group on the road, under the direction of Duane Hamilton, became known as Heritage Singers USA and continued touring all over the United States. It was a tough transition for Duane, learning to adapt to his new responsibilities. But in spite of all of the changes and difficulties, Duane said he would always treasure his time in Heritage. "In looking back, I can see how it exposed me to so many things, so many people, and so many opportunities."

"The day-to-day experience of being a Heritage Singer shaped our character in ways we didn't even realize," said Joanne. "When we were not at our best, God gave us the strength we needed. When you see God working through you day after day, expanding your mediocre efforts into something that changes other peoples' lives, it gets your attention. It changes who you are."

CHAPTER FIVE

Staying in Tune

Do all of these things; but most important, love each other. Love is what holds you all together in perfect unity. Let the peace that Christ gives control your thinking, because you were all called together in one body to have peace. Always be thankful.
— *Colossians 2:12-15, NCV*

Being a Heritage Singer meant spending hours a day on a bus. We were a typical bunch of college-aged kids trying to entertain ourselves. Some of us read, others slept, many talked endlessly, and some just zoned out under headphones. At times we drove each other crazy and other times we had a blast. We just did whatever we could to get through the day. Whether it was playing practical jokes on each other, writing letters, playing games, working on new songs, or finding new positions to sleep in, we all managed.

One of the things Heritage II did to pass the time was form a kazoo band. They each got a kazoo and worked out their parts and did rousing and zany renditions of some of our more lively material—made truly amazing by Steve Evenson's snappy solos and counter melodies. They even made a recording of it! Imagine, eight kazoos doing a Dixieland jazz version of "I've Never Loved Him Better than Today."

Heritage II Kazoo band (front: Rick, Judy, Carole Lynn, Barbie, Frank John back: Duane, Mark, Pam, Louie)

Kevin Hale and Ron Edgerton put together a radio show. Their traffic and weather report was classic. Of course, their favorite part was the interview with various members of the group. They even got together in the motel rooms on our days off with sound equipment and recorded spoof jingles and commercials.

Mark Honaker entertained with his "Spies in the Night" puppet show. He used the puppets we had for children's songs in our concerts and stuck them out between the curtains hanging in the back of our bus, putting on a whole show for us.

To help pass the time, the singers also had Rook tournaments on the bus. Jennifer Schmunk and Lucy were the champions. The guys had a hard time getting over the fact that the girls always won. They were forever calling for a rematch.

Eric Haapalo said, "After an adrenalin-pumping concert, some of us would cluster around a few bus seats and start singing a traditional gospel song, such as 'Will the Circle Be Unbroken.'"

"We were a mischievous bunch," said Terry Mace. "I remember when we were in Chicago for a big Saturday night concert. We were staying in a high-rise hotel,

Max and Lucy, Rita and Jerry

right downtown, which was quite a unique experience for us. Jim McDonald, Pete McLeod, Greg Mace, and my brother Perry Mace and I got into a shaving cream fight that encompassed two floors of the hotel. We were up and down the stairwells shooting shaving cream all over the walls and floors. Fortunately, Max caught us before the hotel management did. We were still in trouble though. But that's just the kind of thing we'd do after being cooped up on the bus all day."

Throughout the years there have been many times when the ability to forgive, and to ask for forgiveness, has helped the group survive life on the road. We all had to learn how to be tolerant of each other's different personalities and how to give people the benefit of the doubt, as well as try to see the best in people. It was how we stayed in tune with each other.

Looking back on the early days, Max remembered the differences he and Jerry Leiske had. Sadly, things did not work out between them, and the Canadian singers split off to form their own group, The Heritage Family. This resulted in some

confusion among their audience about the two groups' identities. Over the years there remained some unresolved feelings between the two groups. The situation remained a burden for Max. He prayed about it and longed for closure and healing.

One day while traveling down the road outside of Nashville, Tennessee, the Heritage Family bus pulled out right in front of them on the freeway. "Let's follow them," Max said. The two groups ended up meeting at a restaurant where Max and Jerry were able to talk and work things out. They remain good friends today. Understanding and forgiveness opened the way for healing to begin. The odds of running into each other were small, considering the two groups traveled in different parts of the country.

Max talked a lot about forgiveness and how it kept him in tune with God. He says it has become very important for him to ask others for forgiveness and to be able to forgive. Only when we understand what's standing in our way, can we open ourselves to healing and true inner peace, said Max. "Forgiveness is not something you do for the other person," he said. "It's something you do for yourself."

Max wanted to ask his former schoolteacher for forgiveness for something he had done many years earlier. He had lied to his teacher about doing work that he really hadn't, and it continued to bother him. He decided that if ever he were given the opportunity, he would make it right. That opportunity came one night after a concert when he and Lucy met the people they would be staying with for the night. Their hosts turned out to be Max's former teacher and her husband! He didn't allow the opportunity to go by without asking for her forgiveness. After many years, the guilt was gone.

Max continues to look for opportunities to talk about the importance of forgiveness. During a recent concert in the

Northwest, Max felt impressed to encourage anyone in the audience who might be struggling to forgive a family member, a pastor, a co-worker, or whomever, to let go and make things right. Little did he know, the Holy Spirit had been working on a woman's heart in the audience that very night. After the concert was over, the woman shared her story with one of the singers. Apparently, ever since she was a little girl, she had carried hatred in her heart towards her father. He had molested her and she was unable to forgive him. This internal bitterness had caused her great heartache throughout her life. However, that night as she heard the words to the song "Forgive Me," she was finally able to let go and completely forgive her father. She said she felt peace for the first time since her childhood.

Former singer Conna Bond said she too had to learn a lesson in forgiveness. For years she held a grudge against Val Mace. Conna always dreamed of becoming a Heritage Singer. She attended the group's concerts, and when she was only nine years old, she met Val Mace for the first time.

"Val was about 14-years-old and a very visible part of the group," Conna said. "I wanted to be just like her. After the concert I marched up to Val to talk to her and the other girls in the group, and I told her, 'I'm going to sing with the Heritage Singers some day!' I'm sure they had heard it all before from little girl groupies like me. Val turned to me and said in a teasing voice, 'Which part are you going to sing? Bass?'

"I was hurt and decided she was the meanest girl I'd ever met. It's painful to admit now, but I harbored resentment against her up into my late 20's. The last thing on my mind was singing with the Heritage Singers.

"Then one day, my Heritage Singer friend Dave Bell called

Val with Conna Bond on Val's wedding day.

me and invited me to come to a concert and to audition. He and I had sung together quite a bit in high school. Dave told me Heritage was looking for a second soprano and he thought of me. I told him I was settling down and wasn't interested and was too old to be gallivanting around the country. The truth was I was determined to avoid getting stuck on a bus with Val, who wounded my little girl spirit all those years ago.

"Well, Dave had other ideas, and apparently so did the Lord. The next time Heritage was in town, Dave called me again. He was getting ready to go back to his teaching profession, but told me that singing with Heritage had been one of the best experiences of his life. He knew I'd never get the opportunity again. The group was planning to stop their full time tours after that year. The next day I went to the concert and auditioned for Max. A month later I was headed for Placerville to begin practicing for the upcoming tour. It all happened so quickly it was almost surreal!

"The most surreal part of all was finding myself rooming with Val night after night in the same hotel room. We had plenty of time to talk! I told her my little story about how she had hurt my feelings when I was a little girl. She was shocked and appalled and apologized profusely. Suddenly I realized how ridiculous it had been for me to hold a grudge against her all those years!

"Val became one of my dearest friends and companions on that tour. What a blessing! And to think that I might still be holding that grudge today if Dave hadn't been so intent on recruiting me, even against my will! That grudge could have poisoned my life permanently. But God knew exactly where I needed to be to take care of that little matter of forgiveness, and my heart was healed on a deeper level in the process.

"While I was with Heritage, I spent six hours a day on the bus reading my Bible and a little book called 'Christ's Object Lessons.' During that time I experienced a true heart conversion and gained an understanding of my personal need for the Savior.

"Toward the end of the tour we spent Thanksgiving in Orlando. At one of our Florida concerts, I met the man who would become my husband. My dear Heritage friends were there for our first date, and I will always love them—especially Val, Nita and Lauren.

"We've not kept up with each other much in recent years. I moved to Orlando, got married, went to law school, had four children, and now I live in Texas. Nineteen years have gone in a flash, and I've seen Heritage maybe three or four times. But it's always a happy reunion. Their faces are just as precious to me now as they were then. Seeing the Heritage Singers is always a huge reminder that God's ways are so much bigger and better than our ways. As my grandmother used to tell me, 'He is silently planning for thee, in love.' This really rang true for me when I was honored to be one of Val's bridesmaids when she got married!"

God's presence was always with the Heritage Singers. Sometimes the group needed an extra measure of God's protection too. One day when the group was doing a concert on the south side of Chicago, Steve Evenson left to take a nap on the bus before the concert because he wasn't feeling well. The bus was parked on a city street in front of the church. The door had two vertical panels that separated from the center when opened. In order to lock the door, they had to use two separate padlocks, one for each panel. To let himself onto the bus that day, Steve unlocked only one of the panels.

Soon after Steve had settled in for his nap, he heard some loud banging. He got out of his seat and walked to the front of the bus to see where the noise was coming from. Standing just outside the bus door was a very large man with a hammer and chisel trying to smash the locked padlock. Apparently, he hadn't noticed the unlocked one! Steve, who was also one of the group's bus drivers, knew exactly what to do—he leaned over and just

GRACE NOTES:

"Sunday night at Calvary Temple in Seattle, I was the one for whom the Heritage Singers sang 'Someone is Praying for You.' It was a special request from my family because I have cancer.

"Thank you for that very special evening—not only for the special request, but the wonderful inspirational concert. It was the first time we have attended one of your concerts and it certainly will not be the last. Thank you for your prayers. I will be praying for you too. I know God is in control of my life and I am trusting in His word. I know the day of miracles isn't over."

———

"I am writing to share this praise report. One of the women in our church brought her niece to your concert. Her niece is not a Christian. She was afflicted with a malignant tumor in her neck. She says that toward the end of the program she was deeply moved by one of the songs. She went forward at the end of the concert and accepted Christ as her personal savior. When she returned to her seat, she was full of peace and she put her trust in the Lord.

"She received a touch of the Master's hand, for when she went to see her doctor, not only was the cancer gone, the whole tumor was missing! Praise God! Our God does a complete and perfect job. Who says the Lord doesn't perform miracles of healing? He's the same yesterday, today and forever. We are the ones who must boldly cling on to His promises."

laid on the air horn. The guy jumped up so fast that he smacked his head on the side mirror, breaking it off. Peering into the bus and realizing Steve was inside, he yelled, "Hey! How did you get in there?!" His attempted break-in foiled, he stuffed his hammer and chisel into his bib overalls and took off down the street, no doubt thinking someone else had beat him to the job!

Life on the bus was always interesting. Frank John Salas remembered what it was like to travel for hours on end, day after day on that bus. "Those were tough times. That old bus got so cold in the winter! I was the driver, and I'd have the heat on full blast. Then someone would yell up from the back of the bus, 'Hey, Frank! Turn up the BTUs!'

"We also didn't always realize how far away our next concert was, until we got on the bus the next morning and looked at the map. One time we were booked at a place that was at least a 10-hour drive from where we were the night before. By the time we got to the church where we were supposed to be singing that night, it was packed full of people waiting for the concert to begin. We hauled in our equipment, set it up, changed our clothes, and came back and did our concert. The people waited for us the whole time!"

Dave Mauck recalled arriving at a hotel after a long day on the bus and finding out that Clint Eastwood was staying in their hotel. "The girls gasped!" Dave laughed, "and so did most of us guys. It's amazing how a possible celebrity encounter can revive a tired group. We unloaded our things and moved into our rooms. I'm not sure what everyone else did that day, but Tiger (Dick Bird) and I had a singular strategy—find Dirty Harry! We walked all over the hotel and, sleuths that we were, found out that he was staying in the Barbra Streisand Suite. We quickly headed in that direction. We didn't really think we'd see him; we were just having fun. As we proceeded up the stairway, engrossed in our conversation about all things Clint Eastwood, we suddenly stopped dead in our tracks. Coming down the steps toward us was the man himself!

"Mustering as much nonchalance as I could, I greeted him.

'Hi, Clint,' I said. He looked so much taller in person. 'Hi, guys,' he said, as he continued down the stairs. Not wanting to look like stalkers, we continued up the stairs as if we really had someplace to go. Tiger was quick to reprimand me for not referring to him as 'Mr. Eastwood.' At the top of the stairs we came up with a new strategy. We decided to turn around and follow him to see if we could talk to him, at least for a minute. We saw that he was headed for the pool. As we narrowed in on him, we could see through the pool fence that he had taken off his shirt and was getting comfortable in a chaise lounge. It was a beautiful sunny day, but not very many people were at the pool. Tiger and I saw our opportunity, and we approached Mr. Eastwood. Never being shy, Tiger opened the conversation by telling him that we were Heritage Singers and that we were in town doing a concert. You know, a casual conversation between celebrities—like, 'Yeah, we're important, too. Just another day in the life.'

"Gracious under fire, Clint told us that he was in town scouting sites for a movie he was making. He told us he really enjoyed music and asked us where we were 'playing.' We couldn't believe we were having a conversation with Clint Eastwood! Somehow, we had the presence of mind to invite him to our concert.

"Now feeling totally at ease, Tiger mentioned that he was also a television personality. He had been on the *Come Alive with the Heritage Singers* television series. Somehow, in the course of that short conversation, they discovered that they had the same make-up man. I jumped in and asked Clint if he would like some of our music. He said 'yes,' so we ran off to the bus to grab some albums. When we returned to the pool, Clint was standing next to a lady getting his picture taken 'for her daughter.' We said our goodbyes and left, convinced that was one of the coolest encounters we could ever have.

"A few months later we were in Los Angeles singing at a series of meetings," said Dave. "I was walking with Max when we met the pastor and one of his deacons. The deacon looked very familiar to me. He was a middle-aged African-American who sported a small afro and a full mustache. I knew I had seen him somewhere, but I couldn't think of where. As we were walking away, Max turned to me and said, 'You know who that was, don't you?' 'No, who?' I asked. 'That was Little Richard!' replied Max. I quickly turned to see what I had possibly missed. Even though he appeared different than his 'normal' look, it was definitely Little Richard. You just never knew what was going to happen or who you were going to meet!"

To help cope with living on the bus, the singers also would make up funny songs. Pete McLeod, a natural comedian, would come up with funny lyrics at the drop of a hat. One of these songs, sung to the melody of "Through it All," had to do with what Heritage Singers did on their days off. It was called, "Through the Mall!" At the Heritage Singers 30th reunion concert, Pete (who was the emcee for the night) pulled out his guitar and sang another of his famous silly songs. This one was written to the tune of the theme song from "The Beverly Hillbillies:"

Come on and listen to a story of a man named Max.

Wanna hear the details? Listen to these facts.

One day he went to quite a fuss,

He loaded up his family and moved 'em on a bus!

Old Blue.

Scenic Cruiser.

Well, the first thing you know, old Max is on the air,

Singing gospel music; you could hear it everywhere!

With the Heritage Singers,

Through blood and sweat and tears;

It's hard to imagine,

That it's been 30 years!

There are as many stories of life on the Heritage bus, as there are mile markers along the road. What we did on that bus was live our lives. We were like family, cringing and rolling our eyes at each other one minute and laughing together the next. And when someone would give their heart to the Lord at a concert, our hearts would be humbled and our little annoyances would melt away. We would again be reminded of why we were there.

Section II

A Bus-shaped Life

CHAPTER SIX

Friends Along the Way

"It's the friends we meet along life's road who help us appreciate the journey."

— Lucy Mace

ART LINKLETTER WAS INTERVIEWING BILL TRUBY ONE TIME AND ASKED HIM WHAT IT WAS LIKE TO BE A Heritage Singer. It was in the 1970s and the group was very excited to be on television. "Where do you stay?" Art asked. "We stay in peoples' homes," Bill replied calmly. "Really?" Art seemed interested. "How many nights a week do you stay in peoples' homes?" "Six," Bill said. Then just to add a little background, he added, "And we stay in motels two nights a week."

In typical Art Linkletter style, the quick-witted host didn't say anything or even break a smile. He knew a good opportunity for a laugh when he heard it. A master of comedic timing, he just turned and looked directly into the camera with a look that said, "Huh?" It wasn't until after the interview that Bill realized he had eight days in his week! Without even meaning to, he had perfectly described the life of being a Heritage Singer!

Singing on the Art Linkletter Show

"Singing with Heritage was truly an amazing experience," said Dave Mauck. "I can just envision the classified ad that Max and Lucy would put in a newspaper!"

Max Wants YOU!! Would you like to travel in an old bus for numerous hours each day? Push the bus when it breaks down? How about practicing your weight lifting by man-handling a heavy sound system two times a day, and sometimes four times on Sundays? You'll get to carry records and

GRACE NOTES:

"I just want you to know how much the Heritage Singers have meant to us over the past 30 years. I know you have heard this many times, but our family grew up with the Heritage Singers. We have lost quite a few of our close family members, but I was blessed enough to be able to bring my Grandmother to a concert recently. The show was wonderful as usual, and I know my Grandmother enjoyed herself very much. It brought back so many wonderful memories."

"You and the group came to our town of Mt. Shasta back in the 1970's and stayed at my uncle's house one weekend. What a blessing that was for all of us! I am now 37 years old and the Lord has given me a singing ministry in my local community. I get to sing at our local Christian coffeehouse, local churches, and various community events. What a blessing it is to share the good news of Jesus in song!"

"As children, my cousins and I would gather together in the bathroom, of all places, and we would practice our Heritage Singers songs over and over, hoping and dreaming of one day becoming a Heritage Singer. Well, that didn't happen, but we always have and always will cherish those wonderful songs. I can honestly say that the Heritage Singers are the reason that I became interested in singing, and I thank you for this wonderful blessing in my life. I can't think of anything I would rather do than sing for Jesus. I am planning a night of gospel hymns from the past Heritage Singers albums at our local Christian coffeehouse soon. I know it will bring back a lot of wonderful memories for my family and also for the people of Mt. Shasta who have come to know you."

tapes, tables and stands, and talk to thousands of people you've never met. You'll get to sleep in a different bed each night—or on a bus when we have long drives. You'll eat potluck food every day (created by many loving hands), sing for hours and hours—practicing the same songs over and over—and perform concerts in many small venues and a few large ones. You'll learn to smile until your face hurts and sing until you drop. And, you'll get to live with the same people 24/7 for 11 months out of the year—people you may not even like—all cooped up on one bus. Does this sound too good to be true? Then the Heritage Singers are for you! Of course, we'll need you to do all of this for very little money. The emotional and spiritual advantages, however, are beyond comprehension!

Laughing, Dave said, "Even though most of us were not aware of these conditions when we joined Heritage, we decided afterwards that this was the life we wanted. We just kept coming back for more. Obviously, we didn't really perceive the negatives!"

Rick Lange said, "Being a Heritage Singer was a big adventure. People treated us differently simply because we were part of Heritage. I think there was a certain mystique about being a Heritage Singer. It kind of made you feel like a star."

The people who hosted the singers in their homes were understandably intrigued by the group's lives and what it was like to be a Heritage Singer. They were curious about the ministry and couldn't help but ask questions and we enjoyed getting to know them too. Rick recalled, "They'd keep us up talking, wanting to know all about us and hear our stories.

Most of our experiences in peoples' homes were great. We had a comfortable night's rest, a good breakfast, and great company. We often met people we liked very much and tried to stay in contact with them afterwards. It was great for those of us who stayed in Heritage long enough to return to some of the places we had been to before, because we often were able to see these people again. We were shown such wonderful hospitality.

Whenever a church invited the Heritage Singers to perform, they were responsible for finding housing for the singers. People in the local congregation would sign-up to have two or three singers stay with them, and then those singers would go home with them after our concert. We never knew what kind of home or family we were going to get. We could be staying in a beautiful home with an indoor pool and stacks of thick white towels in a marble bathroom, or we could be in a mobile home or crumbling farmhouse with rusty water for bathing. It really was quite an adventure, mostly because we knew if we survived the experience, we'd have a good story to tell the rest of the group the next morning. But no matter what kind of amenities or comforts our hosts could offer, they treated us wonderfully. We got to eat delicious homemade food and relax in a cozy home environment, which often was quite comforting to those of us who were homesick.

Dave and Amanda Mauck

The group deeply appreciated the hospitality and generosity of their hosts. They could not have toured without these people opening up their homes to the singers. It helped make the Heritage ministry possible. We couldn't afford to stay in hotels every night, and the people who so generously took us into their homes kept our ministry on the road. We will never forget their kindness to us.

Joanne said "There are a few memorable moments we still laugh about to this day. Kim and I will never forget the time a host's cat came into our room playing with a cute little mouse toy. Kim reached over to grab it so she could play with the cat—only it wasn't a toy! Then, there was the time that the head of our bed totally collapsed onto the floor, leaving our feet waving in the air. We just lay there screaming and laughing until someone came to help us. Another time we got so cold in the night that we grabbed an area rug off the floor as there weren't any extra blankets in the room. We were as snug as two Heritage Singers in a rug the rest of the night."

"I remember one morning waking up to a cow looking in the window! I thought: Kim, you really have to stop using that peel-off mask stuff, you're starting to scare me! That same morning our hostess made scrambled eggs in a cast-iron frying pan that probably hadn't ever been washed. When she poured the cooked eggs out onto our plates, she made sure every drop of grease from that pan, scrapings and all, drizzled over our eggs. We assured her that we just never ate breakfast; that she didn't need to worry about waiting on us.

Most of the time, the singers were paired off in groups of two. For girls, that usually meant sharing the same bed at whatever home they ended up staying in. "We got used to this after a while," Val said. "In fact, even on our days off when we stayed in motels, we girls often had to double-up and share a bed. Imagine our surprise one night when the lady who took us home with her only had one bed—the one she slept in! Insisting that there was room for two more, we saw no choice but to snuggle-in for a sleepless night. After a few nights like this, even the most sociable among us longed for privacy and dreamed of having one night in a big bed all by ourselves!"

Bill Truby recalled staying in people's homes, too. He said, "The one difficult thing about staying with people was how tired I always was. I had been driving the bus all day, then I had to help set up the sound system, sing, give my testimony, pray with people, help take down the sound system, sell records, load up the bus, and make sure everyone was assigned to a home. Then I'd grab my bag and get into someone's car. Once we arrived at our host's house, I would just want to collapse, but, of course, they would want to visit with us and we were happy and thankful for their kindness to us."

Terry Mace particularly enjoyed staying in people's homes. He loved meeting new people. In fact, he still runs into people he stayed with during the early years. Many have become dear friends. "I have always had a problem with hotels. It's just a square room with a television and a bed. It is so inhospitable," said Terry.

Lucy remembered one old hotel they stayed in during a crusade in Glendale, California. "Max and I had to pull the mattress off the bed and put it on the floor every night, just so we could sleep on it. The elevator there didn't operate correctly, either. It never quite lined up with the floor it was supposed to be lined up with. When the door would open to our floor, we didn't know if we'd have to climb up or jump down to get out. One time we were waiting in the lobby for the elevator door to open, and when it did, Rudy and Ginny's chins were about level with the lobby floor. All we could see was their heads!" laughed Lucy.

Charlotte and Bobby Brody

When Lee Newman first joined Heritage back in the early '70s, he wasn't so excited about staying in peoples' homes, and in fact, he was dreading it. "I am normally an introvert," he explained, "although people say I cover it well! I was not looking forward to staying in peoples' homes, but I quickly warmed up to the situation and got to where I actually enjoyed it.

"Years later, I realized that staying in peoples' homes was one of the Heritage Singers' secrets of success. The people who took us into their homes became our most devoted supporters. If anyone would try to criticize us, these people would stand up and say, 'Hey, those singers are my friends! They slept in my home and they ate at my table. I know them personally, so if you have anything bad to say, then you're going to have to get through me first!' They remain Heritage's most loyal supporters to this day."

Naturally, Max and Lucy have stayed in more homes than the rest of the Heritage Singers combined, and they have hundreds of stories about their experiences. Max told of one time on his way back from a trip to the bathroom, he forgot which room he and Lucy were staying in. Imagine his embarrassment when he walked into his host's bedroom in the middle of the night! He just heard the lady trying to direct him to the door, saying, "Max, a little to your left; no, over a little; no, a little farther down...."

Another time, Max and Lucy had to share a room with a baby. Lucy said upon being shown to their room, they realized that there was a baby sleeping in its crib alongside their bed, which meant they were on baby duty for the night. Lucy had to get up several times and quiet the fussing baby.

Val said that it was difficult, as a kid, for her to be separated from her parents after a concert. Many times she and Greg were assigned to different homes than their parents, even when they were quite young. This was also hard on Lucy who wanted to be with her children.

Over the years, Lucy made many special friends from her travels. She particularly looked forward to the Northwest tour as they had many friends and family in that area. This was where Heritage got its start. Lucy said, "In certain towns we knew exactly who would be taking us home for the night. For example, when we traveled to Yakima, we knew we would be staying with Mrs. Price. She always had the table set for Max and me when we arrived at her home. She had canned Bing cherries for Max and peaches and apricots for me, as well as a loaf of homemade bread for toasting. She treated us so special and always remembered to have the things we enjoyed. It was like coming home to 'Mom's' place.

"In Wenatchee (Washington) we would always stay with Charlotte and Bobby Brody," Lucy recalled. "Bobby and Max were college classmates, and they would spend hours laying on the floor in front of the stereo in the living room, listening to music, all kinds of music. They usually ended up falling asleep there. Charlotte and I would be sound asleep for hours before they would come to bed. Max just felt so comfortable in their home.

"There was also a restaurant in Bend, Oregon, where we always stopped and had blackberry pie. I also remember a watermelon stand in Hermiston, Oregon, where we had some of the best watermelon we'd ever tasted.

"In Olympia, Washington, the ladies of the church would go all out for our evening meal," Lucy said. "They'd bring out their china and cloth tablecloths, so we'd feel like we were getting a real treat. It was a special meal, and it meant a lot to us that they went to so much trouble to make us feel welcome. Wilber and Esther Garner have opened their home to us there many times. They've been members of the Heritage 29ers Club for many years, sending us $29 each month to help support the ministry. Max and I always looked forward to staying with them.

Eating watermelon in Hermiston, Oregon
Connie, Max, Arnie, Annette, Rob, Greg and Tim

Becki and Bolejack family, Catherine, Candice, Carrie and Cathy

"I remember one time when we were singing at a camp meeting in Montana. Our hosts housed Max and me in a room just off the stage in the gymnasium. It was okay until it started to rain, and the roof began to leak. Max and I woke up to water splashing in our faces and dripping all around our makeshift bed. We got up and pulled our bed over a couple of feet, hoping to stay dry. I think it must have been where they counted the offering, because we found a stack of offering buckets that we placed around the room to catch the drips. The chorus of raindrops

finally helped us drift back to sleep."

Another of Lucy's treasured experiences was getting to know Heather and Holly Keyes, who lived in Lodi, California. "I've known these two girls since they were tiny," she said. "When they lost their mother to cancer, they seemed like two lost sheep. We tried to fill some of the emptiness in their lives." Lucy remembered how wonderful it was to help Heather find dresses for her wedding. While on stage at a Heritage concert recently, Max acknowledged the girls, who were in the audience. "We're so glad you're here," he said. "You are a part of our family now." Lucy also remembered the wonderful potlucks at Lodi. She said, "Those German ladies could really cook! I treasure the recipes they've shared with me through the years. I can taste their cheese-button casserole right now."

"When we sang in Indianapolis, Indiana, the Bolejack family took the entire group of Heritage Singers home to their house and gave us their own bedrooms" recalled Lucy. "They all disappeared somewhere. To this day, we don't know where they slept. Whenever we have a concert anywhere within driving distance of them, we know they will be in the front row, and watching their smiling faces just warms our hearts. We always look forward to seeing them.

"We've made so many special friends over the years," said Lucy. "There are just too many for me to mention them all. Hopefully, they know what a blessing they have been to us."

Former singer Barbie Cupps said, "What I remember the

most about traveling with Heritage are the friendships I developed, both with the singers in the group and the people who came to the concerts. Five nights a week we stayed in the homes of those who came to hear us sing, and I still stay in touch with many of them. I enjoyed talking with the people after the concerts and spending time with them in their homes. Everywhere we went, the people would prepare the most delicious food for us. I felt I never went without comfortable accommodations and lots of love by those who enjoyed our music."

Dave Bell's most memorable moment was during a trip to Australia. "I was told that I would be sharing a room with my hosts' five-year-old son," he said. "But what they meant to say was that we'd be sharing a bed. As many five-year-olds are prone to do, my sleeping partner wet the bed. No, he actually wet me. When I woke up, I was soaked."

Eventually, the group phased out the practice of staying in peoples' homes. One reason was because more and more women were working outside of their homes. This meant they had to leave early in the morning to get to their jobs. "They'd bring us back to our bus at 7 a.m. This left us with nothing to do and nowhere to go all day. It was just easier to not expect people to entertain us the next day," said Terry.

"Our time on the road has not always been easy. We have sometimes had less than ideal living conditions, but when we think of the hundreds of homes the Heritage Singers have stayed in and the countless ways people have helped us," said Lucy, "we are overwhelmed with gratitude—gratitude for all of the generous, caring people in this world, and gratitude to God for arranging for our paths to intersect."

Backing Down Hills and Other Cliffhangers

T HE HERITAGE SINGERS BUS WAS MORE THAN JUST A MEANS OF TRANSPORTATION; IT WAS OUR HOME. FOR eleven months of the year, the singers lived on it together. The original Heritage Singers bus was nicknamed "Old Blue," and it had a lot of problems. Besides the air conditioning not working most of the time, it would refuse to start at the most inopportune times. It even refused to be shifted into reverse. In fact, the only way to get the bus into reverse was to stop, get out, and use a broomstick to push in the gear. Imagine the situations we got ourselves into with that problem! One incident that stands out in Heritage bus lore was at the tollbooth of the Holland Tunnel, entering New York City. Imagine the sight. The embarrassment!

The bus's fuel gauge also didn't work right. It wasn't always accurate, especially when it got below a quarter of a tank. The bus drivers had to use a toilet plunger as a dip stick to check the fuel level. It's amazing that the group only ran out of fuel a few times, but when a bus runs out of diesel, it takes an Act of Congress to get it started up again!

In the beginning, the group didn't have a professional bus driver. John Musgrave, the business manager for Heritage, thought

Driver in training

everyone could be taught to drive a bus. It was in this spirit of self-sufficiency that many of the male Heritage Singers found themselves getting their chauffeur's license. Not all of them were "natural" bus drivers. Let's just say we cut our losses after a few fender-benders and stuck with the guys who were pretty good at it.

Being a bus driver also meant being a mechanic, as well as a navigator. When the bus broke down, the driver had to find a way to fix it. The driver also had to navigate the group to the next concert and get them there on time. Our guys learned to find places UPS drivers have never heard of, and they could park on a dime, give or take a few nearby bumpers. The ultimate test of our drivers was making it up the road to the Heritage ranch in one try. Greg remembered one time when the bus developed a leak in the air line, which affected the brakes. "As long as the motor was running, the brakes were okay, so we didn't think much about it. That was how naïve we were," he said.

Lucy's brother, Lyle Hatley, also traveled with the Heritage Singers, and he too drove the bus at different times. He remembered one scary incident when the bus froze at a traffic signal. He said, "We were on our way to a concert and dressed in our white performance suits with pastel shirts and white boots. When we stopped at a traffic signal the bus froze. I couldn't get it to go into gear. The engine revved up, but we just sat there. I shut off the engine and everyone piled off the bus. I quickly pulled on my coveralls before going to the back of the bus to inspect the engine. I must have looked pretty cool in my white performance suit and overalls!

"I soon saw the problem, a linkage rod that goes from the transmission to shift the gears was gone, nowhere to be seen. It must have fallen off while we were driving down the highway. I crawled back out of the engine and told Max what the problem was. All we could do was pray for a miracle. We had no way to fix the problem. After we prayed, I decided to open the engine up again and take another look. My eyes focused in on the rod that keeps the door closed. It looked about the same size as the one that was missing. We took some pliers and other tools and removed the rod from the door, then took some wire and placed the rod into the transmission. It fit just like it had been made for

Sad "Old Blue"

it! I started the bus and tried to shift gears. It worked perfectly. We had another prayer of thanks and even made it to our concert on time. And, my white suit was even still white—another miracle!"

Bill Truby also had the privilege of driving "Old Blue." He loved to drive and often hung out with the bus driver. However, Bill had only driven the bus a few times when the bus driver quit. Unlike most of the bus drivers, who were quite tall, Bill was shorter in stature. As a result, he received a lot of ribbing about needing foot pedal extensions to reach the pedals. Bill said, "The bus driver just walked away, leaving me to drive the bus. I had a license, but I didn't know the gears well. Everyone was patient with me as I ground the gears to fit! I drove the bus a lot and enjoyed it, but it was tiring. I had to drive and set up for concerts. I didn't get to sleep and probably couldn't have slept anyway.

"We experienced a few miracles while driving 'Old Blue.' One time we were driving on Highway 101 in Northern California. We went down a little hill and around a corner, and then the bus just died. I hopped outside and ran to the rear of the bus to take a look at the engine. There was a piece of metal on the ground and I picked up. Then, I started the bus from behind (you can start the engine at the back). It started up just fine, so I ran back up to the front and took off. We went to see a mechanic later that day when we got to Eureka. He checked things out for us and told us we needed a new part, but it was really hard to find. Well, it just so happened that the piece of metal I picked up off the ground was the exact part the mechanic needed to fix the bus. I believe God knew we needed that part, so He caused the bus to stall at that exact spot.

"Another time we were driving in San Francisco and I had

to parallel-park the bus. I've always been kind of proud of that moment. It wasn't easy driving up and down all those hills with a clutch. The bus was not made for it; it was made for flat highway driving. But, there I was parallel parking it. We measured afterwards and there were only about ten inches in front and 14 inches in back—a tight fit!

"The scariest time, though, was when we were in Southern California near Loma Linda. Dr. Raymond West invited the group to come to his house for lunch. As the driver, I usually asked about roads and turn-around spots whenever we were invited somewhere, but this time I didn't think to ask about the steepness of the hill. He lived up on some ridge. Here we were, climbing up this hill on a windy road, and I am shifting gears to accommodate it, slowly losing speed, until I just can't go forward any longer. It was too steep. At that point we had gone about a mile up the hill. Since I couldn't go forward, I began backing down the entire hill. To demonstrate the faith they had in my driving, all of the singers got off the bus!

"When you backed up that bus, especially downhill, the brakes make a tremendous amount of noise, and I had to use them a lot. I also had to stop a couple of times and let the air pressure build up because they were air brakes. It was an intense moment for me because I had to get that bus down the hill without any mistakes!

"I also remember a tiring non-stop trip we made from Florida back to Portland, Oregon. We were all so tired. We drove through all kinds of weather. Someone helped me do a little of the driving, but I did most of it. We stopped at a truck stop in

Arnie Knapp

the middle of the night somewhere in the South. I needed something to help me stay awake, so I ordered some hot chocolate. The waitress had bad teeth and a dirty apron. The entire place was dirty. She handed me a cup and it had greasy fingerprints on it from truck driver's oil. I just sat there and looked at that. Then, from behind the counter where she was standing, comes this cockroach over to the cup. I'm just so tired. I'm just watching this. I'm not moving. I'm not killing it. The cockroach crawls up the mug. At that point I'm realizing I'm not going to drink that hot chocolate, but I'm going to watch this cockroach and see what happens. It goes over the edge a bit, kind of sniffs the hot chocolate, goes back down the edge, walks back across the counter and leaves. I'm thinking, 'if a cockroach doesn't want this, I'm sure I don't want it, either!'"

Frank John Salas and his wife Carole Lynn traveled with Heritage II. He said, "I not only sang with the group, I drove the bus. I'll never forget my bus-driving test! The Department of Motor Vehicles official kind of looked like Elmer Fudd, complete with a clipboard and a cigar. I remember we drove up the freeway to Placerville, and I drove really badly. But he had sympathy on me and passed me anyway! He told Max, 'Yeah, he passed, but if you let him drive, someone's going to get killed!'"

Lee Newman remembered traveling on the freeway north of San Diego one day when there was a loud explosion and the bus tipped and jumped two lanes. "Tim Truby was driving that day," Lee recalled. "He fought the steering wheel and brought the bus to rest back over on the right-hand shoulder. We exited the bus to find that the side had blown out of the left front tire!"

There were no cars beside the bus at the time, but a Highway Patrol officer was about a quarter mile behind the bus. "He stopped and directed traffic around us while we changed the tire," Lee said. "He came up to us, shaking his head, and said that there was no reason on earth why that bus remained upright. God was looking out for us that day."

Lee also remembered helping the bus driver navigate a few times. "One time we were in a town where they were doing a great deal of urban renewal," he said. "The streets were torn up, buildings were being demolished, and others were being constructed. We were trying to get to the church where our concert was going to be held that night, but we just couldn't find it. We stopped at a service station to ask directions.

"A man dressed in a gas station uniform came out of the service station and asked if he could help us with anything. I told him our situation and he said, 'Follow me.' He then got into his car and led us around all of the construction to the church. He pointed out his window as he passed the church and drove on down into a dip in the road and out of sight. I watched to see him come up the other side of the dip, but he never reappeared. I just assumed he had turned onto another street.

"Later, I actually walked down the road to look at the dip in the road, wondering where the man could have gone. The road went down and up on the other side, but there were no roads branching off on either side where he could've turned. He simply disappeared! I can't help but think it was an angel that God sent to help us that day."

Anyone who has ever traveled with the Heritage Singers has

Paul Hortop

bus stories. The Heritage II bus getting stuck inside an arched overpass on a busy Boston expressway. The bus driver knew it was going to be close; the sign read "Low Clearance." How tall was our bus again? The driver thought maybe if it stayed in the middle lane and just crept through, he'd make it. The sound of the top of the bus scraping the inside of the tunnel was unmistakable. It came to a complete stop. There it was, wedged inside the tunnel—and right in the middle of an everyman-for-himself Boston rush hour!

The only thing the driver could do was put his life on the line and venture out into traffic to let some air out of the tires! Inside, the singers moved over to the side that seemed to be stuck, weighing it down as much as they could. It worked! The inch or so shorter allowed them to carefully squeeze through. With the bus finally free, they made a quick exit and found an alternate route.

Max remembered, "After performing at a camp meeting, we slowly pulled away to leave. People were all around us, so we were creeping along very slowly, but not so slow that a strategically placed speed bump couldn't jostle the holding tank open, dumping the entire unsanitary contents all over the pavement! As it spattered, people scattered. Dare we pretend that we didn't know it happened? What else could we do? Mortified and appalled, we sheepishly slithered away, leaving a little something to be remembered by."

Terry Mace remembered a long trip from Twin Falls, Idaho, to Orlando, Florida. He said, "We drove straight through, and we were open to trying anything that looked like a short cut. We looked at a map and saw an alternate route that looked like it would save us some time. It was called 'Alternate Route 14.'

"First of all, no Greyhound bus has any business on any alternate route, period. Those buses were built for the long, straight, open-road situations, not for mountain climbing. Alternate Route 14 was basically a goat trail over the Sawtooth Mountains. There were cutbacks so steep that the bus scraped bottom as it maneuvered the curves. The road got steeper and steeper and windier and windier until we came to a complete stop on a switchback, and the motor died. We were stuck.

"In order to get the bus in reverse, the guys had to insert a broomstick in the gear mechanism from behind the bus. And to rev up the engine, the driver had to take his foot off of the brake, which caused the bus to lurch backwards. The bus was teetering on a corner, with a steep switchback to the right and a sheer drop-off on the left. The air suspension kept getting lower and lower, affecting the brakes, so the idea was to keep it at a fast idle to build up the air pressure so the brakes would work. It became an impossibility to even rev the engine enough to move the clutch to get it in gear.

"Everyone but Pete McLeod, our driver, got off the bus. We walked to the top of the mountain. There was another mile or two of sharp switchbacks. We were cold and we were scared, but we just kept going. When we got to the top, we realized that the sun had come up. It was a beautiful, but cold, sunny morning. Of course we prayed, asking God to help us get the bus off of that mountain.

"Maybe Pete drove the bus out of there, I can't even remember how we got the bus to the top, but when he got up there,

Pete McLeod at the wheel

we just sat a while, letting the air pressure build up before we continued on our way. After a while an old pickup truck came along. Inside the truck were a gypsy sheepherder and his dog. When the guy saw us, he stopped. We asked him where we were. We told him we were looking for a freeway. He was pretty flabbergasted. He asked us what in the world we were doing out there. No one could drive this road. It was not even safe for his pickup truck! How we got out of that situation without crashing, we'll never know. It was simply miraculous. It had to be the guiding hands of a whole army of angels." Alternate Route 14 will never been forgotten.

Driving the Heritage bus was often a humbling experience. Lucy remembered the time they stayed at the Huntington Sheraton Hotel in Pasadena. "There was a circle drive in front, and one of our employees, Jack Owen, had just had the bus repaired and was returning it to us. He tried driving the bus around the circle in front of the hotel, but the curve was too sharp for the length of the bus. He actually ran into three or four cars in the process, pushing them up onto the curb.

"Another time Jeff Wood backed the bus into a telephone pole and broke the back window out," continued Lucy. "During the days of amateur drivers our bus was known to plow right over fire hydrants, sending geysers of water shooting into the air. It often clipped corners off of overhangs and bumped into cars as we turned corners. Our bus left a path of destruction. If you saw the Heritage Singer bus headed your way, you'd have been wise to keep your distance."

Max will never forget the humility of some of these

experiences. "One time Jay Prohaska, who was driving the bus, came around the corner and ran into a brand-new Cadillac parked in front of a house." Max cringed. "It was so new it didn't even have plates on it yet. I had to go to the door with Jay and tell the owners we had just ruined their new car.

"Another time while on the way to a concert, the bus' fuel level got dangerously low. We were out in the middle of nowhere, and there was no place to get diesel. Knowing the problems we would have getting the bus running again if it ran out of fuel, we had a decision to make. We could stop on the side of the road and wait for someone to come help us, or we could take a chance on making it.

"We had never missed a concert before, so we decided to keep on going. That bus continued going and going on empty until we found a station that had diesel. When we filled the tank, the service station pump said it took one gallon more than we knew the tank could hold! We knew God kept the bus going, so we could make it to our concert that night."

Terry remembered running out of diesel on the way to a concert. "We were in Santa Rosa, California," he said. "After someone helped us get some fuel in the tank, we thought our troubles were over. We didn't know that once the engine runs dry, the lines have to be bled before you can start it up and go. We tried to start that bus for hours. After a while, it was clear that we weren't going to make it to our concert.

"Max took a lot of pride in making sure we never missed a concert, so he arranged for a couple of vans to take us there. A tow truck towed the bus into town for us; however, the tow truck had a hard time getting the bus to move because we had engaged the manual brake. When he finally got the bus moving, a huge cloud of black smoke engulfed him from the manual brake rubbing against the wheel. We ended up having to call a mechanic to come get the bus started and let it run for a while to build up the air pressure. We were constantly learning how to drive that bus, mostly by doing things wrong!"

One time when Lyndon Crabtree was driving the bus in Sacramento and they ran out of diesel. "This was before everyone had cell phones," said Lucy. "He left everyone in the bus and hitch-hiked to get help. When he finally returned with help, they had to bleed the lines and refuel the bus before they could get it started again. Just after the tow truck left and we were ready to pull back onto the highway, Lyndon killed the engine. He couldn't get it started again. The entire group ended up sleeping on the bus that night. The next morning Lyndon went to get another tow truck and start the process of getting the bus started all over again. The sad part was, we were only about 40 miles from home."

One of the scariest bus stories the group remembers was when Pete McLeod was driving on a mountainous road in California. Not really wanting to drive the bus in the first place, he reluctantly found himself at the wheel, doing the best he could. "I needed to make a very sharp U-turn to head downhill," Pete explained. "Coming out of a driveway, I made a sharp left turn, blocking the road. Then I put the bus into reverse to back up a bit, so I could negotiate the turn. What an inopportune time for the bus to run out of fuel! We were stuck. I looked around. A steep cliff was straight ahead of us and behind us was a wall. Traffic had stopped.

"Everyone got off the bus—everyone but me. Apparently I was dispensable. Someone called for a tow truck to come and help us. The huge tow truck hooked a hefty chain to the back of the bus, hoping to pull us back far enough so I could make the turn and head down the mountain. Meanwhile, the rest of the group stood alongside the road and formed a prayer circle. It was a dangerous situation. If I couldn't make that turn, I would in all likelihood go over the cliff. And because the engine wasn't working, I didn't have power steering or brakes. I wasn't very smart back then; I should have resigned my driving duties prior to this episode!

"The tow truck began to pull the bus backward—inch-by-inch—when snap! The chain broke! With a lurch, the bus headed straight for the cliff, picking up speed. I could hear the girls screaming; the guys were just glad that they weren't driving. Just as I was about to careen over the cliff, the bus ran over one of those little road reflector posts, bending it backwards. The front of the bus was hanging over the edge. It started to teeter. Then suddenly I could feel the bus catch on something. The only thing keeping this 40-ton bus from crashing down the mountain was a spindly road reflector—that and several exasperated angels!"

Pete's story is surprisingly familiar. When Heritage II was traveling in Georgia Doug Botimer was at the wheel. Since he was one of our more confident, experienced drivers, we always felt we were in good hands when Doug was driving. Some of us even took turns sitting on the "Botimer Board" in the front of the bus—a square piece of plywood that reached from the dashboard across the steps and over to the floor in front of the first seat. From that perched platform, we had a close-up view of the road and could visit with Doug as we traveled.

The sky got dark and it started to rain. The two-lane road that we were on was curvy and had steep hills. Our old Continental Trailways bus always seemed top-heavy, but especially when we were jostling along a bumpy, hilly road. As we descended a long, straight hill, we could see a car at the bottom turn on its left blinker and stop. Doug downshifted and started to brake, but we kept barreling down on the car. We could have sworn that car had a couple of chances to make its move, but it didn't. We kept coming. Doug kept braking. We weren't stopping. We were going to hit the car, and we were going to hit it hard. We started to scream. As we came closer, Doug began to swerve around the car, but there wasn't much of a shoulder. The ground was soft, and the bus started to tip over to the right. Suitcases, shoes, cassette tapes, and books from the overhead storage rack were flying around, hitting us in the head as we began to roll over.

Suddenly, we lurched to a stop. We seemed to be hanging out over a cliff at a 45-degree angle. The door had flown open, and our belongings were falling out of the door and down the steep cliff. As we were able to, one by one, we let ourselves fall out of the bus and onto the wet ground. Grabbing onto trees and to

each other, we quickly checked to make sure we all were okay. We were horrified to see our bus precariously perched above us—the top front corner teetering against an old wooden telephone pole! A measly splinter of a pole was holding up our bus!

"The bus was tipped so much we had to walk on the sides of the seats to get to the door," Buz Starrett recalled. "When we saw the bus resting against the utility pole, we saw that the lines were pulled very tight and could snap at any moment."

"Scrambling to get out from under the leaning bus, should it fall, the singers climbed up onto the road. They all trembled in a dripping huddle by the side of the road, giving thanks to God for saving them. We spent the rest of the day watching a very large tow-truck pull the bus back up," Buz said. "There was a very large dent in the top front corner of the bus marking the evidence of God's protection. We talked about that miracle for months. Audience after audience heard our famous bus story. We knew, beyond a shadow of a doubt, that God had protected us that day."

An article in a 1979 Heritage newsletter chronicled a similar story:

On a cold morning in Marietta, Georgia, we arrived at the church expecting to get on a warm bus and head to our next destination. But, the bus wouldn't start. We decided to use the time wisely while we waited for a repairman to come, so we went inside the church for a practice session. As we were nearing the end of one song, Garth [Gabriel] just happened to look out the window and was horrified to see our bus rolling backwards toward a 60-foot cliff overhanging the highway below. Our new bass player, Bob [Griffiths], along with Garth, dashed out the door of the church and ran after the bus. They both grabbed the open door and pulled back as hard as they could. Garth jumped on the bus and put it in second gear, but it wouldn't hold. He then jumped off and, along with Bob, pulled on the door. They were actually able to bring the bus to a stop, but only about 10 feet before the drop off! There was no way two humans could stop a fully-loaded bus on a downhill grade! Yes, the Lord is even stronger than our bus. He has all the power in the whole universe!

It's hard to believe, but it's true that in all of the millions of miles the Heritage Singers have traveled, there never was one major accident, and no one was ever injured from an accident on the road. But, there were plenty of adventures!

Almost every Heritage Singer has experienced the wild and daring drive up or down the Heritage Ranch road. In the early days, the road was extremely steep, unpaved, and had some sharp turns. One cutback was so tight that the bus driver had to rock the bus back and forth a few times to inch around it. As we headed down the hill, you did not want to be standing in the front of the bus for this! The front wheels were set back from the front of the bus, and you would be hanging over the edge of the cliff!

Push!

Cindy Haffner said, "We always worried about making that turn. I can remember all of us praying that we would make it around the corner. One night we didn't make it. It was raining, and we all had to get out of the bus. We watched Steve Evenson, our bus driver, as he edged and rocked the bus in the slippery mud. One tire was already off the road. We were so afraid that he would slide right off the edge of the drop-off. But he finally did make it, and once he got going, he wasn't about to stop! We walked the rest of the way up the long, winding drive, mud and all.

"A couple of years later, Max had the drive straightened out a bit. It was now shorter and had fewer turns, but it was actually steeper. Every night when returning to the ranch from a concert, our hearts would begin beating faster as we headed down New-town Road and got closer to the ranch road. As we approached the cut-off, the bus driver would pull over to the side of the road and rev up the engine and say, 'Okay, guys, hold on!' Then he'd just floor it, giving it all he had to get that bus up the hill.

"The scariest times though were when it rained, and we didn't make it up the hill. We'd get about half way up and start to slow down. Rocking and jerking to a stop, we would sit there a minute, and then start sliding backwards down the muddy, unpaved drive. It would be pitch black outside, and here we were sliding down the hill in a very heavy and hard-to-stop bus. And, it usually was somewhere around two o'clock in the morning!

"Before it was too late, we would all jump off the bus—the girls would walk the rest of the way up the hill to the lodge, while the guys would stay behind with flashlights and help guide the bus driver as he backed down the hill and tried again. He'd usually make it the second time, having lightened the load by several passengers. Those were good times."

Sometimes when the group stopped at rest stops on long trips, they wouldn't leave with the same number of Heritage Singers as they brought with them. Someone would often get left behind. The outcome of these incidents was largely affected by the ingenuity of the person who had been stranded.

It was the middle of the night when Paul stopped for fuel. Most of the singers were asleep and didn't notice that Becki had gotten off the bus to use the restroom. She handled the situation with typical Heritage-style grace and dignity. Quickly befriending a truck driver, she asked him to contact the Heritage bus driver on his CB radio to let him know he was missing a passenger. When the driver got the message over the CB radio, he immediately pulled over to the side of the road and one of the singers ran back to accompany Becki to the bus.

When Garth Gabriel got left behind, he actually hitched a ride with someone and they raced down the highway after the bus. When they caught up to the bus, they slowly passed it, and Garth waved at everyone as they went by.

Cindy Haffner remembered the day the group got its new bus, which Heritage still uses to this day. "What an exciting, long-awaited day!" she said. "The bus driver rolled up to the lodge and we stepped inside to take a look at our new home on wheels. It was an empty shell, all hollow and full of echoes. We actually traveled in it that way for a while with all of us sitting on beanbags and pillows. We had our dresses hanging on a freestanding coat rack in the back of the bus. If the driver hit the brakes too hard, down would come all of the clothes, totally burying whoever happened to be sitting back there. It's a good thing we were all much younger then!"

The "new" bus was built in 1981 and is becoming less reliable, needing more and more repairs. While on a recent trip from Placerville to Los Angeles, the bus broke down in the middle of a freeway exit, blocking traffic. It was 104 degrees outside, no air conditioning, and horns honking all around. The group immediately called for a tow truck, but it was two hours before they could get one large enough to do the job.

While they were waiting, a sweet lady stopped and said she was from a local church. She wanted to take the moms and their children to her home to wait, where it was much cooler. She said, "You know, I never go home this way. This is the first time I have ever taken this route." The singers knew God was looking out for them and had impressed her to drive past them.

Meanwhile, Greg Mace had spotted a car rental office less than a block away. He walked over to see if they had a van he could rent. There were about 15 people in line and by the time he made it to the front of the line, they were out of cars. Greg asked if they could call another rental agency. They were also out of cars. Just about that time, the agent behind the counter got a call from another office, and he asked if they had any vehicles. There was one car left—an SUV that would hold seven passengers. The only problem was it was in a town 45 minutes away. The agent offered to give Greg a ride to go get the SUV.

Tim Calhoun and Dave Bell were still waiting at the bus trying to keep cool. A young man from a car dealership walked over and started talking with them. The guys told him they were part of a gospel singing group on their way to Los Angeles to do a couple of concerts. The other guy said, "I'm a Christian, too. Is there anything I can do to help?" They told him they needed to find the nearest truck rental office. The man said, "There is one just a few blocks away, and I'll be happy to take you there."

While Greg was on his way to pick up the SUV, and Tim and Dave were on their way to pick up a rental truck, the tow truck showed up to tow the bus. Unfortunately several of the boys cell phones were dead and there was no way to tell them where they were taking the bus. It took them a while to figure out just where the tow truck had taken the bus. Eventually, it was found, and the huge task of unloading everything into the rental truck began. Sound equipment, CDs, DVDs, clothes, and all the necessary things to do a concert were all loaded into the truck. By this time, the singers were totally exhausted from the stress and the heat.

As Greg drove the SUV to pick up the rest of the group, he slipped Heritage's newly recorded CD into the player. Once the singers were loaded into the car, Greg started up the engine again and the very first song that began to play was, "God Will Take Care of You." Adriane Mace said it brought tears to her eyes and made her realize how God had once again taken care of them with all the miracles that happened that day. The singers arrived at their hotel at 2:30 a.m. They were able to get a little rest and cleaned up for their morning concert. They thanked God for giving them the energy and strength to do a second concert later that same day.

At the concert that evening, someone wrote a note on an offering envelope. It said, "Sorry I can't help you. I'm homeless and struggling." Max said, "When I read that note, all of the things the group had gone through the day before didn't seem so bad. We all had plenty to eat, a nice bed to sleep in, and we were all safe. I think God allows us to have a few trials in life to make us appreciate what He provides for us. I just wish we knew who wrote that note, so we could help this person."

It was the morning after the Heritage Singers sang at the Crystal Cathedral in Anaheim, California. "At 6:00A.M. our phone rings and Greg, our son, was calling to tell us that the bus engine had just blown!" Lucy said. "Not the best news to hear first thing in the morning. The singers were all on board the bus and ready to drive home. As John Giese, our bus driver for several years, was starting the bus, he saw smoke coming from underneath. Greg jumped out to see where it was coming from and immediately signaled John to turn off the engine. Oil was pouring out of the back of the bus. The engine had blown right in the parking lot of the hotel!

"You're probably wondering how can that be good news? Well, knowing the condition of the bus, John had prayed the night before that 'if the bus is going to break down, please don't let it break down on the road.' Just a couple of days before, as they were driving over the Grapevine to Los Angeles, the bus barely made it because it was lacking power. Preventing the bus from heading back home and from breaking down in the middle of the freeway was definitely a direct answer to John's prayer.

"The singers were all sent back to their rooms while Max and I made arrangements for rental vans and a U-Haul to get

Greg and driver John Giese with a blown engine

them back home. We needed to get fifteen members of our Heritage family back to Sacramento, including three little ones in car seats. By 10 o'clock they were on their way home while we waited for the tow truck to take the bus to the mechanic in Riverside.

"Now here is the second miracle! Just three days before we left for the Crystal Cathedral concert, a generous couple donated money specifically to have our engine replaced. Remember, this was before our engine even blew. God knows our needs even before we ask!

"When Max made the call to our mechanic, Dalton Mastrocolla, he told Max that he wanted to donate his time to replace the old engine and put in a rebuilt one. Dalton said he loves the Heritage ministry and is honored that he can use the talent God has given him to help us. He was also able to find a rebuilt engine for the exact amount of money that had been donated to replace the old one. We are humbled knowing God is still performing miracles today and we are the recipients!"

CHAPTER EIGHT

In the Spotlight

Sing and make music in your heart to the Lord, always giving thanks to God the Father for everything.
— Ephesians 5:19–20

NO MATTER WHAT KIND OF DAY THE HERITAGE SINGERS HAD AND NO MATTER WHAT DIFFICULTY OR DISCORD there was among them at the time, something miraculous happened when they stepped out onto stage each night and began singing. As they began singing and glanced at each other across the stage, a new energy washed over them—a peaceful renewed feeling. Whatever personal issues there were between them, their problems vanished while they were on stage. They could be sick or tired or both. They could be upset or angry with someone. They could be lonely or heartbroken. It didn't matter. When they were on stage, they were united in Christ, and just let Him sing through them.

When we were on stage, we knew that was where God called us to be. We had a purpose and our lives had meaning.

It was also when Max was at his best. He loved being on stage singing, and we loved seeing him there. He would lift his hand and gently direct us as if smoothing a cloud. He'd sometimes move the pace along by raising his eyebrows and putting some excitement on his face. He didn't have to do much for us to know what he wanted. A simple tug on his ear, a shift in his stance, or a raised index finger told us what he wanted to hear. It could be something as simple as a smile or a wink to spark the smile in our voices. Other times he'd just close his eyes and tilt his head

as if gliding along with the music. Max was the cornerstone that held the group together.

Duane Hamilton said, "Although Max may not be a trained musician, I think he is one of the most intuitively astute and knowledgeable musicians I've ever known. He possesses a sense about music, which cannot be taught, superseding traditional learning alone. He is also blessed with a musical charisma, which is arguably more important. His intuitive sense is the basis for his understanding of music, but his charisma is the tool that allows him to draw others into his vision. He possesses an indefinable quality that compels those around him to reach for higher heights. Even today the memory of being on stage with Max and drawing from his energy is still strong."

Max was also a master at keeping a song going, even if he forgot the words. If he was singing a solo and forgot, he'd simply make up new words. Lucy laughed as she remembered some lyrics Max came up with once—something about a big white horse. If Max forgot the words when the whole group was singing, he'd just keep moving his lips as he slowly raised his microphone to cover his mouth or look to Val for the words.

Max was a genius at smoothing over mistakes. He always knew just what to say to get everyone laughing. He mastered the art of delivery. We all have our favorite on-stage "Maxisms:"

"You know, folks, sometimes I feel like I'm in a rat race, and the rats are winning!"

Getting a level before the concert. Max, Kim Bird, Dave Mauck, Amanda Mauck, Jim McDonald, Debbie McDonald and Dunbar Henri

"You know what, folks? When you feel that you're at the end of your rope, do what I do. Just tie a knot and hang on!"

"If you don't like this song, it lasts only three minutes."

"If you'd like to sing along, please don't, because it kind of bothers us."

"If you buy the CD and you don't like it, give it to someone you don't like."

"Folks, I've read the back of the book. And we win!"

When setting up for a concert, Max would have the singers run through a song so Greg could adjust the mix and the stage monitor levels. Max said, "Greggor, would you turn me up a little bit? I'd just as soon hear myself as anybody!"

When practicing or learning a song or warming up before a concert, Max would sometimes have to reach deep into his well of inspiration to get us to give him the sound he wanted. For years, other choral directors have wanted to know Max's secret

for getting that smooth, lush Heritage sound. Max would look at us in frustration and say, "C'mon you guys, BLEND!" Other times he would tell us, "Guys, we got to sell the song," or "Annunciate!"

Max always said, "If you make a mistake, make sure it's a good one, so you can laugh about it!" Lucy remembered one time when Max thought he recognized a friend in the audience. Lucy said, "He was so thrilled to see his friend that he told the audience a bit about the person, and then asked him to stand up. Well, everyone was looking all around and Max was gesturing for the man to stand up, but the man just turned around to see who Max was looking at. It turned out that the man wasn't who Max thought he was after all!"

Performing on stage didn't always go perfectly for the Heritage Singers. Max told of one time when the group was in the middle of a song and all of a sudden his bow tie shot off like a bullet into the crowd! Another time there were beetles bombing the singers on stage, and the singers kept trying to dodge them! Max said, "They were coming in like dive bombers at us!"

Gerry Wood remembered another similar incident when Heritage was performing in Oklahoma. She said, "We were booked into a little hall in a small town out in the middle of nowhere. The building had a low ceiling, a small stage, and a very squeaky screen door. As little kids are apt to do, they began running in and out of the building while we were trying to sing, the door squeaking loudly each time it opened and shut. I think the confusion got to us all because Max forgot the words to 'In the Garden,' so he just made something up and kept going. Of course that is a song that most people know. The audience had to have known he was making it up.

"The rest of us were also having a hard time concentrating.

Then, as one of the kids ran out the door, a huge June bug—sticky legs and all—flew into the room. It began to fly helter-skelter all over the place, eventually finding us up on stage. It flew right at us, almost hitting us. I remember seeing Larry Matthews out of the corner of my eye as he ducked to avoid being hit. It flew by me and brushed my hair. I ducked and let out a little scream, but kept singing. Then it flew at Max and he hit at it with his microphone, but missed! By this time, we had no idea what we were even singing. We were trying so hard not to laugh while singing a soft, subdued song. But it got worse.

"The June bug circled around, taking a big tour of the room, then turned toward the stage and headed our way again. We were mesmerized by its flight and just stared at it as it came in at a low angle and landed on the stage, skidding across the floor for a few feet before coming to a stop in front of us, center stage. This was almost too much for us! Fortunately, it was time for us to exit the stage for a break, and we were able to hold our laughter until we got outside."

Gerry also remembered a time when the group was performing in Yucaipa, California, and everyone was waiting in the wings for the man on the stage to introduce them. Gerry said, "The man went on and on about how he was a good friend of the director and the Heritage Singers. He said he had known Max for a long time and was so privileged to introduce 'Mark Max and the Heritage Singers!' Max looked over at me with a puzzled look on his face and said, 'Did he say Mark?' I nodded, laughing, as we all walked out on stage and began singing. Jim McDonald didn't let Max forget that for a long time. He would start laughing, looking

"Put some feeling into it"

at Max, and say, 'And now my good friend, Mark Max and the Heritage Singers!' Then we'd laugh all over again."

Dunbar Henri remembered the time the Heritage Singers performed at the Crystal Cathedral in Garden Grove, California. This was back in the days before instrumental tracks were used, which meant Heritage had to use live instruments. Naturally, the singers were excited about performing live on television in front of such a large audience. They even arrived early that day to set up their sound system. Each singer had his or her own microphone that was attached to a cord. The microphones were marked with narrow pieces of colored tape so that everyone knew which microphone was theirs. With cords all over the stage, you can imagine that things got a little tricky when eight singers tried to add a little choreography.

Dunbar said, "We were in the middle of the song, 'Nearer, Still Nearer,' when the girls stepped forward for a trio segment. As they stepped forward, one of their microphone cords suddenly was yanked up tightly between my legs, where it remained for the entire portion of the song. I was hoping the entire time that the television cameras didn't pick up on it!"

Tammy Rael Lawley sang with both the Heritage Singers and Heritage en Español from 1991-2000. "My last year of Heritage I joined the Spanish group and traveled with them for one year. Not knowing Spanish very well at all led to many funny stories. One that I remember was during a TV taping at TBN. We were taping the song 'Yo volaré' ('I'll Fly Away'). The music started and everyone started to sing, but something sounded very strange. Everyone except me was singing in Spanish. I forgot that I was singing with the Spanish group and blurted out in English!"

Art Mapa told of a concert that the group held at Southwestern Adventist College in Texas. "The band went out on the stage first to get settled. We saw a little mouse running around the stage. Then, the group stepped out. Of course Becki stepped right on the poor little mouse while getting ready to sing. And, the worst thing is Becki didn't even notice. She didn't even believe us when we told her about it later."

Another time, Judy Mote started a solo Duane Hamilton was singing in the wrong key. It was Judy's first concert playing the piano for Heritage II. She was an excellent piano player who could play any song in any key. Duane and Judy had practiced "The Savior Is Waiting" earlier that day. Duane said, "When Judy started the introduction in concert, she was in the wrong key. It was way too high for me, but I just went along with her

Heritage visits Tijuana, Mexico

and did my best. After a while, Judy got this look on her face like she realized what she had done, so she added a little musical interlude and tried to transpose the song down to a lower key. However, instead of going down, she actually transposed it into an even higher key! I was already at the top of my range, and I could feel the sweat dripping down my face. I ended up sliding down an octave and finishing the song that way. I looked down at Judy and noticed a tear running down her cheek. Out of the corner of my eye, I could see the singers in back of me just shaking because they were laughing so hard. As soon as I finished the song, we left the stage and had a good laugh. Judy never forgot that. Neither did I!"

Performing overseas could be just as interesting. "They'd always warn us not to drink the water or have any ice—you know, those sorts of things," Val said. "I remember one time

when we were in Brazil, all of us thought we were being really careful. Unfortunately it hit us during the concert, the singers were getting sick one by one and began leaving the stage. They were lying down behind the stage curtain just moaning in pain. Our group on stage kept getting smaller and smaller until there were only three of us left!"

"A memorable moment was when we were somewhere back east and sang in a large school auditorium," said Cindi Rael Paige. "I felt fine all day, until 'half-time' when we went to collect the offering. I was starting to feel sick. Jim McDonald was giving the call, and I suddenly started to feel queasy. I tried to get Max's attention, but he was so into Jim's call that he wouldn't look at me. My ears started ringing and I grabbed the sleeve of the person standing next to me. The next thing I knew, I slithered to the floor. I fainted in front of all those people! They carried me off stage and to the bus. When I came to, I started crying, and I remember Max telling me, 'at least you went down gracefully. You could have gone face first!' Thanks Max."

Dunbar Henri remembered preparing for Heritage's first trip to Central and South America. The group only had two weeks to put together a Spanish concert for their upcoming trip. They practiced for hours every day, working with a Spanish coach who had been hired to help them learn their songs in Spanish. There wasn't time for interpretation, although, they already knew the songs in English.

"Max was very busy doing other things to organize the trip, so he wasn't always able to attend the practice sessions," said Dunbar. "Shortly before we left for Central America, we had a concert in California. By this time we felt fairly confident singing some of our songs in Spanish, and we decided to surprise Max with how well we were doing. The first song on the program that night was 'Plenty of Room in the Family.' When the instrumental introduction began, we walked out onto the stage, grouped into our 'threes,' looked over at Max for our opening cue, and began singing. You should have seen the look on Max's face! He didn't know the Spanish words, and here we were putting him on the spot in front of an audience. His face got beet red, but always the professional, Max just lifted his microphone up a bit to cover his mouth, moved his lips, smiled, and pretended to sing as if nothing was wrong. The audience didn't know the difference. Throughout the song he kept looking over at us like, 'I'll get you later!'"

The singers didn't play tricks on each other very often—at least not on stage. In fact, when they were in concert, they tried to look out for each other. When someone wasn't having a good night and couldn't sing their solo, someone else would step in and do it for them.

Max remembered a concert they did in Dayton, Ohio in 1989. "There were about 1,500 people in the audience, and we were well into our concert when the power suddenly went out. The entire neighborhood had no power. Well, we can't do much of a concert, at least not with that many people, without power. Our bus driver, Arnie Knapp, called the power company to see what was going on. He was told that a main substation transformer had gone out and that it would be an hour before the power would be restored. Talk about being put on the spot!

"Well, I led the congregation in singing and prayer. We sang a few songs and had just finished praying (maybe ten minutes had passed) when suddenly the power came back on! We were so thankful for that. We ended up starting our concert over so that the radio station could record it. We went on to have one of the most inspiring concerts. The audience shared in the experience. It was a concert they'll never forget. Many decisions for Christ were made that night."

"One of the best concerts I remember was in Everett, Washington," said Terry Mace. "There was an old, beautiful auditorium there. Another great place was Symphony Hall in Portland, Oregon. In those venues, we had access to bigger sound systems. They had lighting people and a stage manager. We played to full auditoriums every night. It was something I'll never forget.

"I also remember a concert in Portland, where Ron Edgerton joined us on stage as a guest artist for the song, 'To God Be the Glory.' It was just an incredible thing to be there and feel the energy of that song as only Ron could sing it. What an amazing talent! The audience's response was incredible. People literally jumped to their feet after the song."

Marcelo Constanzo, a current Heritage Singer recalled a concert that the Spanish group held at the Adventist college church in Chile. "We were in the middle of the concert and the power went out in the church. A huge storm was raging outside. The vice president of the school and a former Heritage Singer, Magdiel Pérez, was able to get a generator for us to run our sound system, but we still didn't have any lights. We couldn't sing in the dark. The people of the church came up with a solution. They went and got their cars and drove them up to the glass windows of the church. Then, they turned their car lights on and we finished our concert. They were willing to do anything to hear us sing. God worked in spite of the storm."

"Being in Heritage gave me a chance to feel like a real musician," said Rick Lange. "Max gave me my first chance to write orchestration scores. I worked on the first three Heritage II albums. We recorded the third one at Pinebrook, Bill Gaither's recording studio. It was a thrill for me—although not without some rough spots.

"We had the studio full of musicians and were recording the tracks that I had orchestrated. Everything was going along fine until the horns came in, and they were playing in the wrong key! Realizing that their scores had been written out incorrectly, I grabbed Mark Becker, our tenor singer, who was also working on getting a degree in music. He was able to quickly transpose the horn charts in another room, while we worked on another section. That was how we all worked together as a team. It was a fantastic experience, and I'll always be grateful to Max for giving me that opportunity.

"Max also asked me to arrange the background orchestrations on two Heritage children's albums. I loved that experience! I am amazed at the faith Max and Lucy showed in me, and I'm amazed at the talent there was in Heritage. They made it happen, both in the recording studio and on stage.

Heritage Singer Scott Reed said, "I've been in recording studio settings of all kinds, some of them high-profile, and I can tell you that there's nothing harder than recording with Heritage. The way we work on pitch and tone, you think you can sing, until you're in that situation. It's been really great vocal training for me.

Heritage Singers with performers from the Mexican Riviera cruise

"It's not just Max's musical vision that I admire; it's his philosophy of sharing the spotlight. It's a reflection of Max and Lucy's vision and attitude of ministry. That's why good musicians are willing to sing for Max for not a lot of money; people want to partner with that kind of vision and philosophy. Observing Max as a leader and seeing how he totally trusts and respects the people around him has been inspiring. He just brings out the best in people. He's totally shaped me."

Scott recalled a cruise that Heritage took in 2000 to the Mexican Riviera. The devotional speaker for the week was Pastor Morris Venden. During the week, the Heritage Singers held a few concerts. They were able to enjoy the cruise entertainment during the evening, and got to know several of the young dancers that were working on the ship. One night the Heritage Singers even gave up their seats in the formal dining room so the dancers could experience the fine dining.

"The dancers could relate to us because we were all together in the culture of performing arts. They saw us as normal people, not fanatics. We got to know them, and then told them about God," said Scott. Some of the dancers even began to come to the devotional talks. Scott equated this to parenting. "As parents we have to tell our kids not to do something, and sometimes crack down on them. Eventually, they thank us for giving them boundaries. These dancers needed boundaries too. We were able to paint a picture of God that gives freedom in our boundaries, and in that we have joy and life. The dancers saw us as a group of people who were fully alive yet free.

"The beauty of Max's ministry is that it tells of the power of a strong dad. The gospel of Jesus gives us freedom. We are blessed to be able to be used by God through the Heritage Singer ministry. It is humbling to be in the spotlight. Our prayer is always that people will see less of us and more of our Heavenly Father."

CHAPTER NINE

International Travels

Heritage Singers at the Malacañing Palace with President Ferdinand Marcos and Mrs. Imelda Marcos

U P UNTIL THE LATE 1970S, THE HERITAGE SINGERS PRETTY MUCH WENT WHEREVER THE BUS COULD GO, which limited them to North America. Then, the group started doing international tours, and a whole new world opened up to them. Terry said, "I was with the group when we went to the Philippines for the first time. People just loved us. They treated us like royalty. We sang outdoors in a park in downtown Manila, where 40,000-50,000 people gathered to hear the concert. These kinds of crowds were unheard of in the United States."

Lucy said she would not forget the sight of all those Filipino people gathered outside. "It was an incredible visual—a sea of black hair for as far as you could see. And then, it started to rain. Suddenly, umbrellas began to pop up, one at a time, throughout the crowd of people. Imagine, 40,000 umbrellas popping up in all different colors. It was like watching a colorful flower garden bloom before your eyes!"

While in the Philippines the group was invited to sing for Imelda and Marco Marcos at the Presidential Palace. Each of the singers was given a gold medallion, engraved with the faces of the presidential couple.

Touring internationally not only expanded the ministry of the Heritage Singers, but the group's hearts too. "As we were exposed to people from foreign lands and their many different philosophies and worldviews, our hearts were opened," said Joanne. "We learned to be more tolerant and accepting of differences, and we developed a genuine appreciation for different cultures. We also discovered first hand that music is truly a universal language. The generosity and kindness of people all around the world, along with their joyful way of meeting life's difficulties, won our hearts. It was an education we could've never received from books or classrooms."

At one point during the Central American tour, the group was crunched for time and wasn't able to fly to a neutral country when traveling between two countries that were at war with each other. If the group was going to make it to their next concert on time, they needed to fly directly there. Joanne said, "An unmarked cargo plane and a few creative passport entries later, we were on our way. I can still see us in our matching shirts, sundresses, bandannas and espadrilles, standing on the tarmac, ready to climb up the steps onto an old two-engine plane. Never mind that the plane's paint was peeling. All smiles and feathered haircuts, we had no worries about hauling thousands of pounds of equipment aboard a plane that had obviously seen better days. For us, it was a wild, crazy adventure, complete with drama and romance. More stories for the folks back home!"

When the Heritage Singers were in Nicaragua, they visited a small hospital in the hills, near where their concert was being held. All around them, they could hear gunshots in the distance. Sniper fire, they were told. "The hospital reminded me of M.A.S.H. reruns on television," said Joanne. "The facility was quite primitive and the patients, even children, were mostly gunshot victims. I felt overwhelmed at what God deals with. There was so much trouble in the world. How can something as insignificant as a singing group even put a dent in solving these kinds of problems? How relevant could we really be to these people?

"But then, we noticed the hope in the eyes of each person we saw. They had been looking forward to this day for a long time and were just soaking up every minute they could get with us.

We obviously were the bright spot in their lives. So maybe, that's why we're here, I thought. Maybe just being here and doing what we do is enough to help them get through this day and give them some hope for their future. It was important for us to know that we were doing some good, or else it just didn't seem worth all the trouble. We had to look beyond the futility of it all and trust that God was using us to bring hope to this remote corner of the world. We had to believe that we were there for a purpose greater than what we could humanly do for these people."

Lucy remembered going for walks with Max every morning in San Salvador. Each morning there was a shoeshine boy sitting outside their hotel. "He couldn't have been much older than five or six," Lucy said. "Whenever we'd walk by, he'd look up at Max and say, 'Shoeshine, Mister?' Max would give him a dollar and have him shine his shoes. One day Max and Jim McDonald had to leave early in the morning to do a radio interview, so Max didn't come with me on my morning walk. When I approached the shoeshine boy, he said, 'Where Mister?' Then, even more emphatically, 'Where Mister?' He must have followed me for two or three blocks saying, 'Where Mister?' 'Where Mister?'"

Dunbar Henri remembered the group's first trip to Central America and what a rough schedule they had. "On most days we had two concerts," he said. "That, in itself, was draining, but I was also in charge of the speakers and setting up the sound system. In those days, the equipment was large and bulky, and the speakers were very large. There was a lot of physical work involved in setting up and then tearing down the system twice a day! We worked very hard, and we got tired, but we didn't fight. Maybe we did some things we shouldn't have done, but we did the best we could to get along with each other."

During the Central American trip, Joanne remembered another unforgettable plane ride. She said, "This time, we seriously didn't think we were going to make it. We were taking off from a runway on the top of a mountain. We were on a smaller plane, heavily loaded with sound equipment, and dangerously over the weight limit. Our equipment was strapped with cargo netting along one side of the plane and all of us squeezed onto the few seats on the other side. The curtain between the cockpit and the passengers remained open. I sat with Bob Folkenberg, the president of the Central American Union, who was accompanying us on the tour. We looked out the front window of the plane, seeing what the pilots were seeing—the end of the runway quickly approaching.

"The engines roared as we tried to pick up speed, but we weren't lifting off the ground. The sweat was pouring off Bob's face. He was leaning over into the center aisle, trying to say something to the pilots. His face was pale and he looked very scared. I saw the surrounding mountains getting closer and closer as we approached the drop off that was obviously the end of our runway.

Pastor Bob Folkenberg, Max, Kim Bird and Joanne Mullin in Central America

"We approached the drop off at the highest speed possible for our poor overloaded plane. The engines screamed as we bumped over the end of the runway and saw the ground drop away beneath us. The plane just kept going straight ahead. It was the only way we became airborne. However, we didn't seem to be climbing at all as we approached a nearby mountain. The plane banked sharply and just missed the mountain. We strained and pulled our way around it and through a narrow pass, gradually easing into our flight.

"The Heritage Singers sang with new enthusiasm and joyful relief that night. It just felt so good to be on stage singing about the God who had protected us that day. After what we had just been through, every word we said and every song we sang came to life. It was so very real and meaningful. As we looked at each other across the stage, we wondered what would happen next."

While in Brazil, the Heritage Singers visited Iguacu Falls. Far larger and steeper than any falls they'd ever seen, they were in awe of the massive thundering beauty and intimidating power of it. Not far from the falls was a monument where the borders of Argentina, Paraguay and Brazil met. There was a market in Paraguay that the group wanted to visit and in order to get across the water to it, they had ride in a little canoe-like boat.

Joanne said, "Our boat had a small outboard motor and a large rudder to steer it. There were so many of us in the boat that it sank down to only about two inches above the water. If we tipped a little this way or that, we'd be taking on water or flipping over. The man steering the boat told us we'd better keep our hands inside the boat because the waters were infested with flesh-eating piranhas.

"Suddenly, the motor stalled. We started to drift in the silence of the calm water above the falls. The man who was operating the boat couldn't get it started up again. We could hear the rushing water of the falls getting louder and louder, working its way up to a thundering roar. As we drifted toward the brink, we prayed that that engine would start. We looked at each other fearfully, realizing just how precarious our situation was. Then, as suddenly as it had stalled, the motor started up again, and we were safely taken ashore.

We had a great time at the market, but we had to get back in that same boat again to get to our side of the water. Thankfully, this time the trip was uneventful."

Cindy Haffner remembered traveling with the Heritage Singers in the early 1980s. "I think we went to Australia, South Africa and London three years in a row," she said. "It was such a great experience meeting people in other cultures and seeing how they lived."

Lucy always prepared individual servings of snacks for each trip in case anyone needed a quick energy boost. Cindy said,

"We took these snacks with us everywhere, even into the heart of Africa. Some people there allowed us into their home, which was nothing more than a hut made of straw and mud. We gave the children our peanuts and crackers, and you would think they'd won the lottery! I will always remember the looks of joy on their little faces! It brought tears to our eyes as we saw what a huge impact our small gift had on these little children. We didn't know how spoiled we were until we traveled and saw how other people lived. There's nothing quite like being there with those people."

"I took individual packs of almonds with me to South Africa," remembered Lucy. "They were wrapped in shiny foil. When I handed them out to the children they were so excited about the foil and being able to see their reflections in the packets, they wouldn't even open them!"

The Heritage Singers first trip to South Africa was in 1983. The 14 travelers had 32 pieces of equipment, weighing almost 2,000 pounds, plus their own baggage and records and tapes. Talk about excess baggage! When the group left New York, it was snowing and cold. When they arrived in Johannesburg, South Africa, it was 115 degrees. The combination of long hours of traveling, the jet lag and the vast climate change caused many of the singers to come down with fevers and nausea. After a couple of days of rest, the singers bounced back and enjoyed the six-week tour in good health.

The government officials warmly welcomed the group as it went out into the villages and cities of South Africa. In just one week of concerts, the Heritage Singers saw 100 people take their stand for the Lord. "One of the pastors told me that he had never

Becki preparing for her ostrich ride

seen anything like it!" Max remembered. "God wanted us there at that time. He opened the doors for us to go."

One day, the group spent the entire day at the television station. There was only one station, and the government ran it. "We taped six songs and several interviews," Max said. "South Africa had very little Christian programming. The station broadcasted only three hours a day, so when it is on, everyone was watching. We knew this opportunity to present Christian music on South African television was a miracle. We sang about Jesus, His love and His soon coming. We prayed earnestly for the Holy Spirit to give us the right words to say."

Even with a heavy concert schedule, the Heritage Singers were able to see some of the natural wonders of the continent of Africa. Although the group didn't have time to tour any game reserves, they did get to stop at an ostrich farm for a ride! The braver members of the group quickly found out that ostriches were not like horses! There is no way to guide the birds, and the only way to stay on is to grab the wings.

While in South Africa, the Heritage Singers were also able to perform at the Adventist colleges in Transkei and Cape Town. Hundreds of students dedicated their hearts to the Lord. One of the college instructors said he had never before seen such an outpouring of love on campus. He said, "It's a miracle that so many lives have been touched!"

The group also performed for two camp meetings, where thousands of people gathered. There were even some impromptu concerts in the bush country of Transkei. Despite the vast cultural differences, music bridged the gap. Within six months of the first South African tour, plans were being made for a return tour, to take place less than a year after the first trip! Since then, the Heritage Singers' have returned to South Africa several times.

In March of 1983 the Heritage Singers made their first trip to Australia and New Zealand. In the span of one month, the Heritage Singers presented more than 17 concerts in the major cities of these two countries. Their concert in Melbourne was standing room only, which prompted the group to add another concert. The Lord truly blessed the Melbourne programs and many people came forward to acknowledge Jesus as their personal Savior.

The Heritage Singers with Beverly Read and her family in Australia

The group planned to travel between cities by air in Australia, but when the airline wanted to charge them a larger than expected excess baggage charge, Max and Lucy didn't know what they were going to do. "Fortunately, we met a man at one of our concerts who worked for a rival airline" Lucy said. "He made the necessary arrangements to change our tickets, and they accepted our 2,000 pound sound system for a minimal charge."

In Sydney, as in Melbourne, the two concerts were filled to capacity and a third one was added. Then, in Brisbane the concert was held at the 1,500-seat Sports Complex where the Commonwealth Games were held.

Before they left Australia, Val was granted her wish of being able to hold a cuddly koala. One of the sponsors arranged for the group to go to a koala park and hold several of the 100 bears.

When the singers visited Sydney, they were hoping to see a special little girl who had been sending them letters for quite some time. Eight-year-old Beverley Read's greatest wish was to hear the Heritage Singers sing, "The King is Coming" in person.

She didn't think her wish would ever come true, not only because she lived on the other side of the world, but also because she had leukemia.

In her letters, Beverley described in detail her life-threatening disease and the painful chemotherapy and bone marrow transplants. She told the group that during these treatments she would listen to the Heritage Singers album *Heaven is for Kids* on her tape player. As she was lying alone in the hospital room, her mind would be on Heaven as she sang or hummed along.

Her doctors couldn't understand why she didn't scream during the treatments, like the other patients. She was a living witness of the Great Comforter to the non-Christian medical personnel. They even learned some of her songs.

When Beverley first started sending her letters, the Heritage Singers had no plans to visit Australia. However, when they arrived in Sydney, there she was, along with her sister and her parents. The group spent the evening with Beverley and her family, and she had front-row seats for both Sydney concerts.

Beverley's wish to hear "The King is Coming" came true. The group asked her to come up with them on stage as they dedicated the song to her. Some of her doctors and nurses also attended the concert and were visibly touched by her witness that evening. Beverley challenged the Heritage Singers to meet her in Heaven if she didn't meet them again on earth. That night over 70 people came forward to accept Beverley's Jesus as their Savior.

Many years went by and the Heritage Singers lost track of Beverly. However, 18 years after that memorable concert in Sydney, Max and Lucy received this letter:

Dear Lucy and Max,

Hi! It's been a long time! I'm Beverley Read, the girl with cancer who you visited on your tour to Australia many years ago. I walked into a Christian bookstore yesterday and they happened to be playing one of your CDs. It was my all time favorite song, "The King is Coming." It sent me on a trip down memory lane, recalling those years I was sick. I was always listening to your music during my treatments and when I just had to lie still.

The Heritage Singers music still means as much to me today as it did then. I remember how you called me onto the stage during one of your concerts to give me your "Dove" pin. Looking at it now reminds me of you and the fun we had.

A lot of water has gone under the bridge since then. I am in good health and have been married for nine years. I work at the local pharmacy. Mom and Dad are well and send their regards. I just thought I'd drop you a line to see how life is.

God Bless,
Beverley

"What a wonderful heartwarming surprise for Lucy and I to get this letter—and after 18 years!" said Max. "The Bible says, 'He who began a good work in you will be faithful to complete it.' What God started during those first international trips has grown and continues to have an impact on peoples' lives."

Following the Heritage Singers concerts in Australia, they traveled to New Zealand. Upon arriving, they discovered a $6,000 import tax on their records and tapes, which had been shipped to New Zealand four months before. Lucy said, "We prayed about it and went to the Appeals Board to request they lower the tax. To our relief, it was cut in half!"

Pieces of luggage and sound equipment headed for Australia

While in New Zealand the Heritage Singers toured in a mini-van and towed a trailer with their luggage and sound equipment. Since the sheep in New Zealand outnumber the people by about three to one, there were always flocks of sheep wherever the group drove. One time while driving, it suddenly began to rain, and then it stopped as unexpectedly as it had started, leaving a Technicolor double rainbow. Lucy said, "The colors were so vivid and intense. It was like nothing I've ever seen."

In September of that year, the Heritage Singers began their first European tour—six countries in two weeks! After arriving in Amsterdam, all 30 pieces of their sound equipment and luggage were loaded onto a waiting bus for the ferry to London. Their first two concerts were in the cities of London and Manchester. Then it was back across the channel to the next concert in Amsterdam. "We were pleased to find out that music is indeed the universal language—especially when the theme is the universally appealing love of Christ," Max said. "Even though we used an interpreter at some of the concerts, the audience responded to what we were saying before the interpreter could finish, so we knew they understood us."

At the French border, the group experienced a delay when inspectors found a problem with Ecuadorian singer Fernando Quinde's passport. Apparently, he needed a special visitor's visa to enter France. The singers prayed about it while the customs officials decided what to do. After 20 minutes, the inspectors issued a rare temporary permit. Very thankful, the group continued on to Paris.

On the day of their first concert in Paris, the group awoke to find that all of the sound equipment had been stolen from the bus, which had been unmarked and carefully locked the night before. The thieves didn't take it all, but pieces of Heritage's sound equipment were scattered all over the ground. They had no speakers, no electric guitar, and no electric bass. Thankfully, members of the audience came to the group's aid by bringing pieces of their own home stereo systems to the concert, which left Greg trying to figure out how to wire all of the bits and pieces of equipment together to create a sound system for the concert!

The group didn't have time to buy new equipment, so with the help of local residents, Max was able to find rental equipment to carry on with the tour. Heritage's loss amounted to $22,000 and included many personal items that could not be replaced. This was a real blow to the group, but the tour continued as planned. They gave two concerts for capacity crowds at The American Cathedral in Paris, an ecumenical and international church uniting Protestant denominations.

The Heritage Singers ended their tour with three programs in West Germany. The final concert was held at the U.S. military base in Darmstadt for servicemen and women. One serviceman told the group, "I really needed this Christ-centered concert. Please remember me in prayer. I'm having problems and it is great to know that there are people and a God who cares."

The response to the Heritage Singers international tours that first year was tremendous. More than 1,500 people had made a new commitment to follow Christ. The singers had experienced different cultures and people, and they were humbled yet again as they saw how God worked through them in their concerts. It was just the beginning of many years of worldwide ministry for the Heritage Singers. The Heritage Singers have now traveled to over 70 foreign countries to share the gospel of Christ. Although traveling can be stressful and challenging, Max said, "As long as the Lord opens the door for us to go to foreign countries, we will continue to go where He is leading."

CHAPTER TEN

Brazil—God's Power Over Evil

"For our struggle is not against flesh and blood, but against the powers of this dark world and against the spiritual forces of evil in the heavenly realms. Therefore, put on the full armor of God, so that when the day of evil comes, you may be able to stand your ground, and after you have done everything, to stand."

Ephesians 6:12 & 13

THE HERITAGE BUS FLOWED DOWN A RIVER OF RED TAILLIGHTS, WINDING ITS WAY AROUND RIO DE JANEIRO to where the group was to perform. Layers of city lights twinkled against an abrupt wall of black mountains that surround the city, and ocean breezes ruffled palms along the boulevard as the moonlight reflected off the waves on the beach.

"We were in awe of the beauty that surrounded us. We were so thrilled to be there, a place that none of us would've ever seen if we weren't in the Heritage Singers," said Joanne. "Anticipation grew as we got closer to the auditorium where we were scheduled to perform and realized it faced the ocean. It was an ornate and beautiful building with balconies that had French doors opening to the ocean air. Upon stepping off the bus, we could hear the ocean waves and feel the balmy breezes on our faces. We suddenly felt energized as we prepared for our concert."

This was an important concert for the Heritage Singers as several singing groups from around Brazil had traveled to be there, so they could see in person the group that had inspired their own. The group was treated like they were celebrities. Fans followed them around to their concerts. They were constantly being bombarded with requests for autographs. It was very different from anything they had ever experienced in the United States.

The hall was filled with people, the stage lights bright, as we walked out to perform. As the evening progressed, we were full of energy and we could feel the Holy Spirit working. We felt renewed and invigorated after the grueling schedule of the last few days. The audience was enthusiastic and receptive. Toward the end of the concert, as we always do, we invited those who wanted us to pray with them to come to the front. Many people came forward, including a young girl named Suzanne.

When the concert ended we made our way to the lobby

to sell records and talk with the people. Our new album *I Am Willing, Lord* had just been released. The albums sold as fast as we could unpack them. People ripped the plastic off the albums as soon as they had paid for them and presented them to us for autographs. Some of the young kids were actually climbing the wall just so they could touch the singers' blonde hair. It was very chaotic.

"I was beginning to feel claustrophobic," said Joanne "I looked up toward a doorway that opened out to a small balcony overlooking the city. I could hear the ocean. The breeze coming through the lobby was so inviting that I found myself wanting to head in that direction to get some air. Just then, our interpreter, Joe, came up to me. 'Why don't we go outside? There's a girl out there who is asking us to pray with her.' Seeing it as a means of escape from the crowd, I gladly followed him out to the balcony.

"The girl was hunched over like she was ill. Three or four men dressed like they could be pastors surrounded her, already praying in Portuguese. Max was there, too. The balcony was small. We were all tightly squeezed against the iron railing. It was then that I got a good look at her. She is not a girl at all! She must be an old woman. Her face was distorted. It looked as though she was having a seizure or something. Then her writhing body, clearly in torturous pain, was on the floor of the balcony. Her eyes were white with fire as they rolled back into her head. Foam was actually coming out of her mouth. And her hands, her hands were rigid, like claws. I began to feel nauseous.

"The men surrounding her rushed to hold her down. I remember wondering what was wrong with her. I held a tall stack of Bibles and stood in the corner against the railing not knowing what to do. I looked at Max. He looked scared too. This did not look like a girl. It was more like an angry person full of agonizing pain and fierce, demonic rage.

"We suddenly realized that what we were seeing was, in fact, demon possession. We had heard about this phenomenon. We had been told that it is very common in Brazil. But what I was seeing with my own eyes was humanly impossible. I felt my knees go weak. The Bibles scattered as I felt everything start to spin and suddenly go black. I passed out."

After Joanne fainted, Max sent someone to get Dave Mauck. Dave had theological training and pastoral experience. He was more prepared to handle something like this. Dave approached the terrace and was stunned by what he saw.

"I saw a woman on the floor being restrained by five or six men. At first I couldn't tell what was happening," said Dave. "This wasn't the way Jesus met the demoniacs in the Scripture. He didn't call for his disciples to use their combative skills to restrict and restrain those demented men. This just wasn't the way it was supposed to be. The men who were trying to restrain her seemed as frantic as the small woman they were trying to hold down. One or two men were on each limb, each one having intense difficulty holding her still. All the while, I heard her screaming, 'I am Satan! I am Satan!'

"She spoke in other languages, as well. I later found out that she could only speak Portuguese. As I beheld this horrific scene, I prayed that God would let His love flow through me as I knelt

Heritage in Brazil

beside her. I looked into her face. It was aged and creased with deep lines. She looked like an incredibly old woman. Her eyes blazed with bizarre viciousness, appearing to flash fiery red with rage and hate wherever she looked. I touched her arm as lightly as you would glide a feather over a child's face. When the hideous 'old woman' felt my touch, she immediately stopped struggling and abruptly turned her head to look at me.

"Suddenly her expression changed. Her attention was entirely focused on me and she got a shy, almost bashful expression. She didn't once try to move her arm, even though her other arm, legs, and body were writhing and flailing about. It was as if God's tender touch of love was holding her arm to the floor. No doubt it was precisely like the extraordinary, supernatural love that constrained Jesus' arms to the cross for you and me.

"A momentary calm came over her face as she continued to gaze at me. It seemed as if she could see into my mind and knew what I was thinking. I wondered if she was the one looking at me or if the tormenter within her was sensing another Ruler, almighty in nature, whose infinite power was light years beyond his own.

"After a moment of tranquil, timid eye contact, she swiftly turned her face away from me. Then, the demon within, collected himself and seized immediate domination of the woman in the same vicious manner as before, shrieking accusatory indictments to all those around her.

"As if being electrified, she started thrashing about, even more intensely than before. She addressed one of the men in Portuguese. I saw his face fall as if informed that his only child had died. Mortified, he stood and left the terrace. By then, Joe our translator, was by my side. He explained that she was speaking as if she were the demon himself, accusing the man of sexual sins. 'Why are you touching my leg?' she demanded. 'You've belonged to me for many years!'

"Once again the woman became still and asked to go inside the auditorium. The men held onto her as we stood and slipped into the main hall. We entered through the side double doors and sat in the back row against the wall. A couple of men scrambled over and around the theatre seats to continue their grasp on her left arm and legs. Only a few men remained in the auditorium. I was still by her right side, restraining her arm simply by a gentle touch. She screamed again. 'I am SATAN!! I am SATAN! I am so high on SATAN!'

"She also shouted accusations at the singers who had gathered on stage quietly singing and praying. As she screamed, she kept grasping Joe's wrist and looking at his watch, as if to see what time it was. The voice coming from her got weaker. 'I can't stay much longer.'

"I continued to pray for God's power to expel Lucifer from her life and restore her to physical, mental and spiritual health. I was so focused on her that I didn't even hear the group singing. I turned to see them on the stage, standing around the piano, singing the most beautiful song I've ever heard. I'll never hear a sweeter sound on this earth. They sang, 'Peace, peace, wonderful peace, coming down from the Father above. Sweep over my spirit forever, I pray, in fathomless billows of love.' The building was filled with a clear spiritual splendor as this magnificent music floated to the ceiling. I know the angels have sung with Heritage before, but at that moment, their blended voices never sounded so beautiful."

As Joanne came to, she could hear voices swirling in and around her. She said, "I could feel that someone was carrying me and even heard Joe's voice. He was telling people to get out of the way and let him through. I could hear the strange voices all around me, but everything was still black. I couldn't bring myself back. The first thought that came to me was a nauseating fear that the demons had come into me, and that I was now saying and doing things I could not control. I was horrified that I was the one who now may be possessed.

"I struggled through the darkness and regained consciousness just as Joe sat me down in the back of the auditorium. As I began to realize where I was and could see once again, I still wasn't sure if I was okay. I put my head down and tried to return to my senses. I realized that people were actually using our record albums to fan my face and that people were still trying to get my autograph! Joe tried to keep the people away from me as I gradually realized that I was okay. I wondered about the woman on the balcony.

"The rest of the singers were gathered on the stage. Several small groups of people remained in the auditorium, as word spread quickly about what was happening. Through an interpreter, we were told that what we needed to do was go to a small room backstage and pray. This is what would cast the demons out. They had experience with this sort of thing. We should pray, confess our sins, and say the name of Jesus, because the demons couldn't stand to hear the name of Jesus. We couldn't get to that room fast enough.

"We found ourselves in a back room with chairs like a classroom. We began to pray. We searched our hearts, like we were told to do. What were we supposed to be looking for? We tried to remember our sins of the day. Then we went deeper and started confessing everything we could remember. We said the name of Jesus over and over. Then we began doing what we knew best how to do; we began to sing soft, simple hymns that we grew up singing."

Dunbar Henri recalled, "There was a lot of emotion around us, but I remember feeling very calm. The night before, I'd spent several hours walking on the beach—getting right with God. I knew I was right with God."

Realizing that many people were still in the auditorium, the Heritage Singers returned to the stage. Holding hands, they formed a circle, all the while continuing to quietly sing, "Amazing Grace, How Sweet the Sound," "Jesus, Jesus, Jesus, There's Just Something About that Name," and "Just As I Am, Without One Plea." And, they kept praying, praying that God would get them through this and cast the demons out of the poor woman.

Dunbar said, "Then we heard it, an inhuman sound that will haunt us for as long as we live; the voice of Satan himself! Unmistakably male, it was a horrible, angry sound, full of hatred, coming from the depths of evil. Speaking in languages we didn't understand, the possessed woman stealthily entered the back of the auditorium and gradually made her way to the side aisle. As she crept forward toward us, she continued to shout in anger, pointing to specific people in the auditorium. We had no idea what she was saying, but it was obvious that other people understood her.

"Several people in the room suddenly left. Even some of the ministers I had seen earlier on the balcony were leaving, quickly and quietly, as if ashamed and trying not to be seen. Our interpreter told us that they were leaving because their sins were being named and their private lives revealed. One by one, as their secret sins were revealed, they got out of their seats and left the room. The interpreter explained that the demons were saying, 'You hypocrites! You singing groups sing about one thing and live another. You are false. You can't hurt me!'

"I remember some of the things she said. I was standing close to a minister who was praying for her, and the demons said, 'What are you doing here? You belong to me!' I also recognized some of the languages the demons were using. Having spent some time in Beirut earlier in my life, I recognized the Arabic language, for one. The thing I most remember is the look in her eyes," recalled Dunbar.

Duane remembered the woman exclaiming in a low, ominous voice, "I am Satan!" A Brazilian theology student happened to be there, and he told Duane that she was speaking in Portuguese, Hebrew, and Greek. He interpreted some of what she was saying to Duane. "I don't care what you sing about. As long as you live the way you're living, I'm not afraid of you."

Suddenly, the group could understand what the demons were saying, remembered Max. It was in English, loud and clear. The woman stiffened and roared in her demonic voice, "I'm going to make all of you pay!" She slowly approached the stage where the singers huddled and prayed. "You can't have her! She's mine!" the voice screamed.

"You!" she growled, pointing at Joanne. "You, with the

GRACE NOTES:

"I just happened to tune you in on my television right after I received word that my mother had six months to a year to live. I knew Jesus at one time, but had fallen by the wayside. The song you sang when I saw your program was 'Someone is Praying for You.' It really touched me because I know both my mother and grandmother have gone down on their knees many times to pray that I would return to Christ. I need your prayers because I'm breaking up inside."

"My sister and I were introduced to your music very early on by our grandparents, with whom we lived when we were children. I was probably six or seven when I heard 'Hymns We Remember.' My sister and I knew every song.

When we were eight or nine, you came to our church in Hawaii. I was so thrilled! I remember giving Lucy a red hibiscus flower from my grandmother's garden, and we have pages of pictures in our photo album of my sister and I with the Heritage Singers.

Over the years all of our Christian influences, including the Heritage Singers music, faded away. It would be almost 20 years before we would find our way back to spiritual things. What I want you to know, because we don't always know how we touch the lives of those around us, is that during those years of denying my faith and my God, one of the few things that would stir the memory of my Christian beliefs was the sweet sound of hymns sung by your beautiful voices.

Your music called out to us over the decades, through the darkness, in spite of Satan's best efforts to keep us from hearing. Your ministry saves lives every day, just as it saved my life and my sisters'. Mr. Mace, thank you for having the faith and the courage to continue on after so many years. God bestows His blessings on each of us every day through your work, and we are truly grateful for your influence in our lives."

blonde hair! I'm going to get you!"

"She was looking directly at me with a look that pierced my very soul," recalled Joanne. "Whatever private thoughts and secret sins I had that I had not already confessed were surely going to be announced right here in front of everyone. I thought I was going to pass out again as she crept up the steps to the stage and crawled across the floor toward us. I wondered, when is God going to cast out those demons?"

Kim heard her say, "I am Satan! I am Satan!" Max heard her say, "I'm going to make all of you pay! You will pay!" Dan Mundy heard her say, "I'll give you everything you want in life—a successful career, whatever you want, but it can't have anything to do with God or religion."

"We heard the voice of Evil attack each one of us individually as the eyes of Satan burned right through us to our very souls," said Joanne. "We heard what we heard. Maybe each of us heard what Satan intended for each of us to hear."

"Satan's power was slowly losing its hold upon her," Dave recalled. "The terrible voice would exclaim through the woman that we couldn't have her, that she belonged to him. Yet, he would follow by saying that he couldn't stay much longer. Then she asked if she could go up to the stage. I remember her reaction as she reached the stage and saw her reflection in the polished black grand piano. She slowly stroked her face with her hands as if trying to smooth the lines from her face. I turned and noticed that Dunbar had a Bible and was reading promises out loud."

"Then it happened," recalled Dave. "While the demon-possessed woman was on the floor of the stage, Satan fell upon me with immense force! He accused me of sins ranging from my youth to the present. Every sin I'd ever committed was as clear before me as if I had just committed them—sins, both confessed and unconfessed. He knows them all, for they find their foundation in him. He gave no ground. His accusations wouldn't cease. He pressed heavily upon me the sense that I knew more than what I was living up to, that I had no right to be there. I felt the burden of guilt for permitting myself to be careless in my relationship with God. He made it appear as if I was worthless and undeserving of the love of God.

"Even in that moment of intense Satanic censure, my loving Lord brought to my attention that even if I felt hopeless and helpless and sin overwhelmed me, as long as I looked to the cross of Christ, and asked Him for pardon, and trusted fully in His promises, He would be faithful to forgive ALL my unrighteousness right then and there! So, I immediately knelt and prayed, this time not for the woman on the floor, but for my own sinful heart. I confessed all that Jesus revealed to me. And even though I didn't feel forgiven in the slightest way, I stood from that prayer in the strength of Jesus Christ, remembering His words, 'If I be for you, who can be against you?' Lucifer's so-called authority is puny and pitiful when compared to the powerful strength of the Almighty God!"

The demon-possessed woman gradually began to calm down. It seemed that the demons were leaving, or at least getting tired. She didn't look so wicked now, more like an exhausted young woman. Dave and Amanda Mauck knelt down next to her. There was a brief lull as she began to look tired and weak with exhaustion. She was quiet for a few moments, then she slowly sat up and grabbed Joe's arm to check his watch. Was it almost over? She suddenly became lifeless and limp as the demons left her wrung out like a dishrag on the stage floor. It was midnight.

"It was only then that we got our first glimpse of what she really looked like. We were shocked to see that this horrible inhuman creature that had earlier been so full of evil and hatred was actually a pretty and petite young sixteen-year-old girl," said Dave. "We learned that her name was Suzanne and that she was a ballerina. She spoke only Portuguese. Even in her exhausted and disheveled state, she was beautiful. Our hearts broke for her as she was carried out, lifeless and limp, silently sobbing."

"We took her off the stage to a side room," recalled Dave. "No one restrained her now. We continued to pray in that small back room as Dunbar read promise after promise from his Bible. Our faith had greatly increased and we claimed those promises

now in the renewed strength God gave us. There were still small groups of people praying all throughout the auditorium. Then, in the almighty authority of the precious name of Jesus, we commanded the evil one to be banished from her life. Satan had no choice. He was totally vanquished. He completely left the girl's body, and she slumped to the floor. At first, she didn't appear to be breathing, but we soon realized that she was still alive, just totally exhausted. Joe picked her up in his arms and carried her to his car and took her to the hospital where she spent the night."

"Speechless and exhausted ourselves, we somehow made it back to our hotel," recalled Joanne. "None of us had ever seen anything like this before, and we didn't know what to think about it."

Max asked the singers to meet and share their thoughts and feelings about what had happened. "What came to my mind at that time," Dave said, "was how important it is to stay close to God every day. Maybe it wouldn't take so long for God to claim victory over a demon-possessed person if our own souls were already surrendered to be used of Him."

Although it was obvious that God was more powerful than the demons, the singers were surprised at how long it took for them to be cast out. "We saw firsthand how powerful our God is," said Joanne, "but in order for God to work through us, we had to have clean hearts. Our sins had to be confessed. It wasn't as easy as just saying the name of Jesus. We had to be cleansed of all sins and all doubts before God's power could overcome the evil.

"Some of us were so scared that we slept with our lights on for a long time after that. Some of us actually slept with our Bibles, thinking we'd be safer. We continued to pray for Suzanne and for ourselves as we resumed our daily schedule. Never far from our minds, we found ourselves searching for her among our audiences, partly hoping, yet also dreading to see her. We wondered what had become of her.

"As the days went by, we learned more about Suzanne. We were told that she was part of a large family of devil worshippers and that her brothers were very involved in spiritualism and her father was one of the leaders. Suzanne was being groomed to become a leader in spiritualism herself, but she didn't want that life. She wanted to be a Christian and had accepted Jesus as her Lord and Savior. She was reaching out to the Heritage Singers for help, trying to break free from the bonds of Satan, but she was facing an overwhelming struggle. And it wasn't over. It was far from over.

"Our Brazilian tour took us to many cities, some of which were far away from Rio. Our central location was São Paulo. Suzanne began showing up at our concerts and at our hotel in São Paulo. A sweet, shy girl, she was pleasant and loving, a joy to have around. Although she only spoke Portuguese, it was clear that she loved the Lord and wanted a different kind of life for herself. Maybe she thought that as long as she was with us she would be safe."

Dave remembered seeing Suzanne again for the first time when he was walking through an underground parking area at another concert. He said, "As we got closer, someone translated for the young girl, asking, 'Do you remember me?' My heart sank because I'd seen and talked with what seemed like thousands of people since being in Rio. I simply couldn't remember her face. I apologized for not remembering her. Then the petite young woman stepped towards me and said, 'I'm Suzanne.' I was shocked I had thought she was a much older woman, but she was only 16 years old! We embraced. And as I held her in my arms, I thanked God again for caring so passionately for all of us. I was seeing Suzanne, the real Suzanne, for the first time."

"However, the truth was that whenever Suzanne showed up, we got nervous," remembered Joanne. "Not having the spiritual maturity of Dave and Dunbar, some of us were very worried whenever Suzanne was around. We were certain that any minute she was going to flip out again and turn into Satan. We kept waiting for that satanic look in her eyes. We truly wanted to help her, but we were a bit uncomfortable around her. Her kindness and sweet ways eventually softened our guard, and we gradually grew to be more comfortable around her."

Dave remembered experiencing four more episodes with Suzanne's demon possession during the rest of the tour. "Each time it happened, Satan's power had deeply dwindled," he said.

In the meantime, Heritage traveled miles and miles over mountainous roads to their various concerts in South America. Often times they saw familiar faces in the audience, faces that had traveled from far away cities to hear Heritage again and again. Greg said, "It wasn't unusual for the same group of kids to show up hours away from where we had previously seen them. They loved surprising us. They even rented their own bus, which had a hand-painted banner on the side that read, 'We cannot bear the pain of separation!' Their bus passed ours on the highway one day and pulled us over for a little reunion on a Brazilian mountain road. It was great having friends, actual fans, who followed us around and cheered us on. That kind of thing never happened in the United States!

"One night, we were preparing for a concert at a very large auditorium. We were backstage having our quiet prayer time, pausing to reflect and asking God to be with us on stage, which is what we did before every concert. Suddenly we heard a terrible and frightfully recognizable sound. To our horror, there she was, Suzanne, once again possessed by a satanic power so intense that her body was totally out of control!

"She's got that look," Dunbar said. "Her eyes started to get that satanic look again, and that voice, that terrible voice! I'll never forget the absolute superhuman strength that young girl had while she was possessed. It took several men to hold her down!"

The group huddled in prayer, knowing full well what was happening, but still afraid. Max led everyone in prayer as he calmly, but intensely denounced Satan, calling on the name of Jesus. It wasn't long this time. The demons were soon quieted. Suzanne collapsed into the arms of the men around her. The men then helped escort her out, so the Heritage Singers could proceed with their concert, feeling newfound confidence in the Lord's power over evil!

Suzanne sat in the audience that night. She even hung around with the singers after the concert, as if nothing had happened. The language barrier between the singers and Suzanne limited their full understanding of what she was feeling, but she seemed like a normal sixteen year-old. Joanne said, "We were still a bit uncomfortable around Suzanne, and we found ourselves looking into her eyes for 'that look.' She could snap at any moment. Her eyes were always the first indication. She wanted so badly to free herself from her family's legacy of evil that she clung to us like a small child clings to its mother.

"One day she wrote me a note in her neat foreign handwriting, thanking me for praying for her. Another day when we were checking out of our hotel to go to another city, I gave her a vase of flowers that had been in my room. Later I learned that she had tried to commit suicide by taking an overdose of sleeping pills. She had used the water from the vase of flowers I had given her to swallow them."

Max will never forget the day when a few of the singers took the rented bus to the beach. "Somehow, the bus got stuck in the sand," Max said. "Joe, our interpreter, and I were trying to get it out. He jacked up the rear of the bus and was looking underneath. Suddenly, the bus came crashing down, barely missing Joe's head as he jumped out of the way! 'Somebody's trying to kill you,' I said, as he realized just how close he had come to being crushed."

The last night the singers were in São Paulo, Suzanne showed up at their concert. They didn't even know she was there until they were already on stage. She sat right in the front row. The singers prayed through the entire concert, asking God to not let her become possessed by demons while they were singing. They also prayed that their concert would bring her some peace and hope.

Dunbar remembered giving the appeal that night. "I spoke directly to Suzanne," he said. "It was as if no one else was even there. When I saw her start to get that satanic look in her eyes, I just looked at her with as much kindness and love as I could. I

was speaking directly to her and to her alone. When it became obvious that the demons were clearly taking over, Dave and Amanda took her back stage, so our concert could continue."

"Dunbar joined us a few minutes later, after he had ended the call. He began reading promises from his Bible again," Dave recalled. "I held her and prayed for God's Spirit to deliver her from this dreadful spiritual disease. Suddenly, two of Suzanne's relatives burst into the room and demanded that we stop praying and reading scripture. They grabbed at Dunbar's Bible and the woman head-butted me in the chest, trying to shove me away from Suzanne."

"She was very upset," remembered Dunbar. "She took the Bible out of my hand and threw it across the room. We were able to get her out of there, leaving Suzanne with us."

Dave said he's not sure who escorted them from the room, but in a few moments they were gone. "I continued to plead for Suzanne to have the strength to resist the devil and give herself completely to Jesus," Dave said. "Then, as in Scripture, Jesus cast the evil one out, and Suzanne was at peace. This was our last traumatic experience with her." It was too late for Suzanne to catch a bus home that night, so he and Amanda took her to their hotel room to stay with them for the night.

Joanne said, "We were definitely close to God that night and to each other, as we gave an intensely sincere concert. We truly felt God's presence. However, it was emotionally exhausting. The rigid demands of our schedule, the pressures of being in a non-English speaking country, and our frightening experiences with Suzanne began to take its toll on our health. Some of us became quite ill. Max was vomiting for no reason. I passed out on stage one night and was so exhausted I couldn't eat. Max and I both ended up in the hospital by the time our tour was over. Mysterious illnesses, unexplained weakness and fatigue plagued us. We limped through the rest of our tour and went on with our lives, putting the experiences away somewhere in the archives of our Heritage stories."

In later trips to Brazil, the Heritage Singers did try to find out what happened to Suzanne. They were told that she had taken Bible studies at one point and tried to get out of the life of devil worship, but whether or not she was ever successful in breaking away from Satan's hold was never known.

After returning to the United States, Max was invited to speak at a church about their Brazil tour experience with Suzanne. It was a sunny, clear day. It hadn't been raining and the roads were dry. As Max headed down the steep and winding ranch road, his car began spinning out of control.

"I knew I was going to die," Max said. "My car was spinning like a top. There was nothing I could do but pray, say the name of Jesus and demand that Satan get behind me. It worked! My car straightened out as I regained control once again, thanking God as I continued down the mountain to tell our story."

"I know Satan is strong," said Dunbar. "Things in Brazil were very primitive, as far as how people worship. God gave us a period of time with Suzanne, and however much we may have had an impact on her, I believe it probably impacted us more."

"We live in the midst of a great controversy," Max said. "The forces of evil are very real. They are nothing to take lightly. Satanism is not something to play around with." Max also said he was surprised at how long it took for the demons to be cast out. There was nothing easy about it. You don't just say the name of Jesus and they're gone. Everyone had to confess their sins and get right with the Lord before Satan leaves.

"God always wins in the end," Max said. "God always triumphs over evil. Even though Satan meant to stop us, and I believe he even tried to kill me, God did not allow it. The thing to remember is that God is always there besides us, even in our darkest struggles. He has promised to turn all things, even our bad experiences, around for our good."

"It doesn't matter where you've been or what you've done," added Dave. "There is no sin that can keep you from the Father's love except the one you chose not to give to Him. It's time for us to let God have every part of our lives. Take a moment right now to claim the promises of God's love."

During Heritage's initial trip to Brazil in 1977, a movement started among the Brazilian young people. They loved the Heritage music and wanted to continue singing those songs after the group returned to the United States. This resulted in several new singing groups, similar to the Heritage Singers.

The Heritage Singers returned to Brazil in 1982, where they were greeted by many of their friends from the first tour. The group traveled by air to their concerts in different cities. One time, they had to send their sound equipment on a bus because the plane they were traveling on was too small for it. The bus carrying the sound system had to take an all-night journey through the mountains. The group also decided to send their performance clothes on the bus to lighten the load of the plane.

However, on the way to the concert, the bus had an accident. A big boulder rolled down a mountain and hit the bus. Naturally, this delayed the arrival of the sound equipment and the group's performance clothes. The group performed that night with whatever sound system was already in the hall, in addition to an assortment of home stereo equipment people brought for them to use. They also had to wear whatever clothing they had on from the plane ride.

Heritage returned again to Brazil in 1995. "This was when we really saw the impact of our previous trips on the Brazilian young people," said Max. One of the young men who had attended some of the early Heritage concerts in 1977 was deeply moved by the music and the message. He promised himself that when he got out of college and became a successful businessman, he would bring the Heritage Singers back to Brazil, and that's just what he did. Thirteen years later, he flew from Brazil to California with an interpreter to start working out the details of the tour. "I want you to bring Jesus to my people," he told Max. He paid for the airline tickets, hotels and ground transportation. That January, the Heritage Singers left the United States for a 20-concert Brazilian tour—from São Paulo, to Rio de Janeiro, to Brasilia, to the Amazon. More than 50,000 Brazilians attended.

Max remembered their return trip to Brazil in '95. "We were

greeted in São Paulo by about 50 smiling faces bearing signs, flowers and lots of hugs. I'm not sure how we looked after our 15-hour flight, but it didn't seem to matter to them.

"Our first concert was in São Paulo to about 3,500 people," said Max. "When Tim Davis gave the invitation for people to give their hearts to Jesus, the response was overwhelming! Families walked down to the front together, young people came for prayer to be set free from one type of addiction or another, and as the singers were praying with them, one could feel the Spirit of God.

"Curitiba held a double surprise for Lucy and me. Not only did we get to see Bruno and his family, who had helped with our last tour, but we also got to meet his father-in-law, Everton Santos. We found out that Everton had come to the Lord as a result of the Heritage Singers ministry. He shared his testimony at the concert that night and invited the group to eat lunch at his restaurant the following day.

Everton Santos and Max in Curitiba, Brazil

"We were met at the airport in nearly every city by at least one singing group that had started up as a result of our last visit to Brazil. Our flight to Aracaju was delayed four hours. Instead of arriving at 9:00 P.M., we arrived at 1:15 A.M. To our surprise, there were still more than 75 excited singers and friends waiting to greet us at the airport! They had a keyboard set up, singing for us while the rest of the passengers at the airport looked on in amazement.

"We learned that Joel, the leader of the group, had accepted Christ at one of our concerts 15 years earlier. Now he, his brother, and the other singers travel throughout Brazil witnessing through song and testimony.

"Just watching these young people sing was an inspiration. One group that really stands out in my mind was the group Integraçao from Victoria. You could see the love of Jesus in their faces! It was obvious that their music was truly coming from their hearts.

"While in Victoria, we met Walter. He told us he had given his heart to the Lord after listening to the song, 'Jesus Is the Lighthouse.' Throughout the tour, more than 3,000 people dedicated their lives to God. More than 1,000 people accepted Christ for the first time!

"When we gave a concert in Campo Grande, there were several people who came forward and gave their lives to Jesus. As they left the concert, five of these people were involved in a terrible car accident. They were all killed. We were very saddened to learn of this unfortunate event. We must make sure that we live for Jesus every day. We have no assurance of tomorrow.

"While in Brazil, I received a call from our travel agent who set up the flights for our tour. She said, 'I made a pledge that every time I heard a Heritage song on the radio I would stop what I was doing and say a little prayer for you. I have never heard so many Heritage songs played on that station in all my years of listening. I guess the Lord knew you really needed our prayers!'

"One miracle happened in Belem on our way to Manaus. We supposedly had confirmed seats, but the airline had overbooked the flight by 100 seats. We were told that we could only send five people. Lucy said, 'But we confirmed our seats yesterday. I have a confirmation number. Doesn't that mean anything?' The man just said, 'I'm sorry. There are no seats available.' We began to ask God to intervene for us. We had a concert that night and there was only one plane a day going where we needed to go. What would we do if we couldn't get there? We didn't have to wait long. Within 30 minutes we were on the plane. Somehow, the seats had become available. It was just one of many times we thanked the Lord for working things out for us.

"So much is out of our hands on these international trips. When we can't control situations, we really find out what trusting in God is all about. That's when we can't help but be humbled by seeing the way God gets involved in the details of our day-to-day lives. It helps us realize that God is in control and that He really does care about what happens to us. We just have to learn to let go sometimes and let Him show us what to do.

"About halfway through our Brazilian tour, the hired bus drivers got drunk and stole the bus! We were to fly out to the next city the following morning. Without the bus, we had to resort to taxis to get us to the airport. Our tour organizers soon found the stolen bus and arranged for two new drivers to meet us at our next destination. You never know

Heritage arriving in Brazil.

what's going to happen! After more than 18 flights around Brazil and several overnight bus trips, we were thankful when we arrived safely back home," laughed Max.

Melody Davis remembers the trip to Brazil too. "I had only been in Heritage for less than a year when we went on our six-week tour of Brazil," she said. "What an initiation that was! It was a grueling schedule with only one day off the entire time we were there. There were numerous flights and concerts that went late into the night, leaving us all exhausted and weary.

"I think it was about half way into the trip when we were all instructed to put our luggage on the bus while we took an hour flight to the next city. We each had only a few essential items and clothes. I think I had my purse, my make-up and my concert outfit, but not much else. Upon arriving at our destination, we were informed that our 'luggage bus' was going to be delayed,

and we probably wouldn't have our suitcases until the next day. Well, one day turned into seven! We traveled and sang a whole week with not much more than the clothes on our back.

"I remember I had on a pink t-shirt and white short overalls. I wore that same outfit every day for an entire week! By day seven, the overalls were no longer white. With the very hot and humid temperatures, you can imagine how we all looked and felt!"

Tim Davis said, "The ministry that took place in Brazil was the most spiritually rich time for me in my years with Heritage. Seeing the people come forward, broken before the Lord, and seeing the plans of the enemy thwarted in a country he has long held a stronghold over was exciting. Although it was exhausting physically and emotionally, I am grateful that the Lord chose us to go on this spiritual journey through Brazil."

Months later, Max was still receiving letters from the Brazilian people telling him how their lives had been changed because of the Heritage ministry. Almost immediately, upon the Heritage Singers' return to the United States, plans were yet again made for another trip to Brazil. In May of 1996, the Heritage Quartet returned for a 15-day tour. The quartet included Bill Young as lead, Shawn Struckmeier as first tenor, Max as baritone, and Duane Hamilton as bass. The trip went well and many people made decisions for Christ. Time and time again, people told the singers how the music Heritage brought to Brazil 20 years earlier blessed their lives. Numerous groups were still springing up all over Brazil as a result of the Heritage visits.

In October of 2006, the Heritage Singers once again returned to Brazil, with concerts in São Paulo, Rio de Janeiro, Porto Alegre, Curitiba, Maringa, Campinas and Santo Andre.

Since these trips to Brazil, the Heritage Singers have received many letters and phone calls from the people of Brazil. Here are a few:

"Hearing you sing was like a beautiful dream come true. Certainly all of my country was blessed during the Heritage Singers' stay. The group was a channel of spiritual blessings and beautiful music produced with love and gracefulness. Without any doubt, you embody an efficient and wonderful ministry that God has used to spread comfort, beauty and hope to touch people who couldn't be touched in any other way."

"I was five years old when I attended my first Heritage concert in 1977 when you came to Brazil for the first time. I grew up involved in music ministry and am today part of a singing group. Max, I have to thank you. All of this happened in my life because of your example. I praise God for giving me the chance to meet you."

"I am a young Christian from Brazil. I write you to thank you for your voices and your music that inspires me and takes me to Heaven. If I never meet you again, I want you to know that I always will pray for God to be with you as you go and take the love of God to the entire world."

Max said, "More than ever before it seems that everywhere Heritage goes around the world, people know us and our music. And wherever we go, so many people came forward to give their hearts to the Lord. The gospel is, indeed, being taken into all corners of the world."

Heritage at Christ the Redeemer statue in Rio de Janeiro, Brazil

At the Crossroads

CHAPTER ELEVEN

New Horizons

Stand firm. Let nothing move you. Always give yourselves fully to the work of the Lord,
because you know that your labor in the Lord is not in vain.
—1 Corinthians 15:58

N EW OPPORTUNITIES AND CHALLENGES WERE COMING EVERY DAY FOR THE HERITAGE SINGERS AS THE GROUP entered the 1980s. They now had one full-time performing group and one weekend group. With only one full-time group, they couldn't cover the United States like they had in the past, and they were getting more invitations for international appearances.

At the same time, Heritage was experiencing extreme financial difficulties. The business manager for Heritage left the organization. The ministry was drained financially. Bills had not been paid for two months. Max and Lucy were shocked at the condition the ministry was in. They really hadn't been aware of the situation. Their suppliers had cut them off, their credit cards were maxed out, and their phone bill was two months behind. They were deep in debt, and devastated, to say the least.

Max and Lucy prayed about what they should do, try and pay off the debt or just go bankrupt and quit. They really didn't want to quit because they felt that God wanted the Heritage ministry to continue. New things were happening. It was an exciting time in the ministry, and they did not want to give up

unless they absolutely had to.

Max and Lucy decided to call their creditors and explain the situation. Fortunately, they were able to negotiate new terms that made it possible to pay off the debt over five years. It was from this precarious position that Heritage ventured into new growth.

Following this difficult period, Heritage was invited to participate in some major venues, both internationally and at home. During the 1978–79 season, the Heritage Singers weekend group participated in the World Concern Concert for World Hunger and also held its first reunion concert at Swing Auditorium in San Bernardino, California. Meanwhile, the full-time group performed at the Pentagon near Washington, D.C., and returned to Brazil, Canada, and Puerto Rico. During the 1979–80 season, both Heritage groups returned to Brazil. Heritage Singers USA also hosted a tour of the Holy Land, Israel and Jordan. This was the farthest the group had ever been from North America.

Max said, "Imagine singing 'In the Garden' in the Garden of Gethsemane, and 'When I Think of the Cross' and 'I Believe In a Hill Called Mt. Calvary' at Golgotha. Later, we sang 'Rise Again' at the spot where Jesus rose from the dead. The singers and all of the people with us were filled with emotion, and in awe at the realization that the same Jesus who had walked those dusty roads of Palestine nearly two thousand years ago would soon return in glory to take His children home."

Lucy recalled when the group was out in a boat on the Sea of Galilee, a storm suddenly came up, just as it was described in the Bible when Jesus walked on the water and calmed the Sea. "It was as if we went back in time!" she said. "We could really picture Jesus and His disciples in the boat as the storm came up. We knew how the disciples must have felt. It was as if we were right there with them."

Heritage was honored to be invited to sing at Ronald Reagan's presidential inauguration in Washington, D.C. They also toured the United States from coast to coast, including Hawaii, that year, and participated in three evangelistic crusades in California.

For years Max dreamed about getting into television ministry. He even talked with a long-time supporter of the ministry, Bob Brody, about the possibility. It was Bob who encouraged Max to go ahead and pursue the idea. He said, "Max, you have a tremendous ministry going here. You have a special way of reaching people, and I feel that you should be on television!"

Singing on the Sea of Galilee

"It seemed a bit over our heads," Max said. "Of course, we couldn't argue with his logic. On television, the group could be in a thousand or ten thousand places at a time. Even though we liked the idea, we just weren't sure how to accomplish it."

Bob was not only a man of vision, but also a man of action. In line with his convictions, he gave Heritage a generous donation to help get the television ministry started. Bob's donation enabled Heritage to pay for their first television programs that were produced in Hollywood. That season was a season of "firsts" for the Heritage Singers.

By this time, "Old Blue" was becoming feeble and tired. It broke down repeatedly and was no longer reliable. One day Mickey Allen, a long-time friend of Max, said, "Max, I'm getting so sick of hearing about this bus breaking down. Let me be the first to donate toward the cause of getting a new bus." He handed Max a generous check. That was a real encouragement to Max and Lucy as they were doing whatever they could to set aside money for the bus.

Max kept a framed picture of a new bus on his desk for the next four years before he was finally able to order one. Prior to placing the order, Max had to go to the bank to get a loan. Naturally, they needed some collateral to secure it. Max said, "Fortunately, Gil Labrucherie went with me that day." Gill and his wife, Sandra, owned a construction company and were on the Heritage Singers' board of directors. When the banker told Max they needed more collateral, Gil offered to put all of his heavy construction equipment up for Max's loan. With that loan, Max was able to place the order for the new bus. It would be another year before they would get it because of a long waiting list.

Max said, "Gil was such an encouragement to me. We'd go out in the pick-up truck and pray together. He'd say, 'Max, don't worry. This is going to work out.' I'll never forget how much he believed in me and in the Heritage ministry. We couldn't have made it without him.

"We ordered an American Eagle model Ten, which was manufactured in Brownsville, Texas. We sent Kevin Kenyon to Texas to drive the bus back to Placerville. We had our new bus! Since we had ordered it unfurnished, it was pretty much an empty shell. Lucy put some scraps of carpeting, a pile of beanbags, and pillows in it for the first few trips until more permanent furnishings could be obtained.

"The monthly payment amount on the new bus, however, was quite a shock! When we ordered the bus, interest rates were at 12 percent. By the time we actually got the bus, the interest rate was at 22 percent! Our bus payments were $2,500 a month in the beginning, and that's not counting diesel, upkeep, or customizing the interior, such as getting closets built. After a couple of years we were able to refinance it, bringing our payment down to $1,500 a month, but even that was high for us. We told our supporters, 'We need to get this bus paid off!'

Lucy and I started the Century Bus Club. Those who donated $100 or more toward the new bus would get their names engraved on a plaque among those who helped purchase the new bus.

"Not long after that, we received a check in the mail from Ron and Faith Schaafsma, of Auburn, Washington. We didn't even know them at the time, but that was the beginning of a long and wonderful relationship that continues to this day. Little by little, donations came in. God was impressing people to send money to help pay off the bus. It took a few years, but we finally did pay it off! We are still riding that same bus today."

That was also the first year Heritage made a concert tour by air—a 21-day tour across the United States. Delta Airlines had a special promotion in which a person could fly anywhere Delta flew for a full 21 days for only $400.

By this time, the Heritage Singers had performed for many different religious denominations. Their television

GRACE NOTES:

"Dear Max, I was introduced to your beautiful music when a wonderful Christian lady invited me to attend one of your concerts. What a glorious experience! I came away from your concert walking on air. I had been longing for music like that and had nearly given up on ever hearing it again. What a blessing you were to me that night. My friend has since died of cancer, but her invitation to attend your concert got my life headed in the right direction again. Thanks for bringing this fine music to the world."

"Dear Heritage, I plan on using your music to help treat psychological disorders such as depression and loneliness. I also will recommend to my colleagues to use it to treat mental illness such as bi-polar disorder, clinical depression and even schizophrenia. If successful, I'd even like to use it in a clinical study. The therapeutic value of good music cannot be overestimated. Your music has definitely helped me.

"I have watched the miracles of God performed through your music. We are using your music as therapy for disturbed minds with wonderful success. I've watched hardened men soften; I've watched deeply troubled minds find peace.

"Our music resource base of music consists of 135,000 songs. Of these, 5,000 were considered and 2,000 tested and only 518 approved for therapy use. Of the 518 approved pieces of music, 289 are Heritage recordings. Considering you sent me 293 songs, and 289 of them were approved for the therapy list is totally amazing.

"We all agree that you are not 'just people' but messengers of God and that your songs are messages from God. You all are greatly beloved. We may even get T-shirts and ward posters that say 'My faith and sanity are Heritage-inspired.'"

Our long awaited "New Bus"

show, *Heritage Singers Presents,* was being aired weekly on the Trinity Broadcasting Network. In the fall of 1981, Heritage was invited to join the King's Heralds for a 21-day airline tour. A male quartet group, the King's Heralds was featured on *The Voice of Prophecy* radio program. Both groups felt the joint tour would be a great opportunity to reach an expanded audience.

The goal of their tour was to let people know that they weren't just a music ministry, but also thankful citizens of the United States. The tour was called "A God and Country Celebration" that included patriotic songs, as well as the gospel songs the groups had become well known for.

Max said, "Both of our groups had traveled extensively outside of the United States. The more we traveled, the more we appreciated the blessings we had as Americans. We also felt there was a tremendous need for God to be made the center of our country and of every individual's life." That was the beginning of several joint projects between the Heritage Singers and the King's Heralds over the years.

The night before leaving on the King's Heralds tour, Max sat in his motel room writing his monthly letter for the Heritage Singers newsletter. In that issue he thanked the supporters of the Heritage Singers for helping launch the group's television ministry. He wrote:

Now the three major Christian television networks have accepted our series for release this fall. We just finished filming 13 new programs, and if we supply the networks with two-inch videotapes, they will air the programs free of charge! Praise the Lord! When our program begins on CBN, TBN, and PTL satellite networks, it will reach over five million people with the message of God's love each time it is shown! This has more than overwhelmed all of us. We weren't ready for this much blessing!

Max and Jim with Jan and Paul Crouch, owners of Trinity Broadcasting

It was all very exciting, and a bit overwhelming. There were times the phrase "too much of a good thing" came to mind as Max struggled to face the new challenges coming his way. But even when he didn't know how he was going to keep up with the group's commitments, God found a way. No matter what Heritage was up against, God used its limitations and less than ideal circumstances to turn things around and bring some good out of it.

In fact, just before the television production was to begin, Lucy was involved in a car accident that seriously injured her legs. Cindy Haffner said she remembered that day very clearly. "Lucy was helping Val and Greg move out of a little house they were staying in on the campus of Pacific Union College. I was in St. Helena where I had a job cleaning Victorian houses and had borrowed Max and Lucy's station wagon. I got a call from Greg saying that they needed the car to transport Lucy, so I raced to where they were to help.

"Lucy was forced to stay home for a while. She couldn't walk for three months. We were all so thankful that she did not lose her legs. We all felt that this was a miracle. Although she couldn't travel with the group, Lucy became the lady behind the scenes, a very badly needed function that she continues to this day. She holds things together in so many ways."

Rather than it being a setback, Lucy used her circumstances to become involved in a whole new aspect of the Heritage ministry. It just so happened that the Heritage Singers weekly television program, *Keep on Singing,* was in drastic need of a full-time producer. Lucy was well suited for this position as she had been involved with all of the Heritage productions from the very beginning, including choreography, stage attire, recordings, and photo shoots.

The half-hour show featured the Heritage Singers and

various guest artists. Lucy took on the challenge with enthusiasm and said, "Our goal is to introduce people to Jesus Christ." Lucy enjoyed doing the TV shows so much that she didn't miss singing with the group. At that time, the TV show reached a potential 39 million cable viewers per week! God turned a limitation into strength.

"The Lord saved my life," she said, "so I knew He could heal a little leg! I hope we all can learn from my experience to thank the Lord each day. Not only for the big things that everyone can see, but for the little things as well; the things that we so often take for granted."

Cindy Haffner said that filming the television programs was a lot of fun. "I have always loved the older Heritage songs and enjoyed singing them with the group on these shows. We sometimes filmed on location, which was a nice way to get to see some beautiful places. We did a set of shows near Palm Springs. I remember we had to start filming at 6:00 AM because by 10:00 AM or 11:00 AM it was already more than 100 degrees!"

Taping "Keep on Singing" Bill, Max, Cindi, Cindy, Rhonda, Val, Jim and Mark

Trinity Broadcasting Network in Santa Ana, California, had given the group five days of filming in their studios using their sets, camera equipment, and technicians, at no charge. Lucy wrote the programs, planned the choreography, and made sure the clothes were all prepared. The group taped 13 shows in five days. The expense would have been about $125,000. In exchange for Heritage giving TBN the rights to air their shows, they gave Heritage a ¾-inch tape master of their programs.

With all these new opportunities, there also came new financial obligations. Even though Heritage had been given a tremendous break on production costs, they still needed to produce commercials for those programs. Then the programs had to be duplicated. After that, they needed to be sent out to the independent television stations around the country. Airtime on the stations had to be purchased so those shows could be broadcast. All those costs were more than the Heritage Singers could afford. As they always had, Max and Lucy took on this challenge in faith, trusting God to work out the details. Max said, "We don't want to stand still now that the Lord has brought us this far! It's time to move on and finish His work."

Truthfully, it was becoming more and more difficult to keep the self-supporting Heritage ministry going. The offerings, love gifts, and record sales just didn't meet the expenses. Max truly believed that the offer by the Christian networks was a direct answer to prayer to keep the ministry going.

Max sent an appeal out to his faithful supporters:

I am coming to you, my dear partners in faith. You have been the ones through the years who have encouraged me to keep going. You have been the ones who prayed for us. You have been the ones who have given financially as the Lord has impressed you. Now I come to you again for counsel. Would you like to see our television ministry proceed? We have the programs recorded and the networks are waiting for them. They have already given us primetime slots for showing. All we have to do is send them the tapes. I will be praying for each one of you that the Lord will direct as we move forward through the open doors.

Imagine Max's frustration! Here was the opportunity to reach millions of people with the message of God's love. All he needed was enough funds to duplicate the already recorded programs. Perhaps any other person in this situation would have borrowed money or started selling tickets to concerts, instead of depending on love offerings. But Max couldn't do that. He didn't want to put his family in any more financial risk than they were already in or ask people to pay to hear about God's love. He stood fast in his commitment to never charge for his concerts, except for fund-raisers, and to never borrow money. He turned it all over to God and to the people who wanted to be financially involved in the Heritage ministry.

Realizing he couldn't control the outcome of the situation required Max to rely totally on God's intervention. God had brought the ministry this far, and He would have to do the rest. There simply was no other option. Max truly believed that if God wanted the ministry to continue, He would provide a way.

When the friends and supporters of the Heritage ministry heard about Heritage's financial situation, they began calling from all around the country, offering to sponsor the Heritage programs in their hometowns. This formed a core base of monthly financial support that the Heritage Singers could depend on. They needed it for the survival of their ministry.

Not many people would have been able to let go of the need to control things as Max did. It felt like he was shirking his responsibilities. He was afraid that if he quit, it might look like he was giving up when the going got rough. The Heritage ministry had always been about giving people hope and trusting in God's wisdom—and about letting go of security and being open to whatever God had planned. For Max to let go of the outcome and invite God to lead the ministry was a freeing experience. The future of the ministry wasn't really up to him. This was God's project, and as long as God continued to provide opportunities and financial support kept trickling in, Max and Lucy vowed to continue the ministry.

That season, Heritage again toured the United States with a 21-day airline tour. This time the tour also included Puerto Rico and the Virgin Islands. The group also assisted with an evangelistic crusade in California and shared a two-city concert tour with Danny Gaither. Little by little, day by day, donations came in; enough at least to keep things going from one month to the next.

During the 1982–83 season, Capital Airlines provided air service for the Heritage Singers to tour Europe, Australia and New Zealand, all for the first time. Doug Batchelor's father, George Batchelor, owned Capital Airlines. He offered to help Max and the Heritage Singers by providing air transportation wherever his airlines flew. It would have been impossible for the Heritage Singers to have taken those trips without his generous offer.

Heritage also had a second Holy Land tour. This time it included Jordan, Israel and Egypt. That same year, the group again made a 21-day airline concert tour that included cities in the United States, Canada, Bahamas, Virgin Islands, West Indies, Trinidad and Jamaica. While in the southern states, the group assisted with an evangelistic crusade in Miami, Florida.

The international travel was especially rewarding because so many people gave their lives to the Lord at the Heritage concerts. However, the schedules were intense and the conditions sometimes less than ideal. The singers slept under leaking roofs, drenched by rain. Bats and strange large insects dive-bombed the singers on stage and animals wandered into their concerts.

The singers never worked harder than they did on international trips. It seemed that every waking moment was filled with events and interviews, and getting from one place to another. Whatever "time off" the group did have was hardly free time. Instead of relaxing in their rooms or venturing out to see their surroundings, the singers often found themselves climbing onto a bus and going off to do a television or radio interview, or some kind of extra performance. They tried to catch up on their sleep whenever they could.

Sometimes, some of the singers found their enthusiasm waning. The idea of getting out of bed after just two hours of sleep, getting dressed in their matching wrinkled "travel" outfits, and waiting in a hotel lobby for a couple of hours for a driver to show up, didn't seem all that appealing. The singers were expected to be "on" from morning to night. Even meals were planned gatherings. The "glamorous" life of a Heritage Singer was not what people thought it was.

GRACE NOTES:

"Dear Max,

"I had the pleasure of attending both your concerts this weekend. It's through music that God communicates with me. He uses groups such as the Heritage Singers to touch the hearts of people such as me, and I thank Him and you for that.

"Today is my birthday. I'm 37 years old. When I was in high school and college I was an outstanding athlete with professional aspirations. I was a high-ranking officer in a large national bank. I had a nice family, a nice home, and two cars in the garage.

"Now it's all gone -- the aspirations, the home, the cars, and the family. I'm separated from my wife and three beautiful children. I'm unemployed, I've filed for bankruptcy, I'm broke, hungry, tired and desperate.

"I share this with you not to depress you, but rather to help you understand how important your ministry is. Thank you for allowing Him to use you last weekend to communicate to my heart through music.

"I don't know what's going to happen in my life. It would be so much easier to just give up. Thank you for reminding me that I should try and hang on a little bit longer. Please include me in your prayers."

Sometimes we don't even know the impact a single song can have on someone's life. Just recently we heard about a young father who had been into drugs and alcohol who was touched by Alanna Yost's song, "Something Happened to Daddy," which was recorded back in the 1970s. He has re-committed his life to God, and has been reunited with his daughter.

"I hope you will be caught up in the vision God has given for this ministry for reaching people with His life-changing power," Max said. "We are His voice to those without hope."

Upon returning to the United States, Heritage participated in the Athletes for Christ banquet in Florida. Later that year, they sang the National Anthem to open a California Angels' baseball game in Anaheim. In addition, the group returned for a second time to South Africa, Australia and New Zealand, performing at the famous Sydney Opera House for the first time. In just 30 days, the Heritage Singers presented more than 17 concerts in the major cities of Australia and New Zealand!

One of the most bizarre experiences happened closer to home. Heritage was scheduled to perform at Whitman College in Walla Walla, Washington. The morning of the concert, they found a note on the windshield of the bus. It was rolled up inside of a small plastic film container and said, "One of you is going to die!"

That night the singers proceeded with their concert. Up until the intermission, nothing happened, until the singers were gathering in the lobby preparing to collect the love offering. Steve Evenson rushed over to Lucy and said, "Don't look now, but there's a girl on the other side of the lobby who has a gun! It's in her purse. I saw it myself! She says she's going to shoot Val!"

Lucy quickly stepped inside the auditorium to see if there was anyone she knew who could call the police. Just as she stepped inside the door, a man was coming out and asked if he could help her, and she asked him to call the police. To her relief, he said, "I'm an off-duty police officer. May I help you?" Lucy told him what was going on, and he went over to confront the girl.

Meanwhile, Val was told to stay backstage. The police officer was able to talk the girl into going outside. In the process, she pulled the gun on him and was quickly arrested! Then she began to talk.

She said she went to the concert with a plan to end Val's life. According to her, her boyfriend admitted to liking Val. She became overly jealous and decided she was going to shoot Val. The police officer told the girl she was lucky to be alive, because where he came from, when someone pulls out a gun in a public place, the "police shoot and ask questions later." As it turned out, the police discovered that gun was not real.

The group went back on stage to sing for the second half of the concert, and the audience never knew what had just transpired. After the concert, Val was informed about the incident. She was quite shaken up the rest of the night. Hearing that someone came to the concert to shoot you isn't exactly what you want to hear.

Max and Lucy went to the police station after the concert and the police asked if they wanted to press charges against the girl. They asked what would happen to her and they were told she would be detained for 48 hours and then released. "Then what kind of help would she get?" Lucy wanted to know. "Probably none," was the reply. "Well, we don't want to press charges," Max said, "but we want to be sure she gets some kind of counseling. She needs professional help." Once they were assured that she would get some help, Max and Lucy requested that she be detained until the group left the following day.

Some months later that same girl came to another Heritage concert. This time she didn't bring a gun. She met with Max and Doug Batchelor after the concert. They all prayed together. She asked for their forgiveness and prayed that God would forgive her.

Another frightening incident took place when the group was in Tahiti. Max and Lucy received a call from their office manager saying a detective needed to talk to Greg. Apparently, a disturbed man had just been accused of killing a child and had named Greg as his accomplice. Bonnie Ensminger, their office manager, asked the detective when the crime was committed. She relayed to the detective that Greg couldn't have done it because he had been in Tahiti at the time.

Apparently, the accused man had Greg's business card, which he had gotten at a Heritage Singers concert, and that was how he knew where Greg lived. He also knew what kind of car Greg drove and even had a photograph of Greg. It was later learned that he and Greg had been in college together. Greg was considered a "person of interest" for a while and there was even a warrant out for his arrest!

When the group returned to the United States, Greg had to give his deposition at the FBI office and prove he was out of the country at the time. Of course, Greg was totally vindicated and the perpetrator was in prison. Needless to say, it was a frightening experience.

By this time the Heritage Singers had been on the road full time for 12 years, but Max and Lucy showed no signs of stopping. As plans were being made for a two-week tour to Europe, Max requested prayers for safety and for the Holy Spirit to prepare the way and bring people with special spiritual needs to the concerts.

Max said, "Some people may have wondered how we could afford to go all around the world. It was because individual people had a special burden to bring us to their country and commit to sponsoring us on those trips, including paying most of our expenses. The combination of music and evangelism was a new approach in many countries, and the response was tremendous! More than 1,500 people that year alone made a new commitment to the Lord."

As the Heritage Singers became more widely known, corporate sponsors began to show interest in the ministry. The Hyatt Hotel chain began to provide accommodations around the world for the Heritage Singers for a greatly reduced rate in exchange for acknowledgement on television programs and at concerts. In addition, Capital Air provided transportation for the group when traveling in Europe.

At a concert, a man asked Max to pray for his wife who was sick with cancer. Later, Max called the man to ask how his wife was doing. The man was so touched that Max would follow up on their initial conversation that he told him what his job was and offered to help the group by extending a discount rate at any Hyatt Hotel.

During the 1985–86 season, the Heritage Singers returned to Australia and New Zealand. In addition, they were able to perform in Tasmania, Tahiti and Papua New Guinea, with a stopover in Hawaii on the way home. In Hawaii, they were invited to sing for the Beach Chaplaincy, which has a church service on the beach at the Hilton Hawaiian Village. That is also where they met Don Ho's dancers. Some of them were Christians so they invited the group to attend that night's performance. The singers were surprised when Don Ho asked them to sing a couple of songs in the middle of the show.

That season, during Heritage's Northwest tour, the group sang at the World's Fair, "Expo 86," in Vancouver, British Columbia. That year alone, the Heritage Singers traveled 56,000 miles—from Portland to Paris, Seattle to Singapore, and hundreds of cities in-between. The group performed 300 concerts for more than 175,000 people, in jungle chapels, before presidents and prisoners, and on stages around the world. In addition, the Heritage Singers television ministry reached a potential audience of approximately 38 million people!

Singing on Waikiki Beach. Max, Cindy, Monty, Jackie, Dave, Becki, Fernando and Val

It had now been 15 years since Max and Lucy started the Heritage Singers. In some ways it seemed like a lifetime ago. So much had happened! The ministry's outreach had far exceeded Max's original expectations. And yet, it seemed like only yesterday that they had started out in their rented bus, not knowing what God had in store for them.

"Throughout all of these experiences, God's hand of protection has guided our travel," said Lucy. "There have been no serious accidents in all the travel by bus, airplane, train and boat. Our records and tapes have encircled the globe."

As the Heritage Singers' 15th anniversary approached, Max paused to reflect on how God had led him this far and to thank the Heritage Singers' Faith Partners for their part in keeping the ministry going. Max wrote:

Faith Partners are the life-blood of the Heritage Singers. Each partner makes it possible to share the joyful message of Christ around the world. As team members of the Gospel Heritage Foundation, Faith Partners supply the means to keep the ministry moving. A large corporation does not support this ministry, and I believe this is the way God wants it. Heritage Singers is kept on the road by many people giving $20 or $25 per month. In this way the blessing is shared by all of us. God bless you, Faith Partners, as each month you are there to send not only your financial support, but your love and prayers as well. We receive letters every day telling of the encouragement and joy Heritage music has brought to so many people. You have made this possible!

At the Heritage Singers' 15th anniversary concert that summer, singers from all over the country came to be reunited and perform songs from when they were in the group. The Anaheim Convention Center was filled with friends and families of those who had been in the Heritage ministry and hundreds of others who had enjoyed and supported the Heritage Singers over the years. The six-hour concert was a heart-warming reunion of old friends and presented an overview of the first 15 years of the Heritage ministry.

Like the Bible's account of the Israelites, who, after a long journey through the wilderness, got their first glimpse of the Promised Land, things looked pretty promising for the Heritage Singers' future. From the vantage point of the Anaheim Convention Center stage, things looked very bright indeed.

But, just like the Bible story, it was too soon to celebrate any sort of arrival. The journey was far from over. Just as God sent the Israelites back into the wilderness for another 40 years, God said, "Wait. You're not ready. There's more to learn." The hardest parts of the Heritage journey—the toughest times that ended up teaching them the most—were still ahead.

CHAPTER TWELVE

Breaking the Sound Barrier

The task ahead of us is never as great as the power behind us.
I can do everything through Him who gives me strength.
—Philippians 4:13

B**Y THE MID-1980S, MORE THAN 2,000 PEOPLE EACH YEAR WERE GIVING THEIR HEARTS TO CHRIST AT HERI-**tage Singers concerts. Max always believed that music could reach people in a way that nothing else could. He was committed to reaching people through music as long as he had the strength and the means to do it. Even with the widening exposure and increasing audiences, the Heritage ministry was struggling like never before yet Max and Lucy put a positive face on things. Every time things seemed impossible, God came through for them—an unexpected check would suddenly show up in the mailbox or someone would donate just the right amount of money. Max and Lucy lived the words of the Heritage Singers song "We've Come This Far By Faith." They knew what it meant to get through life one day at a time, putting their trust in God. There were many times when Max and Lucy had moved forward in faith, not knowing where their next dollar was coming from.

But, this time was different. This time Max and Lucy found themselves soul-searching. They realized the seriousness of their financial situation and knew that if the Heritage ministry was to continue, some major changes would have to take place. It was time to reevaluate the direction of the ministry and how it was operated. It was time to rededicate their lives to following God's leading. They had done all they could. Now they were facing so many new opportunities that they not only needed financial support, they needed direction.

One day Max and Lucy went to Val and Art's apartment to pray about their situation. Max was out of ideas. He had listened to all of the other voices out there telling him what they thought he should do, and he had heard the voices in his head telling him why each idea would not work. He needed to silence all of those voices so he could hear what God was trying to tell him. Just as Jesus needed to get away when facing a transition in His life,

Max withdrew to his own wilderness. It was his darkest hour.

By placing himself at the feet of Jesus and fixing his listening heart on Him, Max truly felt the presence of God as he poured out his heart. Max shared it all with God—his financial worries, his fears about the future, his ideas about what the Heritage ministry should be and his role in it, and whether or not the ministry should even continue. He realized that none of these things were really up to him anyway. He would do whatever God wanted him to do. He just needed to know what that was.

That day, as they knelt in a circle in Val's living room, Max recommitted his life to God. He prayed for a new vision for the Heritage ministry, for the wisdom to know what to do to keep it alive, and for the courage to do it. By opening his heart and clearing out his own agenda, he created a space of fertile emptiness where new ideas could begin to sprout and a new spirit could be born.

Max and Lucy's struggle to let go of their own vision for the Heritage ministry and surrender it all to God wasn't as simple as saying a prayer or two. It involved a lot of determination, planning and hard work. They decided to change the things they could to cut costs. It also involved some letting go. It meant working very hard to do all they could do, while, at the same time, surrendering the outcome to God.

They were very familiar with hanging on when things got tough. They knew what it meant to try and try again and to never give up. But sometimes, determination, planning, hard work, business sense and marketing savvy are not the answer. Instead of working harder to hold things together, God gives us the courage to loosen our grip, and then opportunities and situations will start showing up. When we let go, God will catch us and put us in a place better than we could have imagined.

Deanna, Greg, Becki, Lucy, Val, Marty, Cindi, Art, Ted, Max, Charlotte and Bob Brody, Dani and Monty

"I have to admit," Max said, "Sometimes I felt like throwing in the towel. Then someone who had been running from God for 30 years would give his heart to the Lord. Or we'd get a letter from an individual who had accepted Christ from listening to one of our albums. Sometimes it was a sick person or someone in trouble. You know you've got to keep going because there are a lot of people out there that need the Lord."

The demands on the ministry continued to increase. The U.S. Armed Forces had chosen the Heritage Singers to provide Christian programming for military television networks around the world. On the domestic front, parents were asking Max to start a children's ministry. He was also receiving hundreds of requests to sing in new churches, places Heritage had never been.

Just as doors were opening like never before, the overall financial support for the ministry was not growing. They could barely make it on what they were getting from love offerings and album sales. Clinging to God's promise in Philippians 4:19, "My God shall supply all your needs according to His riches in glory," Max and Lucy decided to not let themselves be tempted to rush ahead of the Lord by borrowing money.

At the time, Max told the group, "This work belongs to the Lord. He will sustain it. I have to trust that the Holy Spirit will speak to hearts and that God Himself will gather together enough people to carry His work forward. I've laid it all out to God. I am going to rely on Him to gather the people together who will help us accomplish what He has called us to do."

It didn't take long before donations started coming in. Max wanted, with all of his heart, to be able to meet these new challenges. Besides the Armed Forces opportunity, hospitals throughout the United States had expressed interest in a Heritage Singers channel for their patients. All Heritage had to do was supply the programming. Here was another wonderful opportunity for expanding the Heritage ministry, but the upfront financial requirements were overwhelming. The Heritage Singers needed a "Loaves and Fishes" miracle. They needed a way to multiply their television programs and stretch them to feed people who were hungry to hear the message of God's love. It was the toughest year in the Heritage ministry so far. Yet, Max was filled with hope for the future and believed that the best years were yet to come. The group clung to John 14:27, "Peace I leave with you. My peace I give to you. I do not give to you as the world gives. Do not let your hearts be troubled. And do not be afraid."

By 1988 things were looking up. Some Christian businessmen sponsored a trip to the South Pacific for Heritage. Max said it was a trip that they looked forward to because of the wonderful sights and sounds of those islands, and particularly because of the hundreds of souls who would receive Jesus Christ as their Savior.

The Heritage Singers also developed a prison ministry during this time. The group visited and sang at many prisons. Significant amount of inmates wrote to them saying what a blessing they had received from the concert and how it had affected their lives. It amazed the group to see the wonderful way God worked through them when visiting prisons.

One such visit was to the Nevada Women's Correctional Center. Former singer Sherri Scott said, "As we sang, we watched the tense faces turn into peaceful smiles as the power of God touched them through the music. Singing to the inmates, we were reminded that God loves people that even the world would rather forget. As we sang, we were touched with a new sense of

Heritage praying with inmates who came forward at the alter call at the Nevada Women's Correction Center

God's forgiveness. We assured the prisoners that God loved them in spite of their past mistakes. He is the only one who can put broken hearts back together."

A few months later, Max began focusing on the children's ministry program. Heritage had always been a family ministry. There had always been a children's section in the concerts when all the kids in the audience could come down to the stage for special songs just for them. In fact, Heritage had already produced two award-winning children's albums: *Heaven Is For Kids, Volumes I and II.* But, Max wanted to do more.

He began producing a series of children's musicals, family worship sing-along tapes, Bible stories, and many other character-building products for children. Max shared this side of the ministry with his friend, Rick Lange, former director of Heritage II. Out of this creative union and their passionate desire to do something for kids, came *The Gospel Train* album. It even included the lyrics so the kids could sing along.

Rick also developed *The Adventures of Heritage Bear.* The ten-song package presented an adventure in story and song about a group of kids who go on a camping trip with the Heritage Singers. While camping in the mountains, they go through several experiences that teach them the value of trusting in God and in caring about their friends—and of course, that was where they met Heritage Bear and his forest friends. *The Adventures of Heritage Bear* included a cassette tape, a 24-page coloring book with six marking pens, and the lyrics to all ten songs. Rick Lange also started a newsletter for children, answering all of their letters.

Nothing like this had ever been done before, and Max was very excited about the project. They were reaching children at their level of understanding and teaching them about the love of God. It was a huge need that had long gone unmet.

Max always had a desire to make the story of God's love relevant to young people. In a newsletter he wrote:

We are losing too many of our young people to the world. Somehow we are failing to capture their hearts and their minds for Jesus. I believe that we need to plant more "good seeds" in the children while they are still very young. Truth, and a love for God, needs to take root and become established before they reach the years of challenge. We have always been dedicated to ministering to the family and to the church. Now we have committed ourselves to serving you as you seek to guide the little ones in your life.

Deanna, Becky, Val and Becki with the Heritage Bear

The success of Heritage's children's programs empowered Max to trust his instincts more and to produce the music he felt there was a strong need for in the world. And when it came to music, Max felt a strong conviction to stay with what he knew and loved—the traditional Heritage style that he had developed in the beginning and that thousands of people around the world had come to know and love.

Max's conviction was tested when he was at his weakest. During Heritage's lowest point financially, the largest Christian record company in the industry approached Max with a very tempting offer. The record company loved the Heritage Singers and wanted to carry them on its label, however, they had one condition—the music style would have to be updated to something much more contemporary.

Max struggled with the decision. It would certainly help Heritage's financial situation. He knew that most nationally known Christian music groups performed the more contemporary music. They performed in big auditoriums and charged $15 or more a ticket for their concerts. Some of them even were into

Christian rock music. They had found out you can't please everyone, so they catered to those who buy the records, mostly young people. Record companies, producers, and Christian bookstores all thought that if you didn't perform and record contemporary music, you wouldn't be a commercial success.

But Max wasn't ready to make this change. He knew the Heritage audience wasn't ready for it. He believed that God had called the Heritage Singers to minister to the whole family and to him that meant continuing with the warm, traditional sound for which Heritage had always been known. He didn't believe Heritage should abandon its loyal followers who loved the more traditional music. "Music should draw the whole family together, not pull them apart," he said. But as he walked away from the opportunity, he asked himself how to do it. How could Heritage minister to the whole family? High school and college-age listeners were reached through contemporary music, older adults appreciated the more traditional styles, and children needed character-building fun songs and stories.

Another reason Max and Lucy chose not to accept the record label's offer was because they wanted to maintain ownership of all of Heritage's music for future projects. They would not only lose control of the sound and style of the music, but also of how the music would be used. The whole experience got Max thinking about Heritage's style and about how to better approach it to meet the needs of the group's widely diverse audience.

In the meantime, Max was getting a lot of requests for another traditional album. Max said, "The funny thing was, in the beginning, the people who were requesting the more traditional music thought Heritage was too contemporary. It's interesting how people's tastes and preferences change over time. The folks who weren't ready for our sound in the 1970s were now embracing it."

Max was going to have to choose his audience and focus on creating the music that would reach them. There were now so many contemporary Christian music groups that the audiences were becoming segmented. The best thing for Heritage to do was to continue being what it had always been, right? Or was it, in fact, time to become a little more contemporary?

Max began to notice that fewer and fewer young people were coming to Heritage's concerts. It was becoming apparent that Heritage was no longer reaching them. Greg went to Max and said, "Dad, the reason young people aren't coming to Heritage concerts any more is that we are not addressing the young people enough. If you want them to come, you have to do some songs that they can relate to, that speak to their age group."

Gradually, album-by-album, a more contemporary sound began to make its appearance in Heritage recordings such as the 1985 release *From The Heart.* Still, Max always remained sensitive to the more conservative listeners and worked to avoid offending them. Although this may have held the Heritage Singers back in the world of modern Christian music, Max was not concerned. He remained true to his convictions and didn't allow himself to be lured into the more commercial aspects of Christian music. That wasn't what Heritage was about.

Max explained, "We're not just a singing group. We're a prayer ministry, a soul-winning ministry, a family ministry and a children's ministry. Our programs have a musical variety that is sensitive to the wide range of musical needs of each audience.

God uses our music to soften the hearts of those who listen. At every concert we extend an invitation to accept Jesus as Lord and Savior. After the concert you will find singers back stage crying with those who weep, sharing with those who have needs and praying with those who have just received salvation."

To Max, success hasn't ever been about albums and concerts or record deals and recognition, nor the awards and television appearances—although there were plenty of those. For Max, real success was having a life with meaning through service that fulfilled their passion in life, and the kind of music that brought people closer to God. Real success was being emptied of the need to achieve and letting God work through you to help others.

Many of the Heritage Singers have gone on to be professional musicians in well-known arenas. The talent that has come through Heritage over the years has been phenomenal. Max had a huge impact on many young musicians by exposing them to recording and performance environments. Some of the former singers are now working in the film industry or recording solo albums and touring themselves. Many of them have music ministries of their own. Perhaps the greatest achievement Max and Lucy can claim is the hundreds of ministries that have sprung up as a result of Heritage's ministry, a multiplication of ministries and healed lives. That is true success!

For 20 years, the Heritage Singers lived out of suitcases and toured 11 months of the year. Life on the road was an adventure—sometimes good, sometimes trying. Night after night, the ministry continued in hundreds of cities. Individual singers came and went, the music evolved, and the group became more widely known. Through it all, Max and Lucy continued to marvel at how God was working through them.

"When we first started out, we wanted to have a singing group, but the ministry soon became more than singing," said Lucy. "We saw answered prayers, even miracles! People were giving their hearts to the Lord as a result of the Heritage ministry. It changed how we looked at everything. We were humbled and awed by how God was working through this ministry."

With that sense of purpose, Max and Lucy continued to find the strength and courage they needed to meet each day. It was about being a part of something much larger than themselves; it was about getting out of the way and letting God do His work.

CHAPTER THIRTEEN

Defining Times

I will give thanks to the Lord with all my heart.
—Psalm 9:1

IT WAS BECOMING CLEAR THAT THE DAY-TO-DAY DECISIONS MAX WAS MAKING WERE ACTUALLY DEFINING AND shaping the Heritage ministry. These were very pivotal times, full of difficult decisions and choices that defined what Max and Lucy believed.

When Max's father died, a piece of property was sold and the proceeds were split between Max and his two brothers. The money was paid out over a number of years in the form of monthly checks to possibly be invested for their retirement. Max knew that if Heritage was to survive he needed to put his portion of the money into the Heritage ministry. For the next five years that monthly check is what helped keep the Heritage ministry going.

From the beginning, the ministry survived on donations, album sales, and love offerings at concerts. Whenever possible, the concerts were free.

"We've remained totally independent and are not sponsored by any church or denomination." Max said. "We're the people's people, supported by lay people and businessmen. We don't get the pats on the back or the big write-ups in magazines. We're just committed to going where God leads."

Perhaps one reason why Heritage has so many committed people who love their music is because they know how important and necessary they are to the ministry. Clearly, they are blessed because of their involvement in the Heritage ministry.

However, surviving on donations was becoming more and more difficult for Heritage, especially since some churches were keeping a percentage of the love offering to cover their own expenses. One of the ways Heritage covered concert expenses was to obtain sponsors for the event, in exchange for publicity. Sometimes a program is published with display advertisements promoting these sponsors.

"We had sponsors fund our 35th anniversary concert at the Crystal Cathedral," said Max. "We told our audience that our costs were covered by our sponsors and that the concert was free. Our sponsors suggested that we also take up a love offering to help further our ministry. That was the largest love offering we've ever received in our entire history! The way people responded to help the Heritage ministry was incredible. The people really rallied behind us and showed us that they believed in what we were doing."

On the rare occasions when tickets are sold it is generally for a fundraiser for a church or youth program. It is always well publicized in advance and handled by the concert organizers. Christian businessmen sponsor most of the Heritage Singers overseas concerts. They cover their expenses by selling tickets to the concerts.

Max always felt a loyalty to his audiences. He felt a sense of obligation to the people who supported him over the years. He was sensitive to them and their preferences. Max related on a very personal level with his audiences and made a concerted effort to choose material for each concert that would be the most appropriate.

Since the beginning, some conservative audiences have been critical of the Heritage style of music, although most have embraced it and become huge supporters of the group. Joanne remembered when she was with the group and one of their hosts told her he thought Heritage's music was too much like rock music and shouldn't be played in church. He stood at his kitchen door and placed his palm on it as he said, "The true test of whether music is okay to play in a church is if you can put your hand on a door and it doesn't vibrate with the beat. If the door vibrates, the music is not appropriate."

Most of the time people responded very positively to Heritage's music, but once in a while the group would be surprised by a negative reaction. Dunbar remembered one such time. He was staying at the pastor's home following a church concert. "The phone rang, and since our hosts weren't home, I answered it," said Dunbar. "The lady on the other end of the line was quite upset and completely berated the Heritage Singers. She just couldn't say enough about how much she hated our music. When I asked her if she'd been to the concert, she said, 'No, but I know how they are.' The ironic thing is, I remember that concert, and we mostly sang old hymns."

Dunbar remembered another negative reaction the group received back in the '70s while performing for a particularly conservative audience at Andrews University. "I remember we were singing a big, dramatic song, and as we ended the song we lifted our hands up. The next day the campus newsletter included an article about how inappropriate our concert was, saying, among other things, that we were 'dancing' on stage!"

35 Year Anniversary concert at the Crystal Cathedral. Max, Adriane, Marcelo, Shani, Tim, Ted, Becki, Scott, Melody, Tim, Val and Dave

That story made Joanne smile because she and her husband recently attended a Heritage concert at Andrews University and the group couldn't have been more warmly received. "I noticed immediately that they were performing some of their more conservative material," Joanne said. "The singers moved around a bit as they sang; their bodies communicating the words and feeling of the songs. It was just a natural part of the singing.

"The people in the audience were involved in the music, and openly participated in the experience by clapping their hands and raising them up, signifying the opening of their hearts. Some even stood to their feet, showing their praise to God. As conservative as I was raised, having been a student at Andrews University myself, even I felt at ease letting myself feel the music. The Holy Spirit was so palpable at that concert I had to remind myself where I was. Things have changed since those early days when we were afraid to raise our hands up at the end of a song!"

In recent years the audiences have become more accepting of the current sound, but Max continues to face limitations that constrain his ability to communicate with audiences. Some churches are even reluctant to allow the group to perform to pre-recorded tracks, a necessary cost-saving step for the group. Some might question why he doesn't just take the music to those who love it and get a blessing from it and leave the critics to their more traditional preferences.

Max said, "I love my Church, and although I don't agree with everything, there's a lot that I do agree with. I have no bitterness.

Max and Lucy reading a letter of encouragement

I do feel, however, that music needs to become a more effective channel for presenting Christ. My Bible says, 'Make a joyful noise unto the Lord' and to 'worship Him with song and thanksgiving.' To me—in the final chapter—I don't have to please anybody but God. It's not up to anybody else. In the end, I'm going to stand before the Lord and be accountable only to Him."

Max recently become concerned about the new trend of some church policies that require a percentage of the love offering. This makes it difficult, if not impossible, for groups like Heritage to cover their expenses. Max said, "I'm afraid that they're making a terrible mistake. How are they going to keep young people interested and involved in the church if they are making it so hard for vibrant ministries that appeal to the young people to even cover their expenses? There's a danger that these groups will stop coming, and the churches may see a loss of interest from their young people.

"Young people need something relevant and meaningful, something that will inspire them to dedicate their lives to Christ and get involved with their own ministries. Groups like Heritage appeal to young people and deliver the message of Jesus in a way that reaches their hearts. I'm just afraid that without positive and relevant influences that they're going to find their relevance and meaning in other places, and in other activities that won't have such a positive outcome on them.

"When church leaders are approached by new groups wanting to come to their churches, I would hope that they would realize the opportunity to open their doors and share the love of Jesus with their community. Where has the desire for evangelism for our local communities gone? I realize it takes money to turn on the lights, but wouldn't that money be worth someone being saved? Music softens the heart for an invitation. Music brings people to Jesus.

"Our churches should say, 'I want to support these young people. These young musicians could be doing a lot of other things, but they've chosen to serve the Lord.' Some church leaders just think about the cost. But what is the cost? What is the cost for a soul? Jesus gave His life to save one soul."

Max always appreciated working with pastors who are dedicated to outreach who would ask, "What are your needs in order for us to bring the Heritage Singers to our church?" Rather than, "What's the least amount you'll come for?" The person who really makes us feel welcome—that's the person who encourages us to continue.

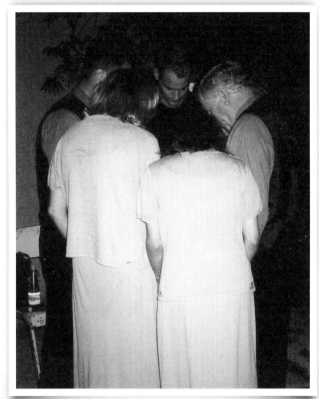

Asking for God's guidance

"We know God is behind this ministry because of how He has provided for us over the years," he continued. "We have received thousands of letters from people whose lives have been changed through the music of the Heritage Singers."

Many of those letters have included requests for the old songs, songs Heritage sang when it first started out. Because of these requests, Heritage digitally re-mastered many of the early recordings and released them on compact discs. This was done around the end of the 1990s and turned out to be a huge

undertaking. But before the project was even completed, people were placing orders for the older albums.

Max didn't realize the impact that these re-released songs would have on people. "We began receiving calls and letters from all over the world." Letters like these:

"I feel like you did these just for me. I grew up on these songs and it brings back such fond memories."

"Back in 1983 I gave away all of my Heritage records and got involved in the occult. Ten years later I came back to the Lord and am so excited to have a second chance to hear all of these songs again. These songs are what brought me to the Lord."

"If it weren't for these songs I wouldn't be in the church today."

"I listened to these songs every night going to sleep when I was a teenager. Now I have children of my own and want them to have the same wonderful experience I had growing up on this music."

"Just when Lucy and I feel too tired to go on, we get a letter or a phone call from someone telling us how the Heritage Singers music has blessed their life or helped them through a difficult time," said Max. "Hearing these testimonies makes all the long bus rides, late nights, fast food, sore throats and sleeping in a different bed every night all worthwhile!"

Recently a concert organizer asked Max what Heritage's denominational statement was. Max paused briefly. "Denominational statement? Hmmmm..." Then, knowing just what to say, he smiled and said, "Jesus, Jesus, Jesus."

SECTION IV

Into All the World

CHAPTER FOURTEEN

Heritage Singers en Español

As the Heritage Singers traveled extensively and were exposed to many different cultures, Max felt that God was calling him to more effectively reach people in their own language. In particular, he had a strong calling to form a Spanish version of the Heritage Singers. "There are so many Spanish-speaking people in the world," he said, "and there is a real need for a professional singing group that can share Jesus with Spanish-speaking people all over the world."

During the 1970s Max had tried to start a similar group in Brazil, but soon found out that the church was not ready. "I guess I was ahead of my time," he said.

Fifteen years later, Max decided to try again. In October of 1992, Max announced he was forming a Spanish Heritage Singers. "It has been my desire for years to be able to share our music with the Latin American countries in their own language. Now the Lord has opened another door for us to extend our ministry to our Spanish-speaking friends through a newly formed group, The Heritage Singers Spanish Edition."

Auditions were held at La Sierra College in Southern California. Max wanted all of the singers to be Spanish-speaking.

Nine singers were chosen to make up the group. They all lived and worked in the Los Angeles area, but represented six different countries: Chile, Colombia, Costa Rica, Honduras, Mexico and the United States. Their first album *Viene Un Milagro* was recorded, and Max was pleased with the sound. He said of the album, "The sound is bright, refreshing and has the warm Heritage style."

Max and Lucy were very excited about the possibilities. Within a few months, a distribution contract with Sony had been signed. The Heritage Singers Spanish Edition was one of only five groups to be selected to be on Sony's new gospel label *La Palabra,* meaning "The Word." Max and Lucy believed this worldwide contract would make it possible to spread the Word through music to thousands of people; people the Heritage ministry would never meet otherwise.

Max and Lucy met the Spanish group in Los Angeles and flew with them to Mexico City, where they sang for 20,000 people in a large bullfighting arena. They held three concerts that Saturday.

"The people were so appreciative!" Lucy said. "They didn't want the group to stop singing. Even though I didn't understand a word of Spanish, I could feel the Spirit of the Lord there and see the smiles on the peoples' faces." Plans were then made for the Spanish singers to go to several Central American countries.

Excitement was in the air. After months of praying, planning, applying for passports, and begging for time off from their respective jobs, the Heritage Singers Spanish Edition met at the Los Angeles International Airport for their tour to Central America.

The agent at the United Airlines counter stared in disbelief as the group stacked up their sound equipment, suitcases, and boxes of product. He told them, "I'm sorry, but they will have to be shipped air cargo and will arrive in three or four days."

Lucy said, "I guess the look of shock on my face and the explanation that we were a gospel group on a mission tour softened his heart. He called the director at air cargo and asked him to come over to the terminal. He put all of our sound equipment, baggage, and product in a large container and said, 'I'll make sure this gets on your flight.'"

There was one small problem—it was going to cost $1,440!

Max, center, with Oswaldo Villalobos, John Robinson, Miguel Yañez, Thony Escotto, Anabel Caro, Amada Andrean, Sonia Vizcaíno and Irma Gallardo

Lucy looked at Max. He knew what she was thinking. This was not in the budget for the trip! "We both knew we needed all of our sound equipment there, so we had no choice," she said. "We offered up a little prayer: 'God, You've brought us this far by faith. You know our needs and we're stepping out in faith that You will provide for this extra expense.' We arrived safely, along with all our baggage, in Guatemala around 5:30 a.m. By 7:00 a.m. we had cleared customs and started the fun job of trying to make everything fit into three small pick-ups and a car!" The group's home for the next two days was a Baptist theological seminary. The dorm rooms came with a bed, a blanket and running water—especially when it rained!

A highlight of the concert in Guatemala was when one of the singers came off the stage to pray with a couple that had come forward. They said they had been away from the Lord for 15 years and wanted to come back and be re-baptized. A father and his young son also came forward. The young boy wanted to give his life to Jesus and be baptized. The Lord was working through the singers.

On the bus ride from Guatemala to San Salvador, the group saw guards with automatic weapons every few miles. "We were comforted knowing our guardian angels were traveling with us!" Max said. No tour would be complete, however, without bus trouble! The group was just one block from its destination when a back tire blew.

The group also had to contend with two earthquakes, power outages, torrential storms, extreme heat, and severe humidity, but the Lord was with them. They held six concerts in four days and over 100 precious souls gave their hearts to the Lord!

It was obvious to Max that there was a big need for a Spanish ministry. He wanted for the new Spanish group to be a success, but after a few months it became apparent that things were not right.

"It seemed that the Lord had stopped blessing the group," he said. "There were a lot of problems. A few members of the group were not living the Christian lifestyle that is required to be a Heritage Singer. You can't get up in front of people and say one thing, then do another." Max made the very difficult decision to disband the group. "It was a very sad day for me," Max said. "Most of the Spanish singers were doing the right thing. I had to disband the group because of what only a few were doing."

Max and Lic. Delfer Gonzales of Sony Mexico signing distribution contract

Disappointed once again, Max decided to put the idea of having a Spanish group aside.

In the meantime, the Heritage music had reached the young people of South America. Throughout the 1980s many singing groups were formed, inspired by the Heritage Singers. They sang Heritage songs and dressed like the Heritage Singers. In Chile, there were several Heritage-inspired groups.

Two individuals who were part of this "Heritage movement" in Chile were Samuel Montero and Carlos Ávila. Both men had their own singing groups that sang Heritage songs. They could see how much the young people in the church loved the music. It encouraged them and inspired them in their day-to-day lives. The Heritage music style and its message of God's love had brought new energy to the young people in the church.

However, the church leaders in Chile were very much against this new kind of music, and their position discouraged the young musicians coming up in the church. By the 1990s the Heritage-inspired groups had almost all disappeared. Music

in the church that appealed to young people was almost dead. The same thing was happening in Argentina and other South American countries.

Samuel and Carlos saw what was happening and decided to go see Max and let him know how much the young people of Chile appreciated the Heritage Singers' music. In January of 1995 Samuel and Carlos visited Max at the Heritage ranch and presented him with a plaque honoring what the Heritage ministry had done for Christian music in Chile. They encouraged Max to come to Chile to explore the possibility of expanding the Heritage Singers' ministry throughout South America. Plans were made to hold auditions in September of that same year.

Max was touched to learn that Samuel and his wife, Ada, named their son after him. Sadly, the little boy, who was only five years old, had leukemia and died in August of 1995, just a month before Max planned to conduct the auditions. The auditions were postponed. Samuel and Ada decided to continue with the plan, and the auditions were rescheduled for October 1995.

Max arrived in Chile and was in for a surprise. "I had no idea that the Heritage Singers were so well known there. People came up to me and asked about the singers by name as if they had been personal friends for years. They told me how they had grown up with our music and how it had kept them involved in the church."

Thony Escotto, the bass singer for the disbanded Heritage Singers Spanish Edition, went with Max as his interpreter. They met with a variety of business people who were excited to help bring the Heritage Singers to their country. Max quickly discovered that the young people of Chile desperately wanted a music ministry like the Heritage Singers. "The pastor of a 1500-member Lutheran church in Santiago welcomed us with open arms to come sing for his congregation. He also invited Thony to preach for the morning service. We also met with the manager of a new Christian television station who was very anxious to have the Heritage Singers programs play on their station."

Word traveled that Max was going to be conducting auditions for a new group and there was much excitement. Some of the people even traveled more than 1,000 miles just to have a chance to audition. Dénar's future wife traveled seven hours by bus to be there. Approximately 60 auditions were held. The singers that were chosen were Miriam Serrano, Izzie Moyano, Gabriela Peña, Rodolfo Vásquez, Alejandro Ambiado, Dénar Almonte, Samuel Montero, and Ada Contardo. Dénar and Gabriel Donoso were the musical directors and Carlos Méndez was the sound engineer. Samuel and Ada were the directors of the group.

Rodolfo Vásquez, Alejandro Ambiado, Gerson Villalón, Dénar Almonte, Luisa Inzunza, Carla Ambiado and Izzie Moyano

Although the church leaders rejected the idea of having a Heritage Singers group in Chile, most of the people, both young and old, supported it. The idea of having a professional group had never gotten this far before and people were very anxious to see the results. Even though some in the Seventh-day Adventist church resisted, the movement was started and could not be stopped.

One day the president of the Chilean Central Conference summoned Max to his office. When Max arrived, he saw that the directors of the conference departments had also been asked to be there. Max immediately felt as if he was on trial for committing a crime. "Who gave you permission to come to Chile?" the man asked. "I am the man in charge of what happens in this conference, and I was not told you were coming." He expressed his dislike for the music style and made it clear he had no interest in having a Chilean version of the Heritage Singers. He told Max

he would not support it.

Max sat and listened. After the man finished, Max said, "You know, I don't need to come to Chile. I am very busy with what I'm doing in the United States. But let me tell you something, if God wants me to come here, I will be here." Then, he went on. "Sir, the young people of your conference are begging me to come here, and if God wants me here, I will be here."

After the meeting was over, the directors of the various departments began to leave the room and some of them whispered to Max, "Please come. We want you here. We need you here to start something for our youth in music."

Max believed that God was behind the new group and continued with his plans. In February of 1996 Samuel and Ada Montero traveled with Max and the Heritage Singers to observe firsthand what it was like to be a Heritage Singer. "They were so excited to get out and start witnessing," Max said. "They planned to record their first album by mid-summer. The mission field in Central and South America was so ripe for spreading the gospel through music. We were looking forward to traveling and sharing with our new friends in Chile."

On June 8, 1996, after six months of rehearsals, Max traveled to Santiago, Chile to help the Heritage Singers Edición en Español kick off their new ministry and introduce them at their first major concert in Santiago. They played to a packed house at Ñuñoa Adventist Church and were well accepted by the people.

During that weekend Max took pictures with the group for posters and advertisements. As he observed the singers and got to know their personalities, Max couldn't help but play matchmaker. He told Dénar and Izzie, "I think you guys would be a great couple." The very next day they started dating and after four years they got married.

Max told the group that they would be traveling on a part-time basis for three years and singing only on weekends. He told the singers, "If you're in the group for the right reasons and you stick together as a group, keeping the Heritage sound and values, then you'll become full time singers at the end of the three years."

For three years the group sang almost every weekend. During the week, the singers were in school or working. Some of them were studying over 300 miles away and had to travel on a bus every weekend to get to the concerts.

During this time, the group had no albums to sell. Samuel covered all the costs of food, travel, equipment and performance clothing. He loved music so much that he wanted to invest his money and time into the project. Because he lived over a thousand miles from Santiago, he had to travel with his family every weekend to get to the concerts.

In 1998, the group performed on a short tour through Argentina. More than 3,000 people saw them at different concerts around Buenos Aires. While on their tour in Argentina, they saw many people come to Jesus—including many drug addicts. The vice president of Argentina attended one of their concerts and told them it was the first time he had ever attended a musical program like it and that he was leaving with a great peace in his heart.

That year the Heritage Singers of the United States also traveled to Argentina, Chile and Perú. In addition to holding concerts, they also held clinics for music groups in an effort to teach them how to be more effective in their music ministries. While in Perú, they were invited to give a special one-hour concert for the congressional officials there.

This was the first time the Spanish group met the American Heritage Singers. They were excited to meet the people who had inspired them through their music, and they learned a lot from their time together.

While he was there, Max needed a bass singer to fill in for three concerts with the English group. He asked Magdiel Pérez, who was the vice president of the Adventist University in Chile,

if he would be willing to sing with them. Magdiel was excited to sing, and before leaving for the weekend he mentioned his plans to his superiors at the union office. They told Magdiel, "If you sing with the Heritage Singers, you will lose your job. We will fire you." Magdiel went with the group anyway, and thankfully he was not fired.

The three-year trial period for the Chilean group was now over. Max felt they were ready for the next step and told them it was time to become a full-time group. Since many of the group members were either in school or working, they had to make a decision about what they were going to do. Four of the original eight singers, plus the original sound engineer, decided to go full time. The group then added three new members - Patricia Barriga, Ricardo Arias, and Luisa Inzunza – and officially became a full-time group under the umbrella of the Gospel Heritage Foundation. Samuel and his wife decided not to continue in order to take care of their daughter. They recommended Dénar Almonte as the new director.

Based out of Santiago, the group began full-time ministry and toured all over South America. To help support them, Max found American sponsors for each of the eight members. The sponsors committed $250 a month to help offset the expense of their salaries. Max sometimes asked himself why he was starting another group. "The only thing I can say is God placed it on my heart. I felt we had such an awesome responsibility to share Jesus."

Max appealed to a congregation in Yakima, Washington to provide ongoing financial support for the Spanish group. They also needed to purchase a bus. Larry and Frieda Soule were in the audience that day. They approached Max after the concert and told him they wanted to sponsor the Heritage Singers Edición en Español. Not only did they send in generous donations to keep the group on the road, but they also donated all of the money to purchase the bus in Chile.

A few years later, after the group came to the United States, Larry and Frieda also purchased a second bus for the group. Larry even drove the bus and Frieda cooked for the singers, which they greatly appreciated. For Christmas and New Year's, they invited the group to their home in Washington. It was the first time some of the singers had ever seen snow.

A man by the name of José Becerra was hired to be the bus driver in Chile for the group during 1999. His wife and three daughters attended church, but at that time he was not sure about giving his life to Christ. While on tour, the group set aside time each day for worship on the bus. José was there for it all. He heard everything the group talked about and was there for all the concerts. He saw how people were moved through the music. After a while he started participating more in the group's worship time.

Larry and Frieda Soule

At the end of every concert the group invited people to give their hearts to the Lord or to come to the front with any burden or problem. The singers would pray privately with each person who came forward. One night Dénar gave the alter call. "I was inviting people to come forward," he said, "and the very first person to come for prayer was José, our bus driver. He said that he saw the joy and passion in the hearts of the singers and wanted to have that in his life. His family was really happy because for years they had prayed that he would make a decision for Christ. Months later José was baptized and we sang at that wonderful occasion."

One foggy night the Heritage Singers Edición en Español were traveling and their bus driver missed the entrance for the freeway. While trying to find the right entrance, they saw another bus on the freeway that was heading south, which was the way they were trying to go. After about three minutes of circling, the driver finally found the freeway entrance.

Dénar said, "We had only just made it onto the freeway when we saw stopped traffic ahead. After stopping the bus, Carlos

and I walked down the shoulder of the highway to see what was going on. Less than a mile ahead was the same bus we had seen earlier. Apparently, a big truck had been coming from the opposite direction and had crossed the median and hit the bus head on. The driver of the truck had apparently fallen asleep at the wheel. We got there before any policemen or firemen had arrived. 'It just happened three minutes ago,' somebody told us.

"We could see that several bus passengers had been killed. We came back to our bus and told the rest of the group what had happened. The realization hit us that if we hadn't missed the freeway entrance, it could have been our bus that was hit. We immediately prayed— thanking the Lord for His protection. It was humbling to see just how fragile life was and how quickly it could be taken away."

The Spanish Heritage Singers continued to tour for eight months. Max was very proud of them. Unfortunately, the church leaders still refused to support them. "They refused to invite the group to any church events," Max recalled. "They wouldn't include them in anything. They were just dying in Chile. Lucy and I decided to bring them to the United States. We were so afraid the singers would get discouraged by how their church leaders were treating them that they'd leave the church. We wanted to bring them to the United States where they could see they were supported."

In January of 1999, the group flew to California and went to the Heritage ranch in Placerville to record two albums - *Campeón de Amor* and *Nuevo Ideal*. They also changed their name to Heritage Singers Español. In February they returned to Chile and toured around South America. The group returned again to the United States in June of 1999 and toured for almost six months, doing five or six concerts a week. Their tour started in Miami and finished in California.

It was an awesome experience for Max to see many Spanish-speaking Americans coming to the concerts and seeing how God was working through the group to reach people. It was really a dream come true. "I was so thrilled to see people's enthusiastic response to the group," he said. "People just loved them."

When Max brought the Heritage Singers Español to the United States, he was certain the Spanish pastors would support them. "I just knew the pastors of the Spanish-speaking churches would be so excited about the group and invite them into their churches. Unfortunately, I couldn't have been more wrong."

Again, the church leadership would not support the group. "The man in charge of the Spanish churches throughout the Pacific Union didn't support us." Max said. "And because of him, other pastors followed suit. There were a few brave pastors who put their neck on the line to invite the group to their church, but even when they were invited, the pastors often wouldn't let them take up a love offering to cover expenses, or they wouldn't let them sell albums. There was just no way for the group to support itself."

Everywhere the group performed the people were enthusiastic—saying they had never heard a sound like this before. By the end of 1999, Heritage Singers Español had signed a three-year contract with Integrity Music, the largest praise and worship distributor in the world. This put their recordings in every Christian bookstore in the United States, South America, Mexico and Puerto Rico.

Bus driver José Becerra with Max

Spanish quartet, Roldolfo, Dénar, Alejandro and Shandor singing with Bill Gaither at the Gaither Homecoming Concert in Long Beach, CA

They also recorded a new album, *Santo Santo,* and shortened their name to Heritage en Español. The group went back to Chile in December, with plans to return to the United States for another six-month tour in January 2000. Some of the members chose to stay in Chile, and new members were auditioned and added to the group. They included Steve Olivares, Keyla Vazquez, Shondor Carrasco, Tammy Rael, and Marcelo Constanzo.

In March of 2000, Bill Gaither heard a recording of the group and invited the quartet to sing at his Long Beach, California, Homecoming Concert, where they received a standing ovation from the 20,000 people in attendance. This was a highlight for the Spanish group.

Max still struggled with acceptance of the group in the Spanish-speaking churches. "I had a friend, Ernie Castillo, who was the vice president of the Pacific Union. He was kind of my mentor. Since he was Hispanic, I relied on him to give me advice about how to work with the Spanish leaders in the church. He was a Godly man and really tried to encourage me."

Max was worried about Heritage en Español's ability to survive. He prayed for wisdom to make wise decisions on the group's behalf. "I kept calling my friend Ernie, asking him what we could do to get the church leaders to support the group," Max said. "We did everything he suggested that we do, but it just didn't work. We kept trying and trying, but we just weren't getting the support we needed to make it financially."

Following an exhausting United States cross-country tour

that year, several of the singers decided to return to Chile to finish school. The group returned home and primarily held concerts on the weekends. God continued to bless their outreach.

Plans were soon made for the group to sing to a crowd of more than 20,000 youth at Picarquín, Chile. Young people came to the event from all over South America. The concert was held outside. "It was amazing to see the vast sea of young people worshiping God through our concert," Marcelo stated. "God was blessing."

In addition, seven songs recorded by Heritage en Español were chosen by Integrity Music to be included on a new album, called *Songs 4 Worship en Español*. It was a Time Warner album that featured different Christian artists. The album was advertised on television stations in the United States, Central America and South America.

Heritage Singers en Español, Luisa Inzunza, Rodolfo Vásquez, Patricia Barriga, Alejandro Ambiado, Dénar Almonte, Izzie Moyano and Gerson Villalón

In 2001, the group toured once again to Argentina. The group always appreciated the miracles that God worked through them. Dénar remembered, "It was a Wednesday night. The church was packed. People were standing outside of the doors coming into the church for our concert. Then just five minutes before our concert was to begin, the lights went out. There was a power outage in Buenos Aires. We all started praying for the power to come back on. Thirty minutes went by, and suddenly, the power was back. We got through most of the concert when once again the power went out. It was really late and everything was so dark that we couldn't even see our hands. Amazingly, nobody moved from the church. After twenty eternal minutes, the lights came back on. I decided to sing one more song and then end the concert. Then I started feeling guilty for not planning to do the altar call like we always did. When we returned to the stage, I told Carlos, our sound engineer, that we'd do two more songs and have the altar call in between them.

"I knew that the power could go out again, but I thought that maybe this was happening for a reason, so I made the altar call. A few people came forward and we prayed with them, but nothing unusual happened—at least, that's what I thought at that time.

"A few days later, during worship before our next concert, a member of the other church where we had sung previously came to us and told us about a young man who had been at that concert. He was born into the church and had attended the youth programs and most church events, but when he got to be a teenager he started spending time with his friends outside of the church. After a while he stopped coming to church altogether. He started smoking, dancing, drinking and living a different lifestyle. Several years passed, and then one of his old friends from church invited him to our concert. He was curious about hearing our group and came to church to check us out. That night he saw all his friends that he grew up with and they were so happy to see him. During the concert, he felt like every song was written and sung just for him. He was one of the few people that decided to give his heart to the Lord that night.

"After the concert all of his friends prayed with him. He told them that he had been looking for happiness for a long time and that night he had seen seven people on stage full of joy. He saw in the singers the happiness that he had been looking for. He saw in the singers the joy of Jesus. He decided to stop living the life he was living and come back to the Lord.

"Tragically, the story does not end there. Something else happened that night. After the concert, the young man returned to his house. It was pretty late at night. When he was about two blocks away from his house, three men approached him and robbed him. One of them had a knife and stabbed him several times and killed him on the spot—on the very same night that he gave his heart to the Lord. I'm so glad God gave me the courage to make the altar call that night. I look forward to seeing that young man again in Heaven someday."

Unfortunately, the success the group experienced wasn't enough to ensure the financial support of the group. They continued to struggle, and by the summer of 2002, the future of the group was unsure. After much prayer and discussion, Max decided to downscale the size of the group from seven singers to four—two men and two women, plus a sound engineer. By doing this he hoped to significantly reduce the group's travel costs. This meant they did not need a large bus anymore and it was sold to a church. The group purchased a van and a trailer. "I was so proud of those kids," Max says. "They were so talented and totally dedicated. I very much wanted to see them make it."

A new album, *Mejor es el Amor,* was recorded in November and December of 2002, and the group made plans for a tour across the United States, Puerto Rico and the Dominican Republic. A concert promoter in Miami, Luisa Moreno, saw the talents of the singers and worked to book them into new venues on the East Coast. It was a daily walk of faith for both Max and the singers. There were many times when Max was ready to call it quits, but whenever he was at the end of his rope, something would happen to reassure him that God was in control.

Since all of the Spanish singers were citizens of Chile, they had to have visas to work and live in the United States. After September 11, 2001, it became increasingly difficult to renew their visas. When they applied for their visas again, they were told the process could take up to a year, but the singers' needed their visas in one week.

Knowing this was not humanly possible, they turned their worries over to God. They needed a miracle—and they needed it fast. To make matters worse, Catalina Ramos, their new soprano, had previously been denied a visa to the United States. A woman named Esther Morrison worked at the visa office and did everything she could to get the visas processed quickly. She worked tirelessly putting together all of the details. When all of

the singers—including Catalina—were granted their visas in five days, Max praised God and saw it as a sign that God wanted the ministry to continue. "It was just one more reason why I couldn't give up on Heritage Español!" he said. "Dénar, Izzie, Catalina, Marcelo, and Carlos were missionaries to the Spanish-speaking world, and they took this responsibility very seriously."

In order to kick off the group's next tour, Max arranged for Heritage en Español to join the rest of the Heritage Singers at the Texas Conference camp meeting. This event would combine the English and Spanish-speaking congregations. Lucy helped the group get organized. She prepared airbeds and washed sheets and blankets for the many nights the group would be sleeping in church fellowship halls.

Heritage en Español's first concert was in Houston, Texas on May 17, 2003. The tour continued with concerts in several other Texas cities, including Dallas, McAllen, Corpus Christi, San Antonio, Austin and Waco. They performed in Memphis and Nashville, Tennesse, followed by concerts in St. Louis, Missouri. The group went to Illinois and recorded twelve songs in Spanish for 3ABN Television. Plans were made to feature these songs on 3ABN's new Latino television network. The group performed in several other East Coast cities before leaving for Puerto Rico and the Dominican Republic.

With such a busy schedule and close living quarters, it was only by the grace of God the group was able to endure. They rode in a van all day and stayed in peoples' homes. There was nothing glamorous about how they lived. Their sincere commitment and vision were evident. At times, on their days off, the group visited hospitals and sang to patients. One day they gave a mini-concert in a hospital lobby for family members visiting their loved ones.

Art Mapa joined the group for twelve days to shoot a video of the Puerto Rican tour. He commented on the dedication of the singers—telling stories of long drives, little rest and busy schedules. He said the singers never complained.

In addition to all the concerts, there were media appearances while in Puerto Rico. The group's tour promoter, Adalberto

Zapata, made sure the group was featured on the major secular television stations and the Christian radio stations.

The singers said some of the most memorable moments of the tour were those spent with Adalberto. "He worked side by side with us every day. Sometimes we'd begin our day at four o'clock in the morning and work straight through until one o'clock the next morning. Even though the days were long, he never complained. Unfortunately, we didn't realize during his time with us that he and his family were experiencing some problems." One evening after the group's concert, Adalberto shared his personal story with Dénar and they prayed together. "He told me that the songs and messages he was hearing at our concerts were helping to heal his heart."

Izzie, Dénar, Marcelo and Catalina

Back at the ranch Max was encouraged to hear about all the lives being changed through Heritage en Español's concerts. Every night people came forward at the end of the concert to pray with the singers and give their lives to Christ. Even mechanical problems with the group's van presented opportunities to bring others to Christ.

When the group was on their way to San Antonio, Texas, smoke began billowing out of their van. Dénar said, "We made it to San Antonio, but because we were unable to get into a mechanic that same day and because our schedule was very tight, we decided to drive on to Dallas. The smoke had lessened, so we hoped we'd be okay.

"In Dallas—about 300 miles from where we'd first noticed the smoke—we were referred to a Chevrolet auto mechanic. The van definitely needed some work. As we'd suspected, the weight of the trailer had burned out the transmission. The mechanic was amazed we were able to make it as far as we had.

"I told him about our ministry and said our protection was nothing short of a miracle from God. He seemed to listen. The next day we picked up our van, and after reviewing the invoice, we noticed a 50 percent discount on all labor and parts. There were other repairs needed, but because they weren't urgent, the mechanic suggested I do the repairs myself. He wrote down the exact parts needed, as well as where I could go to buy them. This was a huge savings for us. I had only just met this man! Before we left, I handed him a Heritage CD and noticed something different about the look on his face.

"The next day the mechanic called me. He said that he'd been having a very difficult day when we walked into his shop. He'd just asked God to show him where he could find peace for his life. That's when I walked in and gave him the CD, *He Is Our Peace*. It was exactly what he needed. He felt God had answered his prayer through us. Sometimes the Lord allows things into our lives that we don't understand—the last thing we needed at that time was van trouble—but God always has a plan for everything."

Although the group packed churches everywhere they went, it had been a tough year. Despite how well they were being received, the group was barely bringing in enough financial support to cover expenses. Max struggled with whether or not he should continue the Spanish ministry. He waited a little longer, but by 2004 it was clear that he had no choice but to take them off the road.

Max called his friend Ernie and said, "They've won. I can't fight the system any longer. I'm throwing in the towel." Max said he just could not figure out why the church would not want a group of young people inviting people to come to Jesus; it just didn't make sense to him. Ernie felt Max's defeat as if it was his own and apologized on behalf of the church. He knew Max had done all he could do.

Since that time, Max and Lucy have learned that their efforts to bring a Spanish group into being were not wasted. New board members now lead the church in Chile—ones that believe in and support music ministries. There are now many singing groups there and concerts every weekend. The Spanish Heritage Singers helped inspire the young people in Chile to start their own groups. There has been a revival of music in Chile that has given new life to the church and has spread to other South American countries.

The singers of Heritage en Español have since gone their own ways. Many of them are members of new musical groups in Chile. Dénar, Izzie, Keyla, and Marcelo still travel occasionally as Heritage en Español. They have traveled to Mexico and Venezuela, as well as performing for special concerts in the United States. Max still believes there is a need for a professional Spanish group that can share Jesus all over the world. As Marcelo states, "We are still more than willing to sacrifice our weekends and go on long, quick trips where the Lord needs us. We refuse to give up because we know that there is still a need for a Spanish Heritage ministry. We know it is making a difference in the lives of many people."

Bettesue and Marcelo Constanzo

Marcelo's Story

Born and raised in Chile, Marcelo started singing with Heritage en Español and now tours with the United States group as their second tenor. Like many other Heritage Singers, he had dreamed of becoming a member of the group long before it actually happened. When Max went to Chile to audition singers for the new Chilean-based Heritage Singers in 1995, Marcelo auditioned. "I heard that Max was going to be auditioning singers in Santiago, so I went there a day early to get ready," Marcelo said. "I remember I sang, 'People Need the Lord' in Spanish. Right in the middle of the song I forgot the words, I didn't know what to do so I just played like I was emotional and couldn't sing, until I remembered the words."

Marcelo did not make it into the group that time. Instead, he joined a singing group based at the Adventist University in Chile, where he was a student. "In 1998 our group traveled to the United States," he recalled. "We traveled in the U.S. for a whole month, and sang in many cities, including Chicago and Miami, and even in Puerto Rico." This was a time when his musical ability developed and he got more comfortable singing on stage.

Being exposed to the States, Marcelo began to envision himself living and working there. Pastor Boin and his family offered him an opportunity to stay at their place in Chicago, and Marcelo was able to send money home to his parents in Chile. Grateful for the chance he had been given to get a start working in the States, Marcelo went with Pedro and Marly Boin to Florida when they moved there.

It wasn't long before the Heritage Singers en Español came to Florida to sing at a youth rally in 2000. "Naturally, I got together with them," Marcelo said. "One of the singers told me there was a chance they might have an opening in the future. Max wasn't there, so Dénar said he'd talk to Max when they got back to the ranch. Weeks went by. Then one night I got a call from Dénar and Rodolfo telling me that they didn't need any new singers, but they'd keep me in mind. I was really discouraged. Then, only minutes later they called me back and said Max had reconsidered. I needed to make a video of myself singing at church and send it to Max. Of course, I did that right away. This time Max saw and heard what he was looking for, and asked me to join the group."

Marcelo was faced with the challenge of obtaining a visa so he could legally tour with Heritage. He had to go to the US embassy in Santiago, Chile and be interviewed. The authorities there would decide if he would be allowed to enter American soil.

Marcelo described this experience by saying, "I had to prove that I would be eventually returning to Chile; that I owned a business or property, or had some kind of financial incentive to return. I had nothing like that. I had two things: a letter from Max inviting me to join Heritage, and a personal reference letter from my church in Chile. I looked around at the others who were also to be interviewed that day. They had huge folders full of stuff."

When Marcelo's turn came, he gave the man who was interviewing him the two letters. "Is this all you have?" the man asked. Marcelo explained that he was joining a music ministry. The man went inside another room for what seemed like a very long time. When he finally came out, he said, "Come back at two o'clock and pick up your visa."

"I was so excited," Marcelo said, "that I could hardly hold in my emotion. I had passed one hurdle, but I wasn't in yet. When I got to Miami I had to be questioned again. This time it was more intense. Two men asked me what I was planning to do in the states. 'I'm going to sing,' I said. 'And once you're in the country, you intend to stay,' they said rudely. And I said, 'No, I really am going to sing.... with the Heritage Singers.' 'Whoever' they said, 'And then you'll never go home again?' After a while a third guy joined them, and the whole thing turned into an interrogation. I was scared to death. Finally one of the men just stamped my visa, and that was it. I was in."

After a crash course in learning the Heritage songs, Marcelo began touring with the Spanish group right away. When the group later returned to Chile, Marcelo wanted to stay in the States, so Max hired him to work at the Heritage Singers office. He took orders in Spanish and helped maintain the grounds, including keeping the bus clean. During this time he did not sing with Heritage, except for occasionally doing studio back up vocals.

"This was a real testing time for me," he said. "I wanted to sing, but I was doing hard yard work. I was so happy to be staying at the ranch, though, and just stay around the Heritage family. I really felt at home there. Plus, I was learning a lot of English since no one at the ranch spoke Spanish."

Then the weekend came when the group didn't have a second tenor, and Val asked Marcelo if he could learn the songs and join them for the concert. "I not only had to learn the songs and the tenor part, I also had to learn them in English. I only had one day to do it, but I wanted to sing so badly, I did it. I learned around 25 songs in one day!"

Around this time, Marcelo became acquainted with a friend of some of the Heritage girls who visited the ranch from time to time. Bettesue Heid had just moved to Santa Rosa where she was the principal of the Adventist Academy. She had previously been Shani Judd's roommate at Loma Linda, and frequently visited the Heritage ranch. Marcelo really liked Bettesue, but couldn't speak English well enough to really communicate well with her. Yet, despite the language barrier, they began a nice friendship, that soon grew into love.

With the return of Heritage en Español to the States for a six month tour in 2003, the group only had three singers and badly needed Marcelo to go on tour with them. Marcelo was faced with the dilemma of having to leave Bettesue for six months. "I gave Max and Lucy such a hard time. They were disappointed, but really understood my situation and told me that it was up to me, that they just wanted the best for me. I know that was hard for them, and I really am sorry to this day that I put them through that. Now I understand how much they cared about me. That is what a family does. And that is what they are to me, a family."

Marcelo went on the tour, leaving Bettesue behind. They missed each other terribly, but knew that he was doing what God had called him to do. At the beginning of the tour they were engaged. Bettesue planned the wedding with the help of her Heritage girlfriends, and when the tour was over, they were married in December of 2003. Marcelo now began the process of applying for his "green card," enabling him to be legally employed in the United States. He went for a physical, had several shots, and sent in his money and the required documents. The next step was an interview with the authorities.

"I was so nervous about the interview," Marcelo said.

"Bettesue and I took everything we could think of to prove we had a relationship - letters, photos, anything. We were taken to a tiny room and an American-Samoan man came in and took our fingerprints and asked us to tell him our story. He kept asking questions and more questions. This went on for at least 20 minutes. Bettesue and I were getting more and more worried as the time went on. He asked us what we did, and asked us about the Heritage Singers ministry, and how much money I made singing. After a while, he just paused. Then he visibly relaxed and looked up and said, 'Is Max Mace still the director of the Heritage Singers?'

"Bettesue and I just looked at each other dumfounded. Then the man went on to explain that he was a Christian and had grown up listening to the Heritage Singers! 'I think we were lucky to get you!' I said, and he said, 'Yeah, I work in the fraud department. I'm just filling in today for a guy who called in sick.' We left there knowing that God had been looking out for us that day."

Marcelo is currently applying for citizenship in the United States. He and Bettesue live in Sacramento where she is the principal of Sacramento Adventist Academy and he teaches Spanish. Their story is one of integration – a blending of cultures and talents and a love for doing God's work. When Marcelo performs with Heritage, Bettesue travels with him. In June of 2006, they were blessed by the birth of a daughter, Emma Rose and a year and a half later they added another daughter, Madison Grace to their family.

"Our ministry is a family ministry," Marcelo said. "We work full time together, and we travel together on weekends. We take our daughters with us. The singers all know me; they know what I've been through. Our inner lives can be intense at times. My sweet friends have seen my scars and I have seen their scars, and we love each other anyway, because that is what God teaches us

Izzie and Dénar Almonte

about friendship. Like the word says in Proverbs 17:17 'A friend loves at all times, and a brother is born for adversity.' I am so blessed to be able to be a part of this ministry with these people and I am grateful to Max and Lucy for believing in me. The opportunities that God continues to give us are amazing."

DÉNAR AND IZZIE - TODAY:

Dénar and Izzie Almonte have a full time music ministry now that specializes in working with young couples. The name of the ministry is Izzie & Dénar Music Ministry. "We feel that there's a special need among young couples and young adults to improve their relationships and marriages," Dénar says. "With so many divorces taking place, we have a message to give through our music." They also believe that there is a real need for Christian musicians in Spanish churches as they reach out to young people and young families. "As a family, we decided that we are going to be involved in Christian music as long as we can."

Dénar and Izzie had their first son, Dénar Almonte, Jr., in December of 2006. Another boy, Andy, followed him in November of 2008. They are a source of joy for their parents and often travel with them for the various concerts.

Dénar and Izzie travel throughout the United States, as well as to other Spanish-speaking countries with their music ministry. They also have started a recording studio with the goal of helping other people develop their musical skills. "We work with musical artists and teach them what we've learned from our experience with the Heritage ministry," Dénar explains. "We hope that our family ministry will inspire others to trust more in the love of Jesus to help them stay together as a family as they claim God's promise of eternal life."

Dénar and Izzie worked together to write some songs for

their duet album. "We wrote a song together, "Nuestro Amor es una Promesa" (Our love is a promise). It is a very special song for us as a couple because the day after we started dating, Heritage Singers Edición en Español had their first official concert. During the next three years, we were about 250 miles away from each other. We got together twice a month, whenever we had concerts with the group. We wrote each other many letters (not e-mails). We were married two weeks before we came to the States to work full time with Heritage en Español. When we released our first duet album in 2006, we decided to write a special song - our story. We took all the letters we wrote to each other when we were dating and copied part of those letters into this song. It shows how God can lead two lives into one. He definitely used Max and Lucy to achieve that purpose for the Almonte family."

Catalina with her daughter, Cristina

THE SPANISH SINGERS TODAY:

More than thirty singers have been a part of the Spanish Heritage ministry over the past 15 years. Many of them have since returned to Chile and continue their lives.

Felipe Vidal, a second tenor, now lives in Chillán, Chile with his wife, Marly. He is a music teacher and sings with a quartet.

Catalina Ramos lives in Santiago with her husband, Andrés, and their daughter, Cristina. She is a full-time stay-at-home mom for their toddler.

Rodolfo and Carina Vásquez also live in Santiago. Rodolfo sings in a quartet and also has a solo music ministry. His wife is pursuing a career in the medical field.

Carlos Méndez lives in Florida with his family. He owns a recording studio and produces for Christian artists in the area.

Felipe Figueroa lives and works in Molina, Chile. He is still able to travel with the group for some of their international concerts and run the sound.

Alejandro Ambiado and his wife, Patricia, work in the family business of private schools in Santiago. Alejandro sings in the same quartet as Rodolfo.

"It is humbling to see how God has used the Heritage Singers en Español to bless so many lives in the Spanish Christian world." said Max. "I am happy that many of these young adults are continuing to use the talent that God has given them to share the Gospel."

CHAPTER FIFTEEN

Once a Heritage Singer...

Shawn, Melody, Max, Lucy, Thony, Rhonda, Jocelyn, Ken and Greg in Curaçao

"WHEN DO YOU STOP BEING A MEMBER OF A FAMILY? YOU DON'T! I AM PROUD TO HAVE BEEN, AND WILL always be, a Heritage Singer." Lee Newman spoke those words, and he speaks for the 250 or so people who have been a Heritage Singer at one time or another. Once you are a Heritage Singer, you are always a Heritage Singer. It is part of who you are. When you haven't been in the group for a while and suddenly find yourself back on stage, it's like getting back on the bike. It all comes back to you like it was only yesterday.

Some Heritage Singers have left the group and then returned. Others have been invited back for special tours when one or more of the current singers couldn't be away from their jobs or families.

Ken Smith first sang with Heritage II in the mid-1970s. Twenty years later in 1996, Max invited Ken to join the Heritage Singers' on a tour in the Virgin Islands. "It was hard for me to believe circumstances had provided a way for me to sing with the Heritage Singers once again," Ken said. "As we traveled to our destination, my mind wandered back to 1975 when I first met the group. I wondered, would people respond to the group the same way they had in the past? With all that had happened to me, would I still be able to share Jesus through music? Would I be able to learn all the new songs? I looked down at the blue water below and wondered what God had in store for me. Would there be that one special person who would stand out in such a way I would know that was why God had me here? In thought, I said to God, 'Well, maybe this trip is for me.' I thought about all the times I had been blessed when I was sharing Christ with someone else.

"We were asked to sing at an Assembly of God church to encourage their church members to attend the evening concert. After we sang I was wishing I had done a better job and decided I should spend the afternoon practicing.

"As I stood by the van waiting to be taken back to my room, a young man came up to me. Apologizing for his poor English, he told me he was the only Christian in his family and that his family had pushed him away because of his beliefs in Christ. He said his brother had come to church with him for the first time today, and after watching the Heritage Singers sing, his brother said he wanted to have the joy he saw on the faces of the singers. Isn't Jesus wonderful? It's so reassuring to feel the peace and joy of knowing we're okay with our Creator."

Rhonda Green Ramzy

Rhonda Green Ramzy was in Heritage three different times. Her life has not been easy. It was a series of exhilarating highs and devastating lows. Each time she has been in Heritage, the experience has served as a life raft, healing her from what she had been through and strengthening her for the days ahead.

She said, "When I joined Heritage II in 1974, I found myself in a family. I had just graduated from college and was ready for an adventure. I loved singing! However, being with all of those people all of the time was a big emotional adjustment for me. I was very lonely at times."

During this time Rhonda recorded solos on two of the Heritage II albums. Her songs "To God be the Glory" and "Joy Comes in the Morning" became a standard part of every concert. The following season she left the group to get married. However, her marriage soon began floundering. Although two beautiful

children had been born to her, the marriage was a source of much pain and disappointment. Rhonda's husband worked in another city and only returned home every other weekend. She was singing for events and taking her children all alone. Feeling overwhelmed, she knew her marriage was at an impasse.

Then, out of the blue, Max asked her to return to the Heritage ministry. Rhonda said she saw it as an opportunity to take a break from what was going on in her life. "It sounded so good to me to return to a place where I was cared for and nourished.

"I lived at the Heritage ranch, and my daughter, who was two years old during this time, often accompanied me on tour. It was a very exciting time to be in Heritage. We had our own television show. We traveled to many different countries. I was even able to record a solo album, which was nominated for a Dove Award. Those were the best times."

Then tragedy struck. Rhonda received a telephone call from her dad one day and he told her that her brother had been fatally shot. She said, "It didn't really sink in until I heard the word 'autopsy.' I said, 'Is he dead?' and just started screaming, dropped the phone and started running. Thankfully, Garth was there at the time. He talked to my dad and helped me through the initial shock. Only by the grace of God did I get through that," she said. "I left Heritage to go home and be with my family." Not long after she returned home she was devastated as she went through divorce proceedings, but she knew that is what she had to do.

Then, Max and Lucy came to Rhonda's rescue. They offered to help her get her life back together. They sent her an airline ticket and brought her back to the ranch to live with them. Eventually she was able to get back on her feet. Max and Lucy helped her get a car, an apartment and a job. Lucy picked up her two children every weekend so Rhonda could sing with the group.

During Rhonda's first Christmas in Sacramento she didn't have any money to buy Christmas decorations or presents, but Lucy and Val came to her rescue. "They bought us a live Christmas tree and brought it to me, along with $300 and a card," remembered Rhonda. "That WAS our Christmas that year!

"The time I was away from Heritage I felt very isolated and lonely. I missed the camaraderie of the group.

" My life is stable now and I'm at peace. I am enjoying my children and grandchildren. I still love to sing! I do a lot of solo work. As we get older, our voices change, but hopefully, we can still make a joyful noise unto the Lord!"

In looking back, Rhonda said, "As bad as it was, it could have been worse. Nothing but the grace of God got me through it.

"I've always loved singing about the Lord. Being in Heritage gave me a platform to do that. I'll always be grateful to Max and Lucy for all they've done for me. They've been there for me over and over. I love them dearly. I have lifelong friends from my time in Heritage. I wouldn't trade that for anything."

Cindy Haffner joined the Heritage Singers in the 1980's. Cindy said, "I enjoy singing just as much now, if not more, than I did 29 years ago. I am so thankful God allows us to continue sharing His word in song. I am thankful that He makes it possible for me to continue to do what I love most—singing for Him.

"When I returned to the Heritage Singers with my six-month-old daughter Mandy we were just traveling on the weekends. Occasionally our trips would last several days. Amanda became Lucy's first Heritage Singer grandchild. Lucy was 'Grandma Lucy' to Amanda. We traveled with the first crib on the bus. She had her own little heaven in the back corner. Lucy took care of her when I had to sing and Lucy cared for her like she was her own. She just has so much love to give and share. It comes very easy for her.

Cindy and Eddie Haffner

"I am thankful for Max, Lucy, Val and Greg and for their guidance and selfless love for everyone. When you travel with each other 24/7 and still get along, enjoying what you are doing, you know there must be something much more powerful keeping things together!"

"Heritage has not only blessed everyone who has heard its music, it has blessed each and every singer who has been a part of Heritage. Saying thank you to Max and Lucy doesn't even begin to express the gratitude and love I feel for them. If it wasn't for Max and Lucy I wouldn't have met and married my best friend Eddie."

Becki Trueblood also feels the same gratitude toward Max and Lucy as Cindy does. Becki first sang with the Heritage Singers in the late 1980s, after which she returned to her home in Idaho for five years and finished college. Then, she returned to singing with Heritage and has been there ever since. Over the years Becki has become a very recognizable person on stage and a favorite among audiences. It is very hard to imagine Heritage without her.

Becki said, "My aunt roomed with one of the singers in college. Both my aunt and my grandma loved the Heritage Singers. They used to tell me, 'Someday you need to be in the Heritage Singers.' We went to a lot of their concerts.

"I'll never forget the Heritage concert on January 1, 1984. I had just graduated from high school. After the concert Jim McDonald and Max held auditions for singers who wanted to join the group. Bobby Silverman played the piano as I sang 'Amazing Grace.' Later I sent a follow-up tape.

"I know I sang with vibrato, something Heritage didn't do because it made it too difficult to blend voices. I soon got a letter from Bonnie at the Heritage office saying they'd received my tape and would keep it on file. They didn't have an opening at that time, so I decided to go to college.

"Three years later, the day before Christmas, I got a call from Max saying he needed an alto beginning the first of January. I accepted right away. After I hung up the phone, I wondered what I had just done. I was between my sophomore and junior year of college, but all I'd ever wanted to do was sing for Jesus, so I canceled my school plans, packed up my things, and went to the Heritage ranch.

"When I walked into the lodge at the ranch, everyone was back from Christmas vacation. It was the middle of their touring season and they all knew each other. I didn't know anyone. It was overwhelming in the beginning. I moved in with Jackie Leiske and began adapting to the Heritage way of life. We went on the road right away. I was scared. I didn't know the music very well and had a lot to learn about how to sing the Heritage way," recalled Becki.

During her first tour to South Africa, Max decided to do some "isolation tapes." Becki said, "Every Heritage singer dreads this. It's when the sound engineer isolates one voice from the mix of a live concert, then makes you listen to yourself. Sometimes Greg would sample different people throughout a concert and play the tape on the bus. It was brutal. That's when you can really hear what you sound like. You can't always hear yourself when you're on stage singing with the group, but the tapes don't lie! Mine was bad. Max listened to it first, then he had me listen to it. It was so bad that I cried. He said if I didn't get better he'd have to let me go. I was devastated.

"My fellow alto, Cindy Haffner, began working with me on intervals and pitch. We worked hard. At the next concert I was isolated again. This time I was much better. Cindy taught me how to sing like a Heritage Singer. It was hard work! You really had to re-learn how to sing. You had to change your voice, adding so much air and keeping a steady tone with no vibrato. You really

Becki Trueblood, "Miss Idaho"

had to listen to yourself, and each other, to be sure you were on pitch and blending. I'd get light-headed sometimes.

"When Cindy left the group, I was the only alto. I was really scared. It was all on me now. When Val came in, I tried to match Val's sound. I mimicked her breaths, pitch, pronunciation and phrasing. It took me about six months to notice the difference in how my singing had evolved. I couldn't really explain it for a while, but by the time we went back to Idaho for a concert, I felt I knew how to do it. Val, Jackie and my voices were tight and had mastered sounding like one voice.

"Once the music and singing got easier I could concentrate more on connecting with the audiences. Our job was to make it all look easy, but it was hard. Many singers come into Heritage as soloists, but when you sing in a group you have to back off and blend. Also, when you have a bunch of soloists, and the egos that come with them, it doesn't always go smoothly."

Being on stage wasn't always easy for Becki. It often made her feel very vulnerable. She said, "You really have to listen to what God is saying and remain open to what God wants you to say or do. It's uncomfortable and sometimes painful to be so vulnerable. Sometimes you feel inadequate, like nothing you're saying is making sense. But, then someone will later come up to you and tell you how much you spoke to them."

After five years in Heritage, Becki decided to leave the group. She knew she needed to go back and finish college. When she got home, she felt lost. She terribly missed singing with Heritage.

The first day at her new job she received a bouquet of roses from a man who had been stalking her. He had followed her for years, writing her letters, sending gifts, and showing up at concerts and the ranch. Despite a restraining order, he followed her to Idaho and registered at her college. It was very frightening to Becki.

Shortly after that Becki's aunt suggested that she enter the

Miss Idaho pageant. In addition to being a natural beauty, Becki had developed on-stage poise during her time with Heritage. To her great surprise, she won! This new responsibility kept her busy for the next two years. She eventually finished her degree in communications and got a job in advertising. Despite Becki's success, she felt empty inside.

Becki kept in touch with her Heritage friends and would sometimes visit them at the ranch to sing vocals on recordings. Becki said, "I felt so empty. My life was unfulfilling. I wasn't living right. I was trying to keep my feet in two different worlds.

"I kept remembering the peace I felt when I was in Heritage, so I decided to quit my job and take three months off. During this time I went to visit Max and Lucy at the ranch. Max asked me to stay and fill in for a while. I thought to myself how good it would feel to do that. I didn't have to be somebody else. I could just be myself again.

"During that time we traveled a lot and were very busy, but I felt such a welcome peace. I received a great job offer while at the ranch too. It would have been a fantastic career opportunity for me, but Max asked me, 'Don't you want to stay?' I knew I was supposed to be in Heritage, and even though I had a lot of bills from having a college loan, car payment and other things, I declined the job offer. When I hung up the phone, I felt at peace.

"My second time in Heritage was so different from my first. This time I felt comfortable. I felt at home. I had grown up in Heritage. I had learned about life. I had learned about people and about God. Although I had been raised in a good Christian home, Heritage challenged me to really know what I believe.

"I read the Bible and asked a million questions. I made a commitment every single day that I'd connect with God first thing in the morning. It was a necessity for me. I also started journaling. If I ever doubted God's work in my life, I'd just look back at my journals and remember how God has led me through things. He's been so faithful to me."

For many years Becki lived at the Heritage ranch and worked as Max's secretary. Then, in November of 2006 Becki decided to

GRACE NOTES:

"Dear Max, My husband, who has served the Lord faithfully for many years, has turned his back on God and our family. He is talking about leaving us. I was so surprised when he agreed to go to your concert with me. I knew God was leading him there.

"It seemed the songs you sang that evening were centered on the very thing that my husband was battling with. At the end of the service you asked for those who were struggling and needed prayer to raise their hand. I felt my husband's arm lift in response to that invitation. For the first time in a year and a half the hardened heart had been touched and softened and at that point in time a process of surrendering all to the Lord began.

"It has been three years since that time, but the Lord used your ministry that night to heal my husband and our marriage. We are approaching our 20th wedding anniversary together and our lives are not the same. God has given my husband a deeper relationship with Him and with me.

"I cannot thank you enough for being used of the Lord. Your music and dedication and humble willing spirit are tools that God is looking for in these troubled times. Your music is the healing salve for wounded soldiers in the deepest battles. Only God knows who is out in the audience needing healing, restoration and salvation."

leave Heritage to marry Shawn Craig. Shawn is the senior pastor at South County Christian Center in St. Louis, Missouri. He is best known as one of the singers of the popular Christian music group Phillips, Craig and Dean. Shawn is also a great songwriter and has written many well-known songs, including "In Christ Alone." Becki continues to sing with Heritage on special occasions. She will always be a Heritage Singer.

Not long ago Joanne was also given the opportunity to sing again with the Heritage Singers. It had been almost 30 years since she sang on stage with the group. She was at one of their concerts, sitting in the audience, when Max invited her and two other former singers in the audience to come up and sing along to a medley of old songs. She nervously joined the singers on stage and was handed a microphone as the introduction to "He Touched Me" began to play.

Joanne said, "As I looked over at Max's smiling face and then out at the people in the audience, I instantly felt at ease. As I heard my own voice blending with the singers next to me, I fell right into the music as if I'd never been away from it. It all came back to me—the words, the harmonies and the peace I had always felt when I was on stage with Heritage. It was the most natural thing in the world. It was where I belonged."

Yvonne Truby was one of the other singers who joined Joanne on stage that night. She said over the years there are two main things that have never changed about Heritage: the excellent choice of music and the love and generosity of Max and Lucy. "I feel so privileged to have had a small part in their family and ministry. What a happy time it was, and continues to be, when I am with them!

"Max and Lucy have always had a motto: 'Once a Heritage Singer, Always a Heritage Singer.' This is only true because of the open arms of their love and their truly generous hearts. I've watched Max and Lucy care for and nurture their Heritage 'kids.' Their spirit of love, patience and acceptance is beyond measure."

Precious Memories

PRECIOUS MEMORIES:

Responding to a Changing World

These things I have spoken unto you, that in me you might have peace.
In the world you shall have tribulation, but be of good cheer.
I have overcome the world.
—John 16:33

MAX OFTEN TALKS ABOUT HOW THE BIBLE SAYS THAT THE GOSPEL OF CHRIST WILL BE TAKEN THROUGHOUT the world and then Jesus will come and take His children home, and in addition, how blessed the Heritage Singers are to play a small part in this. After each exhausting overseas mission trip, the singers would remind themselves of this. It soon became apparent that God was blessing their trips. Many hearts were being touched.

One particularly memorable trip was the 1985 tour to Singapore and Indonesia. Max said, "That trip was one of the most unforgettable experiences we've ever had. Our host in Indonesia paid all our expenses, and all the concerts were benefits to build a chapel and cafeteria. The vast majority of the people who came to the concerts were Muslims. It was a rare opportunity to present Jesus Christ through song."

Jackie, Greg, Val, Art, Ted, Max, Annie, Art, John and Angie, in Singapore

Both the Saturday and Sunday evening concerts in Singapore were sold out. The enthusiastic response of the people shows that God's Spirit is truly working in the non-Christian countries of the world. Since Indonesia is not a Christian country, the Heritage Singers had to have special permission to sing and could not do any "preaching" there. However, the singers were able to present God's love to the people in song.

When the singers arrived at the airport in Jakarta, Indonesia, they were met by Mrs. Radius Praiviro, the wife of the minister of finance, along with a welcoming committee and the news media. After a reception at the Hyatt Hotel, which included native music and dancers, the group was honored to receive an invitation to Mrs. Praiviro's home. Many of the government officials attended the group's sold-out concerts and banquets. After the last concert, Mrs. Praiviro gave a farewell reception and presented each singer with a gift.

Heritage girls receiving a special welcome at the Hyatt Hotel in Jakarta

While in Jakarta, the Heritage Singers were also invited to have tea at the home of the United States Ambassador John H. Holdridge and his wife. The singers even gave the couple a private performance that day. The Heritage Singers made many new friends in Singapore and Indonesia and were grateful for the opportunity to share God's love.

As time went by, travel became increasingly challenging for the Heritage Singers amid growing uncertain-

Mace Family at the US Embassy in Jakarta

ty and concerns over international travel. Max still remembers waking up on the morning of the Oklahoma City Bombing in 1995 and the shock he felt watching the devastation on the news. He said, "My heart went out to all those families and their loved ones. Just a few weeks before terrorists had hit Japan. There was also the ongoing trouble in the Middle East. My mind went back to Bible prophecy where it says that at the end of time there would be many catastrophes around the world. I really felt, and still do feel, that we are living in the end of time. We must make

sure that we live for Jesus every day. We have no assurance of tomorrow."

Thankfully, with the advancements in media and electronic delivery systems, the Heritage Singers found new ways to share Jesus without having to physically travel so much. In October of 1996 the group was invited to participate in Net '96, a world-wide evangelistic program that was broadcast via satellite. The program was translated into twelve languages and sent to approximately 5,000 churches. In Brazil and South America, thousands of people watched the program on big screen televisions at churches and outside stadiums. "This was a tremendous outreach!" Max said. "Through Net '96 we were able to share the good news with thousands of people at one time, even in smaller countries where it hadn't been financially possible for us to visit."

The following year, the Heritage Singers were able to go to the Philippines. It had been 12 years since their last visit. They also visited Singapore on that trip. At the time, Max said, "We believe that God is calling us to sing in the uttermost parts of the world.

I stand in awe of all that God is doing. He is using the Heritage Singers to bring people to Him. To God be all the glory! Please continue to pray for wisdom and discernment as Lucy and I lead during these unpredictable times."

In 2000, when Max turned 63, the Heritage Singers planned another trip to the Philippines and Indonesia. However, this trip turned out to be very different from their previous ones. The day before the group was to leave for Indonesia, they were told the U.S. Embassy in Jakarta had been closed due to credible threats. The U.S. government was strongly advising Americans to stay out of Indonesia, but if travel was absolutely necessary, they should use extreme caution and keep a low profile. Americans, Christians and large crowds were the primary targets. Max said, "That description fit the profile of our concerts perfectly. To make matters worse, the U.S. Embassy could not guarantee that Americans would have military protection within Indonesia. Basically, we would be entering the country at our own risk."

After much prayer and soul-searching, the group went ahead and boarded the plane for Jakarta, via Hong Kong. During the flight, one of the singers happened to glance at a *USA Today* newspaper. Max said, "On the front page was an article warning Americans to avoid travel to Indonesia, along with many other sordid details. Of course this was quite disturbing to read. We passed the paper around to everyone in the group and decided to spend the next hours praying about what we should do. No one had a good feeling about what was ahead.

"Upon our arrival in Hong Kong, we had a group meeting and decided to stay the night to review the situation before making a definite decision about traveling the following day. Our luggage had been checked through to Jakarta, but when we expressed our concern to the airlines, they quickly acted and held the plane while they retrieved our luggage."

Shortly after, the Heritage Singers got on the phone to their Indonesian sponsors and explained the situation to them. Their sponsors were very disappointed because they had invited the vice president of the country and several Indonesian dignitaries to the airport for a surprise welcome party, as well as many Christians. Despite their sponsor's disappointment, the group felt they had made the right decision to stay in Hong Kong for the night and pray further about proceeding to Jakarta.

"We felt bad about the 4,000 tickets our sponsors had sold for Sunday night's concert," Max said. "They were beside themselves, afraid we weren't going to show up. We assured them we'd do everything in our power to make it to Indonesia, but our first concern was the safety of the singers. Our sponsors told us they would tighten security and move us from a popular, well-publicized hotel to a private, secure condominium."

The Heritage Singers decided to proceed the next day to Jakarta and trust God to protect them. Max said, "It was difficult for us to imagine that God would bring us this far and not want us to follow through with our concert responsibilities. We all decided that we must step out in faith, and that's exactly what we did.

"When we arrived in Indonesia, our sponsors were waiting for us at the airport, keeping their promise of being very low profile. They took us right through customs and to a mini-bus, which whisked us directly to a high-rise condo with heavy security. We stayed in that building until 4:00 PM the next day. We were then driven to the Hilton Convention Center for our concert. Immediately after the concert, our sponsors slipped us out a side door where cars were waiting to take us back to the condominium. Unfortunately, we weren't able to meet with any of the people, but our sponsors assured us that this was the best thing to do.

"The next morning we left the condominium at 5:00 AM and caught a flight to Manila, Philippines. We thought we were finally free from trouble. However, upon our arrival, we learned that the Philippine people were trying to impeach their president. This was causing a political uprising in Manila. Newspapers were full of political statements, and there were demonstrations and hate rallies taking place all around us. Our hotel hosted one of the biggest rallies, drawing huge crowds of screaming people. We heard fights and sirens all night long.

"Despite all of this, approximately 4,000 people came to our Manila concert. At the end of it, Pastor John Lomacang, a former Heritage Singer, gave an inspiring call. Hundreds of people stood to their feet acknowledging Jesus as Lord of their life. There were tears in our eyes as we realized that this was what our tour was all about; people giving their lives to Christ.

"I am so thankful that we didn't allow our fear to overcome us. The people in those countries desperately needed to hear about Jesus, and what a privilege it was to see so many give their lives to Him! It was quite an interesting time to visit Asia. Our heavenly Father proved His faithfulness and kept us safe from all harm."

A year later, terrorists attacked the World Trade Center in New York City and the Pentagon in Arlington, Virginia, on September 11, 2001. At the time of the attack, Max and Frank John Salas were in Tahiti setting up the details for the next Heritage tour. They were supposed to fly home that day, but were delayed for three days because of the moratorium on flights in and out of the United States. Upon his return home, Max wrote this:

New York City fire fighters

There are no words to adequately express the devastation caused by the tragic events of September 11. The sadness has been overwhelming as we've heard of the thousands lost and the families left to carry on without loved ones. We've listened to story after story of heartache, emptiness, and fear. Yet in these devastating times, I have been so proud of the American people and our nation's leaders as they have so confidently turned America towards God.

Our president led our nation in prayer, quoted scripture in his national address to the American people and allowed Billy Graham to share the simple plan of salvation with our world during the National Day of Prayer televised services. It is truly a miracle that even in the midst of such devastation, our God has been glorified.

As a symbol of support for the New York City firefighters, the Heritage Singers sent some CDs and a letter thanking them for all they had done. Heritage also sent CDs to some of the volunteers and the families of victims. The firefighters sent Heritage a note of thanks and a photograph of themselves in return.

Following 9/11, Max and Lucy began to question whether they should continue to travel to other countries. They didn't want to put any of the singers in danger or worry their families. Ironically, the invitations seemed to be pouring in faster than ever. Max didn't feel this was a coincidence. "As a nation, we've experienced unspeakable tragedy," he said, "and from talking with many of you, within your own families, you've had tremendous heartaches and loss this past year. There is no assurance of tomorrow and this awareness has sparked a renewed interest in God and a curiosity about the spiritual warfare that is going on around us. I am convinced that if ever there was a time to put on the full armor of God, it is now.

"I believe we're facing real challenges, but I also believe we will see a tremendous outpouring of people giving their lives to Christ. We are praying that God will use our ministry in a mighty way and that many will invite Jesus into their hearts and experience new life in Him."

The Heritage Singers did reduce some of their international travel, doing only limited touring to countries outside the United States. One such tour was a 12-day trip to Tahiti in 2002. The Heritage Singers hadn't been to Tahiti in more than 15 years and were amazed to see so many familiar faces. In fact, three of the group's sponsors had been children during Heritage's first visit to Tahiti!

"In Tahiti the people treated us like kings and queens," Lucy said. "They were so gracious. They planned so many special things for us, even welcoming us at each airport with large banners. We don't get that kind of welcome everywhere we go!"

While in Tahiti, the singers made many special friends and are still in contact with them today. The singers also enjoyed the island atmosphere and the amazing beauty of their surroundings.

Max and Lucy were saddened to learn that some of the families who had been responsible for their first trip had been through some very rough times. There were stories of divorce and of friends who no longer attend church.

"On our first trip, we became good friends with many of the people," Lucy explained. "One of these friends was Leilani. She and her three children would come to the pool where we were staying. One day her little boy fell into the pool. Max quickly jumped in and rescued him from drowning. He saved the child's life.

"When I heard that she had been divorced and was no longer going to church, I decided to try and find her. With the help of some of our other Tahitian friends, I finally located her. We were able to talk about her life and the choices she had made that had brought her to this place. She felt she had done many bad things. I encouraged her to go back to church and reconnect with her Christian friends."

Five years later, Lucy received an email from Leilani. Lucy was thrilled to learn that she'd gone back to church and had been re-baptized. "She sounds so happy now," Lucy said smiling. "I continue to receive emails on a regular basis from her. She keeps me updated about her family and all of our friends in Tahiti. I look forward to seeing her again someday."

In 2005, the Heritage Singers traveled to South Africa. The

Val, Leilani and Lucy in Tahiti

Max delivering packaged seedlings

Lucy with ladies carrying their seedlings back to their village

group's South African sponsor hired a production team for all three concerts. The sound and lighting director was known for his work with secular artists. "He was funny and lighthearted, yet always professional," Max said. "He focused on the production of our concerts, not necessarily the content. Yet, all the while he was directing, he was also listening and taking to heart every song and testimony. He never commented on the concerts other than to say he was happy things went smoothly."

The third and final concert was in Johannesburg. "As we were saying our goodbyes to the production team and thanking them for their excellent work," Max said, "the sound and lighting director pulled our sponsor aside and told her he'd made a change in his life. He had given his heart to God during our concert. Praise the Lord!"

Lucy and Max returned to Swaziland shortly after that tour with Richard Barnes, the Heritage board president, and his sister Liz Young. They were there to participate in a mission project with the non-profit organization Dream for Africa. It was a fairly new organization founded by Dr. Bruce Wilkinson, the author of the best-selling book *The Prayer of Jabez.* This faith-based humanitarian organization uses volunteers from various nations to bring solutions to issues plaguing Africa, like hunger, orphans, poverty and AIDS.

"We signed up to help with the program, Never Ending Gardens," Max said. "This three-year program teaches people that planting a garden no bigger than the size of your front door can provide 12 immune-boosting vegetables for your family. With the help of several local African youth, we were able to sort and put together more than 6,000 garden packs for delivery the following morning. After the packets had been evenly distributed, the women placed their baskets or boxes full of seedlings on their heads and began their journey over the hills to their homes. The following day, we did it all over again. By the time we headed home, we had packaged more than 14,000 garden packets. That's a lot of onions, cabbage, lettuce and beets!"

Max said that being a part of this mission was a blessing for both Lucy and him. It was a lot of work to sort all of the seedlings and put them into bundles, but they were so thankful that Richard had researched it and arranged for them to join in the project. However, they were saddened a few months later by news that one of the young girls who had been helping them had died of AIDS.

One of their stops while in Swaziland was at an orphanage. Lucy had brought seven suitcases filled with clothes, shoes, toys, toothbrushes and toothpaste for the orphanages. "When we pulled up to the orphanage and started unloading all those suitcases," Lucy said, "the ladies in charge just stood there in amazement! They had all the little children line up along the wall while Liz and I handed each child a toy. We had been told they loved soccer, so we had soccer balls for each of the boys and dolls for the girls. As we were preparing to leave, one of the teachers said, 'the children want to sing a song for you.' They all lined up

and sang a little song in English, 'We're Marching for God.' We were told that about 90 percent of these children were there because both parents had died from AIDS and that they wouldn't probably live to adulthood. It broke my heart."

"Our trips to countries around the planet remind us that no matter where we live in this huge world, people are the same," Max said. "We all hurt. We all feel lonely. We all struggle. We all are tempted. We all are afraid from time to time. Yet through Christ, we are all able to find peace. We are not alone. This simple message is what we try to bring to people everywhere we go."

Whether it be night or day,
Close to home or far away,
I am not alone for God is near.
A stranger in a foreign land,
On mountain peaks or desert sand,
I know I'm not alone for He is near.
I am not alone for He is near me.
Whether it be far on distant shore,
Walking there beside me.
He is there to guide me.
I am not alone for He is near.

In 2003, the Heritage Singers traveled to South Carolina to sing for a Voice of Prophecy evangelistic meeting. The event was to be broadcast by satellite all around the globe. At the time, Max wrote this:

I often have wondered how the gospel would be preached to all the world, but now I have a pretty good idea: satellite broadcast. It's hard to believe that we could be singing in a small convention center, yet through amazing technology, people all around the world can see us within a matter of seconds. I feel so small.

Children from the orphanage sing for us, "We're Marching For God"

God has given us all a great commission. He has told us to go into this unstable world and preach the everlasting gospel, and that when the gospel is preached to the four corners, He will come and take His children to their heavenly home. Some people feel that China is the last big nation to hear the gospel. No one knows when Jesus will come, but we definitely know we're living in the last days. I challenge us all to be ready to meet our Savior. What an honor to be a part of such a huge calling!

In 2003, the group was also invited to perform in two joint concerts with Sandi Patty. Independent concert organizers sold admission tickets for these events, and the sold-out crowds seemed to love the combination of the two artists. Heritage opened the concerts with about 40 minutes of music and

The Heritage Singers singing with Sandi Patty

then joined Sandi Patty in the second half for "Farther Along." "That song brought the house down!" said Max. "We all looked at each other and said, 'Now that was fun!'"

There were times when the twists and turns along the way didn't seem to create much of a pattern. As Max took advantage of the opportunities that came his way, it was often difficult to see a clear direction for the Heritage ministry. But no matter what the future held, Max continued to put his trust in God's leadership. He knew that God had a plan and that someday it would all make sense. Someday, he would be able step back and look at where the Heritage Singers had been and see the beautiful pattern God had been weaving all along.

SECTION V

Behind the Music

CHAPTER SEVENTEEN

Lives Transformed

*"Your music called out to us over decades, through darkness,
and in spite of Satan's best efforts to keep us from hearing.
Your ministry saves lives every day. So to see you again and hear
you sing at this time in our lives is perfect. It's like coming
full circle. It's like being welcomed back by old friends."*
—Letter from an audience member

THERE ARE MANY, MANY STORIES OF HOW GOD HAS REACHED HEARTS AND CHANGED LIVES THROUGH THE Heritage Singers' ministry. There are stories of hope and forgiveness; stories of turning heartbreaking losses into strength; stories of climbing out of sorrow and finding the strength and inspiration for helping other people—even starting new ministries. Many Heritage Singers have shared their own stories of how God worked through them, yet there are so many other stories that we don't even know.

DAVE MAUCK

When Dave Mauck joined Heritage, he was curious to see the kind of spiritual personality that defined the group and to see the influence this musical ministry was having on peoples' lives. He had seen a pamphlet that Heritage had printed that described its ministry as "More than Singing," and wondered just what this meant. He wondered if Heritage was really making a difference

Amanda and Dave Mauck

in how people viewed God or if the group was more about entertaining. What spiritual effect did Heritage have on people anyway?

Dave joined Heritage in 1976. "Max told me that because of my pastoral experience, he was depending on me to plan the schedule for the 'calls,' the short talks at the end of every concert, in which one of the singers would invite the audience to give their hearts to God. Max said that he was depending on me to do a lot of these talks myself.

"I wondered just how much influence I could possibly have on people. Well, it didn't take long for me to realize that God was behind this ministry. Though I don't remember them all, several experiences stand out in my mind and had a huge impact on my spiritual life. Not only were these individuals' lives changed, but mine was, too. One of these people was Mary.

"The year was 1978. Max had started the weekend group on the West Coast, and I was directing the full time group that traveled mostly in the Midwest and East. Mary was a 16-year-old junior in high school when we went to her school to do a concert. After the concert she approached my wife, Amanda, and told her what was going on in her life. Her father had been sexually abusing her from the time she was ten years old. Amanda brought Mary over to me and we both prayed with her. We also prayed silently that God would help us know what to say to her that would encourage her.

"We talked with her for over three hours that night. We encouraged her to give her problems to God. We tried to convince her that Jesus loved her and that He would take this burden from her and bring healing to her life. Amanda and I didn't even know where the words came from. We really felt the power of the Holy Spirit working in us. Mary came to the point of saying she would give her heartache over to God and believed that He would heal her life. We hugged each other and prayed again, and with tears streaming down our faces, we said our goodbyes for the night.

"The next morning, as the singers were hauling our bags to the bus, getting ready for another day on the road, I heard someone shout, 'Dave!' Before I could turn around Mary had jumped on my back, nearly pulling me over backwards. I turned around and looked into her radiant face.

"'God woke me up this morning!' she beamed. 'He asked me if I still had any hatred in my heart for my dad, and I didn't! I mean, I don't! I really don't hate him anymore! And I don't hate God anymore, either!' She had been freed from the guilt and shame and blame that she had held for her dad, for God, and for herself.

"Mary wrote to Amanda and me several times after that. She told us that she had confronted her dad and he had asked her to forgive him. He was moved to seek counseling and take steps toward healing.

"I don't know why I was surprised that God spoke through me. He did it over and over again. Whenever I didn't have the words, I just prayed for God to help me, and He did. I just needed to learn to trust Him more. I also decided to be more prepared, so I wouldn't find myself in these situations!

"Needless to say, my earlier doubts about the relevance and impact of the Heritage ministry had been replaced with a firm conviction that God had called Max and Lucy to a ministry that would touch many thousands of lives. This group was founded and continues to perform on the philosophy of 'More than Singing.' The spiritual heritage that this group leaves behind at each appearance is that there is hope beyond today's hardships and difficulties, and that there is no sin that God cannot forgive. All we need to do is come to Him, surrender to Him, and we will find peace."

Frank Mass

Frank Mass was one of the members of the Rose City Singers right after serving in the military. He lived in Portland, Oregon, where he worked as a fireman. On his day off he was topping off a tree, and he had a terrible fall. He fell about100 feet to the ground, and broke nearly every bone in his body. He was in such bad shape that he wasn't expected to survive. Because his accident happened on his day off, he was not eligible to receive Workmen's Compensation insurance. He could no longer work, and had no income. He was in dire straits physically and financially.

Max and Lucy visited him in the hospital and tried to encourage him. They took the Heritage Singers there to sing to him. For about a year, Max and Lucy made his house payment for him, while he recovered from his injuries.

Today Frank is in a wheelchair and paralyzed, but he is happier than he's ever been. He and his new wife, Barb, have their own music ministry. They write and sing their own songs. Frank and Max have remained friends all of these years, throughout the entire history of the Heritage ministry. They are wonderful people and an absolute joy to be around. Their faces just beam with happiness.

KEVIN POKORNEY

Kevin Pokorney and his wife had been followers of the Heritage Singers for quite some time, and were planning on joining the group on an anniversary cruise a few years ago. But, at the last minute they couldn't go because Kevin's wife contracted cancer and suddenly died. In the process of working out the cruise cancellation details with the Heritage organization, Kevin found himself being encouraged and lifted up during what was a very difficult time.

Since then, he met and married a wonderful Christian woman, Dawn, and the two of them have started a suicide intervention ministry for young people. They operate a 24-hour telephone hotline, and are working to train others to work in the ministry, so it can expand. It is a lot of work, and sometimes overwhelming.

Some of the singers ran into Kevin and Dawn after a Heritage concert. "We were just coming out into the hall to pray together about our ministry," Kevin said. "We're a bit overwhelmed right now, and are trying to decide how we can go on meeting the needs of the people who depend on us, and expand into other areas where we have been asked to help. After being in that concert, we feel encouraged to reach out in faith, and we just wanted to pray about it."

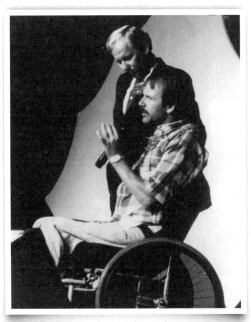

Max with Frank Maas sharing his testimony

They looked at each other for a moment, and then taking a deep breath, Dawn said, "We are learning what it means to walk in faith. We just keep going one day at a time, not knowing where the money and support is coming from but just believing that it is going to be there.

"We feel that we've been chosen by God to do this," Dawn said, as she told a little about her background. She told about a time in her life when she totally lost all ability to speak, and how there was nothing the doctors could do to help her. She couldn't utter a sound. It was a very dark time in her life. Then one day she could suddenly speak.

"God healed me!" she beamed. "And I've never stopped talking since that day! I have been chosen by God to tell my story, and I'm not going to stop. People need to know they're not alone in this world, that they have a God who loves them and will always be there for them."

"Our purpose is to give people hope," Kevin explained, "to just let them know they're not alone. We can't say enough about how much we appreciate what the Heritage Singers are doing. The concerts bring people close to God, and encourage people like us who have their own ministries. They are there for people who are struggling, and are an inspiration to us in our ministry. Their personal interest in me has made a huge difference in my life. Lucy and Becki were especially there for me when I needed encouragement," he said. "They helped me through my grief when my wife died, and I'll always be grateful to the Heritage organization for how they were there for me when I needed them."

DARRELL MARSHALL

Darrell Marshall's singing ministry has been inspired and encouraged by Heritage. Many followers of the Heritage Singers are familiar with Darrell, as he sometimes sings with the group and often is a guest artist at Heritage concerts. His easy-going country boy demeanor and quick wit often have everyone on the bus laughing. His songs are a sincere testament to his love for God through the rough places in his life.

"I first met Max and Lucy when I was introduced to them in May of 2002 at their ranch," said Darrell. "They were so gracious as we sat around their table and visited. Max called me a month later and invited my wife, Gayla, and me to join the Heritage Singers in late August in Chicago and sing a few songs at their concert. Little did we know that two months later my wife would have a tragic accident and fall to her death. Max quickly received a call of the news and he called me and prayed with me over the phone. I have never felt such love and concern as I have from all the Heritage Singers.

"Max invited me out to sing with them and I traveled with Heritage through the northwest singing and sharing my testimony. There are many times Max and I talk every day and he has been the most wonderful friend. He has shown so much love and compassion to me and helped me through my troubled times.

"I have seen all the Heritage Singers inspire and pray for many people all across the world. I know they have blessed many people as they have me. I thank God every day for putting them in my life."

Max and Darrell Marshall

Roger Ryan and Mike O'Brien

MICHAEL O'BRIEN

Mike O'Brien, a former Heritage Singer, shared his testimony in Heritage concerts. He told how he was raised in a Christian home, but when he entered college, he started making some compromises and bad choices. These choices led him into worldly pursuits, including drugs and alcohol. Mike met the Heritage Singers just two weeks after he nearly lost his life from an overdose.

When he began sharing his story, Mike began receiving hundreds of letters from teenagers who said they were in the same situation. They had been caught up in peer pressures and had made wrong choices. Many of them said they had found strength in Mike's words to break away from drugs and alcohol, and to find rest, forgiveness and strength in Jesus Christ to face each day.

Even though Mike had a hectic schedule on the road, he took the time to respond to every letter. It is thrilling to see how the Lord is using the Heritage Singers to change lives!

VAL MACE

"It has been so special to be a part of the altar calls at concerts," said Val. "Recently I prayed with a lady whose husband had just committed suicide. She wanted me to pray that God would show her a way to help her and her two young children cope. Even though I felt overwhelmed with this responsibility, God knew what this woman needed. Somehow the Lord always gives us the right words to say and the wisdom to know how to pray.

"Another time I prayed with a man after a concert that just wanted to thank the Lord for the wonderful doctors and nurses that helped save his life. He had tried to commit suicide but was found in time and taken to the hospital. It was a joy to share with him God's amazing forgiving grace. After singing for so many years, I can tell you that the most significant moments of those years have been spent at the altar with hurting people, watching God work miracles."

Val, Annette and Melody

Annette Morrow Simpson

Annette Morrow Simpson said, "I remember one night in particular when Tim Davis was giving the altar call. He mentioned that there might be someone there who had been sexually abused or perhaps had been the one who had inflicted the abuse. He said God knew their pain, and wanted to help them. This is when a sobbing young girl approached me. She wanted me to pray for her stepfather who, at the same time, had come forward to pray and confess his sin of inflicting this abuse.

"This girl shared her painful story with me, and the fact that her family was being ripped apart. What impressed me the most was the fact that this girl was actually grieving over the man who had caused her so much pain and was praying that mercy and compassion be shown to him. For me, it was reminiscent of our Lord. While hanging on the cross, His heart was breaking for the ones who nailed Him there! This little girl was learning early on what it meant to love unconditionally, as Christ loves us. I will never forget the blessing that I received that night."

Judy Gibson Knapp

Judy Gibson Knapp

"There are so many people hurting with unbelievable trials," said Judy Gibson Knapp. "One night a young woman came up to pray with me because she had just lost her husband to AIDS. I could barely get any words out of my mouth, as I was so overwhelmed with emotion and compassion for her. I am a young mother with two children, and this helped me to remember that I don't really know what tomorrow holds. At any moment, my husband or any other loved one could be taken from me.

"This lady was astonishing. As I remember, she sat throughout the entire concert with a sincere smile on her face! The Lord blessed me through her powerful testimony. She had no apparent anger toward the Lord, or bitterness, but a simple, sweet spirit in the face of adversity. What a testimony to God's overwhelming power to heal and to His peace that surpasses all understanding. The altar calls are vital to us, because God meets the people where they are, and He shows us that He sometimes shines brightest in the quietness of prayer."

Bill Truby

Bill Truby recalled a Yucaipa, California concert in 1973 where he invited people in the audience to give their lives to God. "Only one man came forward," Bill remembered. "His name was Marvin Ray. Marvin had never been converted to Christ and had never given his heart to the Lord. He just wasn't a religious or spiritual person at all. After that call he prayed asking God what He wanted him to do. He believed God wanted him to be in the ministry.

"Well, he did end up going back to school. He attended Andrews University, and after much study and prayer, he became a minister. Eventually, I ended up in one of his congregations. He was my pastor! He always thanked me for giving him the message of salvation and then commented on the ripple effect that Heritage concert had. Many lives had been affected through his acceptance of Christ at that Heritage concert.

"One of the most meaningful times for me was when Mike Madonna, who had come forward in a call, flew to where I was in Florida so I could baptize him. It meant so much to me that he would go to such effort to be baptized in the presence of the Heritage Singers. That's one of the things that is so powerful about Heritage. There are thousands and thousands of people who would attribute their introduction to a relationship with God to the Heritage Singers."

SHANI JUDD DIEHL

"A large majority of the people we pray with, we may never see or talk to again, which is why this prayer time is so important," said Shani Judd Diehl. "I never could have believed the impact that I could have through my simple prayers until I saw it myself.

"I remember a man I prayed with one year on a tour. He needed prayer for just about everything in his life: job, finances, and health, just to name a few. I didn't really know where to start with my prayer, but I went for it in Jesus' name and prayed for

Shani and Byron

Tim, Diana and Aidan

all those aspects of his life. The following year, he came to me at a concert and reminded me that I had prayed over him the previous year. He told me that since that day, his entire life had turned around, and that everything we had prayed for had been answered! I suddenly felt very small but very significant! It was an incredible reminder of the power of Jesus Christ when we pray in His name.

"Perhaps one of the lives transformed the most has been my own. As a little girl, dreaming of singing with the group, I never knew how much more it was than just singing beautiful songs. I have seen the power of God at work through the music and the message not only in others' lives, but also in my own. I have felt and known the power of it as I have overcome my own battle with depression, and dealt with health issues of my son, Matthew. We are more than conquerors through Jesus Christ! I'm one of the many living, breathing examples of it!"

TIM CALHOUN

"One of the most anticipated moments I look forward to in our concerts is when Max extends the invitation to the audience to come up and have the singers pray for whatever is on their hearts," said Tim Calhoun. "With so many different stories that people share with you over the years during this emotional time of the program, one story really blessed me recently. It was last year when a gentleman came to me and wanted me to pray for him. I asked what was on his heart and suddenly he began cry.

"He told me that he was in a serious car accident in which two passengers in the other vehicle lost their lives. He also was seriously injured but soon was consumed by guilt and depression. He proceeded to tell me that he was on the verge of losing his family and friends and he had absolutely no passion to live anymore.

"He heard that the Heritage Singers were coming to town and decided to go, hoping to hear something uplifting. I prayed with him and his family and after the concert gave him my email address.

"In his last email he wrote that he has completely healed from the accident and he has sought Christian counseling for his depression and guilt. His family and friends have been excited and blessed to see his complete transformation. He also wrote that he has renewed his relationship with God and if the Holy Spirit didn't prompt him to go to the Heritage Singers concert he would be dead. What an amazing victory! I'm so glad to be a part of this Heritage Singers' ministry that helps our loving Heavenly Father bring his children back home."

Andrei Barbu and his wife

BECKY GRECCO

Becky Grecco sang with the Heritage Singers in the 1980s. "After a concert a young girl came up to me crying," said Becky. "She was pregnant. Her dad wanted her to get an abortion and she didn't know what to do. We talked for a long time. I shared with her that although her baby was conceived out of wedlock, the Lord loved that little baby so much. It wasn't the baby's fault nor was the child growing inside of her less of a person because of how he or she came to be. It was a very moving time for the two of us as she shared her circumstances. I prayed that the Lord would give her wisdom and strength in her decision and let her know that God still had wonderful plans for her in her life.

"It was many years later at a reunion when this woman came up to me. I had always wondered what happened to that girl and had prayed for her many times. This beautiful woman asked me if I remembered a young girl with whom I had prayed who was considering having an abortion. Of course I did. She told me she was that woman and she had a beautiful boy because of what we had shared together during our time in prayer after that concert. Wow! I will never forget that as long as I live!"

TIM DAVIS

"One of the most rewarding things for me has been the influence Heritage has enabled me to have with people around the world," said Tim Davis. "There have been, to my surprise, many people who have followed me in Heritage. This just humbles me. There have been some who have contacted me through the years asking for advice musically and spiritually. I have developed good friendships with some of them over the years.

"One young man in Romania has really blessed me with his humility and talent. Andrei Barbu is around 22 years old and came to the U.S. for surgery on his back at age 19. His dream was to see Heritage live in concert, so his relatives flew him from Chicago to Los Angeles to see Heritage. That's when we met. A short time later, I received an email from Andrei. His sweet spirit and story captivated me. He was sincere in his questions about faith and his relationship with God. He told me that I was a huge influence on him musically and vocally.

"He sent me some of his work. His singing voice and his talent for vocal arrangements blew me away. As a classical pianist, his music foundation is really strong. Andrei and I are still in contact through e-mails. Although I haven't seen him in four years, I am continually humbled that God would use me in the life of someone who is on the other side of the world."

Tim was later able to secure a job for Andrei on the music staff of the Saddleback Church, the largest church in Southern California, where Tim worked. However, Andrei was unable to obtain a work visa, so he wasn't able to come to the United States after all.

On their recent trip to Romania, the singers were excited to get to meet Andrei in person and invited him to sing a song with them. They learned that he started a singing group in Romania and was using his talents for the Lord.

Another time, the need for God's true compassion became startlingly real to Tim as he prayed with a man who the night before had spent $600 on crack cocaine.

"He was broken, he was weary and he was at the end of his rope," Tim recalled. "He didn't need a lecture and he didn't need to hear scripture about his failure. He didn't need 'the church,' and he certainly did not need condemnation or judgment. He did need someone to listen, someone to care and someone to cry with, and we did just that the entire time. He seemed to hang onto me for dear life as he wept, and when I looked into his eyes, I couldn't help feeling his pain, as if God had given me a glimpse of the pain that He felt for this guy. In that moment, he needed Jesus—just Jesus and nothing else."

DÉNAR ALMONTE

Dénar Almonte recalled a time when Heritage en Español sang in Argentina. "That night a lady brought her husband to our concert. She had been trying to get her husband to come to church and hear about God for many years. After the concert was over, they went and bought a few CDs and went home.

"One day as the couple was getting ready for work, the wife decided to put a CD on. Her husband started to listen to the

Marcelo and Dénar

music and thought it was very good. But, he also was listening to the words of the songs, especially 'Campeón de Amor' ('Champion of Love').

"A few years later, when I was in Argentina again, this man approached me. He told me that because of the message of that song, he started to go to church and gave his life to Christ. Of all of the songs on that CD, the Holy Spirit really spoke to the man through 'Campeón de Amor'. I am so humbled to be an instrument for God. The music alone cannot change a person's heart. It is the special anointing of the Holy Spirit on the lyrics that makes the difference."

BOB MUNSTER

Heritage bus driver Bob Munster told this story. "My wife, Phyllis, and I first heard the Heritage Singers when the group had a concert at a Baptist church in Orangevale, California. One day, just when we needed it most, we found the Heritage television program. We had just lost our youngest son at the age of 21 and I had become angry. I had lost all interest in God, the Bible, church and even the gospel music I had always loved. My love for God was running on empty. This continued for many years. I poured myself into my work, while my wife continued with her church activities. But that Heritage television program really spoke to me.

"Then one day after I had retired I saw an ad in the newspaper. Max was looking for a bus driver, and I was the man for the job. It was only the second concert of my employment with Heritage and I could resist no longer and asked God back into my life. The music was compelling! Who could resist the moving of God?

"I drove the bus for about three years, and cherish that relationship. Phyllis and I believe that those three years were the highlights of our lifetime."

MARCELO CONSTANZO

"During one of our Northwest Tours, we had a concert in Kennewick, Washington," recalled Marcelo Constanzo. "As the end of the concert approached, Max extended the invitation for those that had a burden on their hearts to come forward and we would pray with them. We were able to pray with a gentleman who tragically lost his son in a drowning accident a few weeks before the concert.

"Sitting next to the father in the concert was the girlfriend of his son. Our hearts were saddened by the tragic loss to this family. But, what really blessed us as singers was that this man stood up and shared his testimony and praised God in the midst of the pain he was feeling. No matter what happened the man said he would love God and worship Him.

"Most of the time we, as singers, are the ones that are the messengers of the blessing, but in this situation, we received the blessing as we witnessed the strength and faith of this man. I am so thankful to be a small part of the ministry that Max and Lucy have dedicated their lives to. My life has been transformed through being a Heritage Singer."

Cindi Rael Paige

CINDI RAEL PAIGE

Former singer Cindi Rael Paige remembered a concert where she was sick with a cold, tired and irritable. She didn't feel like singing. "I had just finished singing my solo 'He is Able' and it was time to collect the offering. I backed out of it. When Lucy approached me and told me that there was a gentleman outside on the steps crying that wanted to talk to me, I told her that I just didn't have the strength to speak to anyone that night. Lucy said that I would have the energy to speak to this person.

"I went outside and sat next to the man. What he said to me made me shameful and forced me to remember what my calling was and why God had placed me there. He asked me if I was the one that sang the song about God being able. He said he was walking around town trying to figure out what he was living for. The man had just lost his job, and his wife had left him and taken their children. He had many debts that he couldn't pay.

"The man told me that he was just about to step in front of a semi truck to end his life when he heard singing in this church. He listened at the doors and heard how 'God is Able.' As he sobbed, the man asked me if there was hope for him. I put my arms around him and told him how much God loved him—so much that He died for him. I left him that night with Hope and Peace and feeling very loved by a God who is greater!

"There is nothing on this earth that stirs the emotion and love in my heart that I feel for the Heritage family. It is a privilege and honor to have had the opportunity to stand on the many platforms around the world and sing for Jesus. Thank you Lucy and thank you Max for everything. You hold a very special place in my heart."

MAX MACE

At times people wrote notes to Heritage asking for their prayers. Many times notes were handed to them during our concerts. Max remembered a note written on a piece of paper towel that was dropped in an offering bucket by a young girl. She had wandered into the Spokane Opera House and stayed for the concert. The note said, "I was thinking about taking my life tonight, but after listening to your music I found a reason to live." Another time a man handed Max a note after a concert that read, "Max, you'll never know how much I love your group and how deeply your music speaks to me. This past year has been really trying for me. I had three major heart surgeries and depression followed. Please don't ever quit coming to our area."

The thing that people may not realize is how much encouragement Max and Lucy get from letters they receive. From the beginning of the Heritage ministry, Max and Lucy have gained strength to face their challenges from the many people who support their work through their letters, phone calls and prayers. Every day correspondence arrives from people who have been touched by the Heritage ministry.

"The letters and calls we receive from people give us strength to keep on singing," Max said. "The letters of support and encouragement, their wisdom, and their selfless giving are worth more to us than we could ever say with words. What these people may not realize is just how important they are to the singers individually and to the ministry as a whole."

Just recently Max received a letter from famous radio personality Bill Mack. Bill is known as the truck drivers' friend on XM Radio. He has been playing several Heritage Singers' songs on his Sunday morning program and is planning to do a live interview with Max. In his letter Bill wrote, "I'm receiving lots of good response for the special talent of the Heritage Singers! I want to give extra play for you on my Sunday Social on XM as well as my daily program.

"Max, I hope you realize how the world loves the Heritage Singers! It is my sincere belief that God is utilizing you as never before. Your music is needed now, more than ever. With the critical situation our world is facing, there is blessed strength in the music of the Heritage Singers."

A letter was received from a fan in Fiji. "Since I was a little child Heritage was always part of my family. We had all of your LP records. When cassettes came out, we collected them all. Then, when CDs came out, we replaced our old scratched records with the "Silver Anniversary Collection" of Heritage CDs.

"It's just amazing when you feel a presence that only Heritage music gives. I now have a family of my own, and they are all singing the Heritage songs. A lot of young people here are starting up singing groups inspired by your songs!"

Max said that these letters of encouragement always come at just the right time.

"These people are the foundation of the Heritage ministry," he said. "They are our reason for being out there in the first place. More than they know, they help the work go on. God has perfect timing. He knows when our faith is weak and when we need human encouragement. He knows how these letters give us hope."

"I'd just like to say to each of these people, thank you. Thank you for your prayers and for your stories. Thank you for your support. You are as vital a part of this ministry as the singers themselves.'"

"I will always be overwhelmed by the number of hurting people we come in contact with as we minister from city to city, and country to country," said Max. There are many people, even among Christians, who are exhausted and discouraged. God has called us to strengthen, encourage and uplift His people. People who are weighed down with the concerns of this life need to have their eyes drawn upward. Jesus still offers His vibrant power and life in place of our struggles. And sometimes it takes a song to get that message across. That's the vision I've always had for this ministry. We are His voice to those without hope."

CHAPTER EIGHTEEN

The Heritage Experience

HERITAGE IS SO MUCH MORE THAN THE SUM OF ITS PARTS. THE KALEIDOSCOPE OF STORIES BRINGS ALL OF the odd and insignificant little pieces together; creating a beautiful pattern that is a surprise to all. It can only be God's design how something so beautiful can be made from such different and unique pieces.

LEE NEWMAN

Lee Newman said that over the years many young people have asked him how to get into the Heritage Singers. "My answer was always the same," he said. "You don't choose. Max doesn't choose. Only God chooses who gets to be a Heritage Singer. You may desire all you want, or, as in my case, have no desire at all. Yet if God wants you there, then there is little that can be done to stop it."

Over 250 musicians have been involved with Heritage over the years. Some stayed for a few weeks and others for years. Maybe they

Lee Newman

didn't realize it at the time, but now that they look back on their experience with Heritage, most of the former and current singers would acknowledge the tremendous impact that the Heritage experience had on their lives.

JUDY BOYD

Judy Boyd said, "I learned so much from my experience with the group: tolerance, courtesy, kindness, and patience, to name a few. Our lives were changed and we found a new direction. I think of a song by Ray Boltz that goes, 'Thank you for giving to the Lord. My life was the life that was changed.' These lyrics could easily be changed to 'Thank you, Max and Lucy, for giving to the Lord. My life was the life that was changed.'

"If I could title my experience traveling with the very first Heritage Singers' group, it would be called, 'From the Mundane to the Majestic.' Being one of the original Heritage Singers was an exciting time. I'll never forget the incredible faith that Max and Lucy had when we started out, and all of their many kindnesses to me over the years. But the thing that had the most impact on me was something that happened long after I left Heritage.

"It was one of the worst days of my life. I was packing up my apartment, leaving Nashville. This was long after I was a Heritage Singer, and even after I sang with Doug Oldham. My singing days were over, and so was my marriage, and I was moving out of the place my husband and I had lived for several years. The telephone was to be disconnected that very day. I was devastated, not knowing where my life would take me now. I felt totally alone.

"Then the phone rang – the phone that was to be disconnected that very day. It was Max Mace calling me out of the blue to ask me if I would go on a tour with Heritage to Brazil! It gave me such hope! God knew I needed to have something to look forward to in my life, and Max and Lucy were there for me, even after many years of separation.

"Maybe you don't have a big story to tell. The way you live your life is your story. People can relate to a normal person who just lives one day at a time without any huge extremes. It's about simplicity, the simplicity of God's love for us. It's not about the rules. It's about the relationship you have with God."

Judy, Max and Lucy

Tim and Melody Davis

TIM DAVIS

Tim Davis's experience with Heritage began in August of 1990. "I had just come off of a tour with the Continentals," he said. "That tour was so regimented that we couldn't even go to the restroom without raising our hand and asking permission!

"During my first day with Heritage, the group stopped at a pizza place for lunch, and everyone was sitting at the table, and I actually raised my hand and asked Max if I could go make a phone call. They all looked at me as though I had lobsters crawling out of my ears! Val said, 'What did they do to you in that group?' I quickly and happily adjusted to the more laid back family atmosphere of Heritage.

"I was with the group only four months that year. While with the Continentals I blew my voice out singing with no monitors and had developed a pretty horrible case of bronchitis, which made my voice impossible to control. In December of 1990, some singers were invited to stay for another year. I was not. I was surprised and hurt, but I knew my voice was not working well. God had another group call me to go with them for six months, and then Heritage invited me back in August of 1991. My voice was working better then, and I was so thankful for another chance! I came back and stayed full time with Heritage until 1995."

Tim has been the vocal arranger for the Heritage Singers since 1992. He has taken a lot of the stress away from Max by helping to record new Heritage albums. "Today I have a career in the music industry as a studio singer, which I've been doing for the last ten years. It was with Heritage that I learned the skills of live singing. My work in the recording studio with Heritage equipped me to be able to do what I do today. The specifics of studio singing, vocal arranging and producing are skills that cannot be attained or honed outside of the studio experience.

"I will forever be grateful to Max and Lucy for giving me the opportunity to have such a leadership role in their organization. Were it not for them, I would not be able to do what I am doing professionally today."

MELODY DAVIS

Melody Davis said, "I think almost everyone of us Heritage Singers has experienced the generosity of Max and Lucy, but I'd like to share one more example of the way they so freely give. Tim and I had been back in California not too long, when we were asked to go on a Heritage Singers cruise to Mexico. We were struggling financially as Tim was re-establishing his singing career in Los Angeles. There had not been a lot of work for Tim at this point and money was very tight.

"I remember the last night on the ship Tim and I talked about how we were going to pay the rent when we got home. It was due very soon and we just didn't have the $1700 we needed to pay that month's rent. We prayed specifically for God to intervene and provide. The next morning as we were disembarking, and getting ready to say our goodbyes and go home, Lucy handed Tim a check for $2000 and told him she had just felt led by the Lord to give us that money. She and Max, of course, had no idea how the timing of it all was so perfect. They were a direct answer to a very specific prayer.

"I am always amazed at how they both allow themselves to be led by the Lord all the time, in so many different ways. They

Bill Truby and Pete McLeod

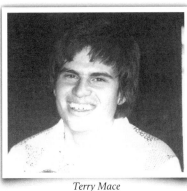
Terry Mace

are examples of obedience to the still small voice that wants to lead and guide us all, if we only have hearts to hear."

BILL TRUBY

Bill Truby said his time with Heritage was the most significant time in his life. "There is no other time in my life, except for the growing up years, that has had such an impact on my entire life. None. I can say that with assurance, with deep conviction. I know that beyond a shadow of a doubt. It's almost as if it happened yesterday. Heritage has that kind of power, I would guess on everyone who's been in the group. Max, Lucy, Greg and Val were literally my family. I felt as close to them as I did to my own family.

"I remember when Pete McLeod joined the group. I used to help with auditions, and there are a couple of auditions that stand out in my mind. Pete auditioned with the guitar. I called him later to hire him. He said, 'Is this the real invitation? Am I like hired? Or...?' I had to talk to him two or three times. We picked up Pete at the airport and that started a great friendship that endures through today.

"That's one of the benefits and positive byproducts of Heritage: the deep and lasting friendships. I appreciate so much everything Heritage has meant to me and done for me. Heritage catapulted my life from where I was to where it is. It was like taking me from the earth in a rocket to the moon. It was that significant of a change and that much of an impact on me."

TERRY MACE

Terry Mace said, "The Heritage experience changed me in profound ways. I was a timid and not very confident young guy when I joined the group. That's the thing Max did for me, and for many others. He built a lot of confidence in young people. The Heritage experience exposed me to so much I would never have seen. I learned about the importance of networking with others, and developed a sense of self-assurance and of being responsible; things that continue to help me in my life and work today.

"During my time in Heritage I developed a new respect for church leaders. We met a lot of conference presidents and worked with church leaders at camp meetings and crusades. Some of those relationships still help me in my work today. It's amazing how many people you get to know when you're a Heritage Singer. You can't be a gospel singer forever, but that confidence and those personal relationships last forever. The Heritage experience helped prepare me for everything else I've done over the years.

"I didn't actually accept the Lord until I was a Heritage Singer. The songs spoke to me. It was a time of constant spiritual impact; something that my own children don't get."

Eric, Shaylee, Alanna, Ginny, Logan and Rudy

Judy and Steve all smiles as they receive their wedding invitations

RUDY AND GINNY YOST

Rudy and Ginny Yost said they would forever treasure the close relationships they formed with the Heritage Singers when they were in the group. "We have so many happy, funny and emotional experiences during the two years we traveled full time and two more years part time," Ginny said. "We lived out of suitcases and stayed in peoples' homes. What gracious people! They took us in and treated us like family!"

After their time in Heritage, Rudy and Ginny decided to settle down in Redding, California. Alanna was home schooled until she was in the fourth grade.

"We have such wonderful memories!" Rudy said. "We can't thank Max and Lucy enough for giving us the opportunity to travel with them and work for the Lord. God used them to help orchestrate our personal lives."

"God continues to bless us in many ways," Ginny said. "Alanna has given us a beautiful family—our son-in-law, Eric, and two most adorable precious granddaughters, Logan and Shayle."

STEVE EVENSON AND JUDY MOTE

Steve Evenson and Judy Mote traveled in Heritage II during the mid 70's, and anyone who was there will tell you that they did not like each other very much. In fact, they could hardly stand to be around each other. Because Steve was the lead guitar player and Judy was the pianist, the two of them were thrown together even more closely than the rest.

"On the personal side of Heritage life, I had discovered that I could really annoy Judy, our pianist, and could usually get a laugh from the whole bus by picking on her," said Steve. "By Christmas I had really done a good job of being a pest. I decided to give her a 'gift.' Well, it wasn't a very nice gift. I had given her a gag gift with the notion that I was being 'nice.' She opened it and was steamed. I have never seen anyone so upset! I knew then that I had gone too far. I tried to apologize, but that didn't work. We soon went our separate ways for Christmas break.

"Over Christmas, I thought about my wrong doing and decided I had better change my ways. When the group reconvened after Christmas I began trying to be nicer to Judy. I sat by her on the bus and talked to her about things. I tried very hard to be kind and thoughtful to make up for how ornery I had been before. We actually became friends. I discovered that Judy was really a very nice person. In fact, I soon found myself falling in love. I had to ask her three times, but Judy finally agreed to marry me. Our wedding day was December 21, 1976.

"Never say, 'Never!' After four years in Heritage, Judy and I began working with Bill Truby, another former Heritage singer, in Southern California as singing evangelists. We worked with Bill for two years. After that we worked with Evangelist Jere Webb in Southeastern California for another year.

"It was about this time that I felt God was calling me into the ministry. I really didn't think I wanted to be a pastor, so I came as close to being in ministry as I could, through our music ministry.

"As Judy and I began raising a family, we found ourselves drawn to a new ministry. We had seen a video that used music to teach Bible verses to children. Judy said, 'This is what we need to do!' We knew nothing about video, but continued to pray about it. At one of our concerts we met a man who produced videos for the U.S. Government and was looking for a way to use his talents for God. We told him of our desire, and he felt that God had led us together. That was how our ministry, 'Plant a Seed' got started. It is now a television show seen weekly on LLBN and on The Children's Channel on 'Sky Angel.'

"After we had been working with children for quite some time, and we were well known at our church, an opening came up for a youth pastor. Judy suggested that I apply for the job. We prayed about it, and talked to the pastor, and now I am a youth

Tammy, Val and Randy with their new found friends

pastor! I never thought this is what I'd be doing with my life, but I couldn't be happier. I've had more fun working for God than anything I've ever done. Had it not been for that phone call from Max Mace inviting me to join the group, I might not be able to tell this type of story!

"Recently I saw Max. He made the comment, 'I never thought you would be a preacher!' Well, I didn't either, but it is proof that God can work with anybody, including me."

TAMMY RAEL LAWLEY

Tammy Rael Lawley first joined the Heritage Singers in 1991, when they were starting to be a weekend group. "I sang for only a few months but that time was memorable to me, because I was able to sing with my sister.

"Then in 1994, I joined Heritage for the second time. Max called and told me that Val was pregnant with Austin and wanted to know if I would step in and sing first soprano while she was absent from the group for a while. This is actually an incredible story to me, because at that exact time, I was going through what would be one of the biggest trials of my life. I know that the Lord had His hand in this, to make everything work so perfect. This opened the door for me to join Heritage and not only have the opportunity to minister to many people with different needs but also to minister to myself every night and to hear songs that told me that I was going to be ok and that the Lord had a plan for me. The one song that stands out in my mind is 'You Are My Song.' Every night we would sing this and every night I would once again, cry tears of hope."

Tammy was able to go on some overseas tours with Heritage. "We went to Vanuatu one year. It was our day off and we wanted to do some souvenir shopping. We took the public transportation van and went on our way. Val, Randy and myself started to notice that we were not on a public road any longer. All we were seeing was dirt road and bushes! This couldn't be right! The driver realized that we were Heritage Singers and without telling us, decided to kidnap us briefly and took us to his house to show us off to his family. They took photos, we signed autographs and they picked fresh fruit from the trees for us to eat! They treated us like royalty! It was a day to remember even though we never got our souvenirs.

"All in all, there were many different experiences while I sang with Heritage. Some were good and, to be honest, some quite difficult. But through it all, I will always cherish my time with the group and know that those experiences helped take me to a closer relationship with my Lord. I thank Max for the awesome opportunity and I thank God for the gift of music."

Scott and Holly Reed

DUANE HAMILTON

Duane Hamilton recalled, "The whole Heritage experience is one of the best things that happened to me in my whole life. It was a magnificent experience. It opened up a world I had never seen before, including being exposed to the professional recording process.

"The Heritage experience taught me things like stage presence and how to properly use a microphone. Professionally, everything I ever learned I learned from Heritage. I am deeply grateful for the blessing of being a part of the Heritage family. As much as my vocal and theory studies at Oakwood College, my experience with the Heritage Singers formed the foundation for my musical education.

"I still run into people who say, 'I was a kid when I came to your concert.' I'm actually still recognized for being a Heritage Singer! It's gratifying. I always knew what our effect on people

Duane Hamilton

was, especially on young people. In spite of the controversy concerning the use of popular music styles, I never took much of the criticism to heart. I firmly believe in the Heritage ministry and I believe that there will be people in Heaven as a direct result of that ministry."

SCOTT REED

"Max and Lucy are incredibly generous," said Scott Reed. "They just open their home to people. It's a refuge for anyone who needs it. They immediately accepted my wife, Holly, and try to include her in everything they can. They are so willing to share with others. For all these years all of their efforts have been about communicating hope and God's forgiveness and love. And they've taken that message to hundreds of thousands of people around the world.

"When I joined Heritage, I was only 19 years old and a student at Pacific Union College in California. I was in a singing group called 'Faith First,' made up of four singers. We were opening for a Heritage concert in Loma Linda, California, and after the concert Max asked us to audition for Heritage. He said he was having a contest, and whoever won would get $1,000 worth of studio time at Turning Point, the Heritage recording studio. Well, Faith First ended up winning the contest, and Max not only gave us the $1,000 in studio time, he fronted us the rest of the money we needed to record a whole album. We eventually paid him back, but that's how we were able to record our first album."

Scott lived at the Heritage ranch for a few months and worked behind-the-scenes in the ministry's operations with Becki and Val. It was there that he was exposed to another side of what sometimes goes on in Christian ministries. "I'm amazed at the number of times Max has just been left high and dry, totally ripped off." Many times people have taken advantage of Max financially, and this is especially upsetting when those people have been professional concert organizers or affiliated with Christian organizations, people you'd think could be trusted. Scott witnessed first hand that, even when blatantly stolen from, Max continued to treat those individuals with dignity. Scott said, "I am constantly amazed at how gracious Max is, no matter what is happening. I appreciate him more and more all the time."

Today Scott and Holly have two beautiful sons. Scott is involved with the Dwell Ministries organization and is the Worship Pastor at South County Christian Center in St. Louis, Missouri. "When I'm not singing with the Heritage Singers, I train other worship leaders, and I talk to them about living a life that is a sacrifice of praise. It's a sacrifice because it's not always necessarily what you feel like doing at the time; it's a choice you make. The Bible says that David made a choice to praise God. I like what Romans 12 says about giving your bodies as living sacrifices to God. It's about putting your whole heart and soul—everything you think and say and do—into praising God. That's what living every day in God's presence means to me."

Dave and Susan Bell

DAVE BELL

At the age of 19, Dave Bell had just started fall quarter classes as a sophomore electrical engineering student at Walla Walla College when he got a call from Max to sing bass with the Heritage Singers. He immediately dropped all his classes and headed out for what he thought would be a one-year adventure. Little did he know that he would continue to be involved so many years later. His rich bass voice has been a perfect complement to the Heritage sound. "When I first joined Heritage," Dave said, "one of

my first concerts was in a large auditorium in London, England. I'll never forget the reaction of the audience when I first stepped out on stage and introduced myself. I hadn't even sung a note. I just said 'good evening' and they started screaming and clapping. It surprised me so much that the other singers told me later that I looked like a deer caught in the headlights!"

At the end of the first year, it didn't take much to coax Dave into staying on with the group for another year. After the second year, he returned to Walla Walla College to finish his degree, but not before vowing "I'll be back!" Dave has been with the Heritage Singers for over 28 years, and his dedication is still going strong. With the exception of Max and Val, he has performed in more concerts than any other Heritage Singer. Often in the background or on the sidelines of what is happening, Dave is a gentle and humble man. He doesn't like to be the center of attention, but when he's on stage belting out those low bass notes, he's hard to miss! His consistent and confident bass line is a strong, dependable foundation for the Heritage performances.

Complimenting Dave's personality is his very sweet wife, Susan. She is a big part of the Heritage ministry as well. Often it's the behind-the-scenes people who really hold everything together. Susan is always the first to ask how she can help and just pitches in and does whatever is needed. The group can always rely on her willing spirit and compassion, as well as her beautiful smile.

Dave and Susan met while Dave was at the ranch for a Heritage music camp. Dave knew he wanted to get to know her from the moment they met after a church service in Sacramento. She asked him to join her at a potluck dinner that the associate pastor was having at his home. What Dave didn't know, was that her friends had already set her up with another guy for the same dinner. "I was seated at a separate table from Susan," Dave said, "and I really wanted to talk to her. I had no idea about the other guy she was supposed to be with. As the afternoon wore on, people started to leave, but I persisted and stayed around, even outlasting the other guy Susan needed a ride home, so I offered to take her. I finally got to talk to her! A few days later, I invited her to go miniature golfing, but I also invited Greg to come along so it wouldn't seem so much like a 'date.' Greg was so funny, I was afraid she would like him better than me!"

After music camp was over the group headed out for a 3-month tour to the east coast and back. Dave was afraid he wouldn't see Susan again, but he started writing his first letter to her as the bus was heading out of Placerville. Their friendship blossomed through the letters they wrote to each other during that tour. Halfway through the tour, Dave scraped up the money to buy a ticket for Susan to fly out and visit the group while doing concerts in the New York City area. "The singers were so nice to me," Susan said. "And, the concert crowd LOVED Dave. They screamed when he hit those low notes." Their young love has stood the test of time. Dave and Susan have been married for 20 years and are loved and respected by all who know them.

Shani and her brother, Marc Judd

"The Heritage ministry has been such an important part of my life," said Dave. "I can't imagine life without it. The part I enjoy the most, besides singing, is hanging out at the ranch with my fellow singers. It's like we're all one big family. Susan and I always look forward to seeing everyone. We all really enjoy being together."

SHANI JUDD DIEHL

Shani Judd Diehl said that being in Heritage has been a wonderful experience for her. "I feel like I have friends for life. We're like a family. I can tell my Heritage friends anything. They've really helped me along the way."

Shani's Heritage experience began when she was just a little girl living in Australia. "I'll never forget the first time Heritage came to Australia in 1982," she said. "We were so excited! I was only nine years old at the time. My parents and I got to spend a lot of time with the singers. And, from that time on, I totally admired them. My dad even set up a microphone and speakers so I could sing along with the Heritage videos. My favorite album was *Spirit of Praise.* I especially loved the songs, 'As for Me and My House' and 'Open Our Eyes, Lord.' Whenever I hear those songs it totally takes me back to that time. By the time we moved to the States in 1986, Heritage had come to Australia two or three times."

Shani's family ended up settling in Southern California, where Shani eventually became part of the four-member "Faith First" singing group, consisting of her brother, Marc; his wife, Andrea; and Scott Reed—all of whom have also been recruited by Max to sing with Heritage at some point. Max saw the group perform, and liked what he saw and heard. Shani said she didn't even have to audition, but, in reality, she had the most strenuous and telling audition of all! Her soulful voice has added some character to the Heritage recordings over the past few years.

"Tim brings it out of me," she said. "He's been like a musical mentor for me, and has taken my singing to another level. He pushed me out of my comfort zone! Now I love singing with the group. Our personalities and voices just click. The recording process is so easy now. Tim knows what to expect and brings out our best."

Her first concert with Heritage was in 1995 in Loma Linda, California. "I was intimidated at first," she said. "But after the first few concerts, I felt more at ease. I still get a little anxious before we sing, but in a good way.

Shani was married in 2000 to Byron Diehl. They are the proud parents of Matthew, who is now four years old. Shani balances her role with Heritage with that of being a wife and mother, which is quite an achievement. "It is very advantageous for me," she said. "I can have fun with my second family and sing for people, and I have plenty of time at home. I only sing with Heritage once or twice a month now, so I always look forward to seeing my Heritage friends.

"I am so lucky to be able to be in Heritage and be married and have a family and a home. It's such a nice balance. My husband is so supportive of my involvement with Heritage. When we got married he knew this was a large part of my life. And now he loves it, too. He has become the resident orthodontist for the Heritage singers and their kids!"

Shani says she hopes to be with Heritage for a while, and hopes that the ministry continues for many more years. "It's going to be a very sad day when Max decides he needs to quit. He is the 'friar' behind it all. He really puts himself out there.

"I wouldn't be where I'm at spiritually if it wasn't for being in Heritage. It's really been a great part of keeping my spiritual life going. I love being part of a team and feeling that I'm a part of something. At the Heritage concerts I enjoy talking to people and praying with them. It's such a thrill to have someone come up to you and tell you that something you said helped him or her. When you realize how God is using you to help others, it's really humbling. I am so honored to be a part of this group."

BRIAN LEE

Brian Lee sang in the original Heritage Singers back in 1971. He said, "My experience with Heritage sent my life in a direction that I would never have chosen for myself. It prepared me for continuing in a ministry to work for the church in a way that made that ministry unique. It's amazing that after 36 years, wherever I go in Canada and meet people from my generation,

people want to let me know that they remember me from Heritage. So even to this day, Heritage not only impacted the lives of others, it had a significant, personal impact on my life and ministry for God."

Brian is now on staff at Canadian University College in Lacombe, Alberta, Canada and has put together a musical group called Rise Above. They visit camp meetings and churches all over Canada. They traveled to China to sing for a musical prelude to the Beijing summer Olympics.

Max said, "Can you believe that after 40 years one of my former singers is in charge of a singing group sharing Jesus? It's a ripple effect, kind of like passing the torch to others."

MARC JUDD

Marc Judd is a part of Faith First, along with his wife, Andrea, Shani Diehl and Scott Reed. He sings and records with the Heritage Singers on occasion, although most of his time is devoted to Dwell Ministries and teaching young people to worship through music.

"Like so many others, the Heritage Singers are a rock-solid memory from my childhood," said Marc. "Growing up in Australia, listening to all their records (yes, records) and then getting to meet and hear them in person was something else. I still remember the concerts in Sydney, and especially getting to hang out with the 'singers' for a meal or two. And, that's what made standing as one of them at the 30th reunion in Ontario so unbelievable!

"There is no doubt that my own music was influenced strongly by the Heritage Singers, and I stand as one of the multitude who have been blessed and encouraged by the Heritage Singers' dedication to declaring the goodness and grace of Jesus Christ!"

DAVE MAUCK

"My dad grew up in a religious home, but it didn't really rub off on him," said Dave Mauck. "Work was his religion. He worked so much that we didn't see him very much. He always wanted me to be a doctor. When I changed my college major to theology, he didn't say a word. He was a bulky, brawny, bellowing type of guy, and I was scared to death of asking him to come to hear me sing or speak at church. But, to my surprise, whenever I asked him, he agreed to go. He never really said anything about my choice of vocation.

"Years later, when Amanda and I were traveling with Heritage, we were traveling in the Eastern United States. One night we were surprised to see my parents in the audience. They had driven quite a ways to be there. My mom loved Heritage music and I wasn't surprised to see her at our concerts, but my dad's response to the Heritage concert really amazed me. I knew he loved music and was a good singer, but this was religious music. I really didn't expect him to enjoy it, but he did.

"The next touring season we returned to the East, and had a concert in Baltimore, Maryland, where my parents lived. This time, however, my dad wasn't at our concert. He was in the hospital with serious heart problems and advanced diabetes. The doctors had surgically removed his right leg above the knee. I went to visit my dad, and for the first time in my life, I saw him cry. A tear rolled down his cheek as I kissed him and prayed for him to be healed. I had never seen my dad vulnerable in my entire life. And now it seemed he needed more than just his family by his side; he needed and wanted God in his life. I bought him a Bible that was easy to read and began sending him lessons. I continued to send him bible study lessons regularly.

Dave Mauck and his father

"We again returned to the East the following year and my parents came to one of our concerts. That night we performed in a high school auditorium with floors that slanted down to the stage. My dad approached me after the concert. He said he would have come forward during the call, but because of the angled floor he decided not to, fearing he would fall. He told me he wanted to accept God into his life. Now it was me who was crying. I embraced him as I thanked the Lord for softening my dad's heart through the music of Heritage. Dad followed through with this decision to follow Christ, and, the next time Heritage was in Baltimore, it was my great honor to personally baptize my own father."

BECKY GRECCO

Becky Grecco said that traveling with Heritage Singers brought a lot of "firsts" into her life and to that of her husband and fellow singer, Bruce. In a letter to Max and Lucy, Becky wrote, "When we look back on how God brought us to you, it is nothing less than a work of His hand. Without you and Heritage, Bruce and I never would have met. Thank you for sharing your hearts with so many of us who have served with Heritage Singers."

Bruce and Becky Grecco

Bruce Grecco stepped in for Max and led the group for a year in 1988 while Max took a leave of absence due to health conditions. He did a wonderful job and took a lot of the pressure off of Max. "I had heavy anxiety on me because of the stress," said Max. "Bruce did a wonderful job. He was a super guy and was able to arrange and direct. I really felt confident that he would be able to step in for me and continue the group."

Bruce and Becky were married at the Heritage ranch. "Thank you for the great year of memories we have of traveling together during our first year of marriage," said Becky. "What a great time we had with you, bobbing up and down in the crystal clear water of Tahiti, while dreaming of the future. Little did we know that Erynne was on her way and our lives would soon take another turn!

"Although we don't see each other often, there is a place forever etched in our hearts that belongs to Heritage and we will always be grateful for your touch on our lives. As we take a walk down memory lane, maybe you will have pictures as we do of some of these memories: Christmas at the Ranch, Tahiti with the private island fresh fish feast, birthdays on the bus, fighting over the clicker, the reunions, surfing lessons in Hawaii, Australia, New Guinea, singing in the rain, church potlucks, making haystacks, and Rehearsal Camp. I remember Bruce asking, 'Who is Ellen White?' to a lady after a concert, and shopping in every mall in America. I also vividly remember Max saying, 'I'm homesick for heaven' at every concert. We experienced long drives, good hotels, great hotels, and not so good hotels. I also remember coming home from our overseas tour to find our bedroom decorated with 'Baby Congratulations' by Lucy. We sang for many, many concerts of which each holds a memory for someone whose life was changed because Max followed through on his dream."

———

So many musicians that were a part of the Heritage ministry have stories to tell of how being a part of Heritage changed their lives and the lives of their loved ones. All that they experienced and learned will stay with them forever. It is a heritage; it is the Heritage experience.

"Going together, enjoying the trip

Getting used to the family

I'll spend eternity with.

Learning to love you, how easy it is

Getting used to the family of God."

—*William and Gloria Gaither*

CHAPTER NINETEEN

Reunions

Fifteen year reunion in Anaheim, California in 1986

"GETTING BACK TOGETHER WITH MY OLD HERITAGE FRIENDS IS LIKE A FAMILY REUNION FOR ME," JOANNE wrote. "It would never have happened if Kim Bird and Kevin Hale hadn't taken it upon themselves to find me. I am so glad they did! We quickly slipped back into our roles of traveling companions full of memories, stories and laughter. It's been only in the last two or three years that I've become reacquainted with some of them, and it has been the most enjoyable, gratifying experience. When I'm with my friends from Heritage, I'm filled with feelings of love, appreciation and understanding.

"As a direct result of being reunited with Kevin and Kim, I ended up going back to the Heritage ranch to see Max and Lucy again, which led to several more reunions, like seeing Judy Boyd again after all these years. We share some overlapping history and will be friends forever. All of this led to something even more unexpected—having Max and Lucy ask me if I would like to help them write the Heritage Story. Thus my reunion with the singers on the 35th Year Anniversary Cruise."

It was breakfast time on the Heritage 35th Anniversary Cruise. Holly and Scott Reed were sitting in a booth on the Lido Deck. As various Heritage Singers wander by, the group expanded to also include them. Pete McLeod and Frank John Salas joined them, then Lucy and Val. Before long, they were laughing and sharing stories like long lost friends. When the singers get together, it is like a family reunion, no matter where they are.

These informal gatherings were their own kind of reunions. But, there have also been several milestone gatherings planned throughout the years when Heritage alumni came together to be reunited, get reacquainted, and to once again sing together.

Reunions are a special time for the Heritage Singers. "Any time we as singers get to all be together at a reunion is so fun for me," said Val. "It's like one big family reunion. I love all the singers so much, and have so much respect for all of them. Their love and dedication for this ministry has meant the world to me and my family."

The 15-year reunion was held at the Anaheim Convention Center in July of 1986. At that time there were 167 current and former singers, and 120 of them actually came to this event. Many of them traveled thousands of miles. They came to sing, to share, and to meet the many friends they had not seen in years.

This six-hour extravaganza featured Heritage groups from 1971 to 1986 and ended with all the singers on stage singing the dynamic, "The King is Coming!" Bill Truby, who sang and recorded this song in 1972, was there to sing his solo part one more time. Max described the event as a real "sing-fest" and particularly enjoyed directing all the singers in singing "Amazing Grace."

"This was a very special moment for me," remembered Max. "Another was when we sang, 'Side by Side,' a song written by our own Jeff Wood. The entire audience joined hands and raised them to heaven with the vow we would all meet again in heaven!"

Taking the opportunity to thank the singers, past and present, and the friends and supporters of Heritage for their prayers and support over the years, Max acknowledged that there were struggles along the way. "It has not always been easy," he said, "but God is good and he has never forsaken us. It is our continual prayer to go where He leads."

"Fifteen years of traveling, singing and sharing the gospel message through words and music had a tremendous impact on our lives," Lucy added. "Our purpose with the reunion was to reflect on how the Lord has led in the past and to recommit the present work to Him."

Ten years later, in the spring of 1996, the Heritage Singers celebrated their 25th anniversary aboard the beautiful Sun Princess cruise ship. More than 30 singers were joined by over 750 people from all over the United States, Canada, South Africa, Brazil, and Japan to help celebrate this very special event. The current and former Heritage Singers presented Heritage songs from the last 25 years.

"What a thrill for Lucy and I to see the singers from the 70s, 80s and 90s come together to thank God for all these years!" Max said. "There were many tears as we talked, reminisced and sang songs from the good old days."

One of the highlights of the cruise was an album presented to Max and Lucy filled with photos and letters from former and current Heritage Singers. Entitled *From the Hearts of the Singers,* it contained many personal letters telling Max and Lucy how the experience of being a Heritage Singer had changed their lives.

By the year 2000, the Heritage Singers had performed over 6,000 concerts, produced 200 television programs, recorded nearly 100 albums, held concerts in every state of the United States, and traveled to over 60 countries outside of the United States. It was hard to believe, but the group had been traveling and singing for 30 years! This was something to celebrate, and another reunion concert was planned.

On August 18, 2001, approximately 125 former and current singers were seated together on the big stage at the Ontario, California, Convention Center for the Heritage Singers' 30th Year Reunion Concert. The singers sang songs from 1971 to 2001, and the auditorium was filled to capacity. Over 4,000 people came from all over the world to celebrate this milestone. The concert lasted over three hours, and the response was overwhelming.

"My heart was full and overflowing as I watched all my 'kids' on stage praising the Lord together!" Max said. "I'm still on an enormous high! We sang over 30 songs and viewed video of

THIRTY-YEAR REUNION, ONTARIO CONVENTION CENTER, *August 18, 2001*

singers and events down through the years. The entire evening was filled with memories. I've just been overwhelmed with the response we've received."

Pete McLeod shared his memories of this special night. "First and foremost, it was a night of pure joy! Laughter, excitement, and happiness were thick in the air. The predominant frustration was that there wasn't enough time to see and talk with everyone. There were too many people to hug and not enough arms to hug with.

"That night I emceed the program. Even though we worked on the program for many months before the reunion, there were dozens of last minute changes. Half of the stage lighting went out which affected the cameras that were video taping the concert. We had to make sure all the singers were in place and all the people that were giving talks and tributes were ready to go.

"When all was said and done, it was a Heavenly night. I know without a doubt that people were inspired, thrilled and filled with longing for the great eternal reunion."

"The reunion concerts are really special times," recalled Adriane. "We get to spend some time with people who love and support Heritage through the years. I'm also very grateful to the sponsors for making it possible for so many people to be there. Ministering to people through music is truly our passion."

Becki Trueblood Craig said it was hard for her to put into words what it felt like to sit on that stage with all those Heritage Singers that night. "Although I've now been involved with Heritage for over 18 years, I was just as much in awe of it all as the people in the audience. I just kept thinking, 'What an honor it is to be here! Thank you God!'

"From early on in the planning stages, our sincerest prayer was that God would use this Reunion and the video that would follow to reach people for Him. I truly believe our prayer has been answered. We serve such an awesome God!

"Those feelings were reiterated to me as I sat at my desk yesterday and watched the video. That huge group of musicians, all together at one time, praising God, sharing their hearts, and loving each other, was made possible because 30 years ago one man, Max Mace, trusted God with his dream. I think Valerie has said it best: 'One man's dream became God's reality.'"

"The 30th year reunion was special in that there were a lot of surprises and tributes for my parents," Val said. "I will never forget their smiles or their tears of joy. It was a night that honored them and their passion for this ministry! It was a night I will never forget!"

Tim Davis recalled, "For me, it was the 30 year reunion that helped me have perspective on the amazing ministry that Heritage was way before I arrived. So often we can only see our current situation, and know little or nothing of the blood, sweat, tears, and prayers that went before us.

"It was important for me to see all of the 100+ singers from the previous years, hear their stories, and realize that though it was my 'current season' in the group, their seasons were just as, if not more, important than mine. I became instantly in touch with the privilege of being a Heritage Singer in a new way, and for me, it was humbling.

"I am just one more person that God chose to bless to be a part of something that would change my life forever. Thank you Lord, and thank you Max and Lucy!"

Larry Soule, a sponsor of Heritage en Español, made it possible for the Spanish quartet to come to the United States to be a part of this special 30th year celebration. As Marcelo Constanzo remembered, "When we found out we were going to be able to fly to California, we only had a few weeks to prepare. It was a long trip from Chile to the United States. We had a 10-hour layover in Panama. It was a small airport with nothing to do, so we practiced our songs for many hours. During the reunion weekend, we felt at first a bit awkward because we didn't know many of the former singers, but by the time the concert began, it felt like one big family reunion. We were honored to be a part of this celebration and were welcomed by the current and former members with open arms."

"I didn't really understand the scope or magnitude of Heritage Singers until the 30 year reunion," said Tim Calhoun. "The stories from those who came before me let me see how truly amazing Max and Lucy are. So selfless, so compassionate, and so passionate about spreading the gospel through what I believe is the best way—singing about the love of Jesus. To be part of this Heritage Family is an honor for my wife and I."

Melody Davis was on stage that night. "One of my favorite Heritage events was the 30th reunion concert in Southern California with more than a hundred former and current singers all on stage together. All of those singers represented 30 years of continuous ministry throughout the world. To be a part of that night was awesome. To be a part of such a wide reaching ministry is humbling."

"To me it felt kind of like Christmas when the kids all come home. Grandma and Grandpa and all the aunts, uncles, and cousins show up that you haven't seen in years. Everyone is talking at once and all crowded in the kitchen kind of atmosphere. Just a lot of warm and fuzzy feelings," Lucy remembered.

In October of 2005, the Heritage Singers gave a 35th Year Celebration Concert at the Crystal Cathedral in Garden Grove, California. It was a packed house, and unfortunately, due to fire regulations, over 300 people had to be turned away. The twelve current singers, as well as a four-man band, were on stage for the entire concert. Also, Heritage en Español contributed to the event by singing some of their music. The three-hour program was a wonderful way to celebrate the Heritage Singers' 35th year.

As Scott Reed remembered, "What a great night of celebration! I was so honored to be part of a ministry that had been so effective and powerful for so many years. I also remember that it was one of the first times Holly and I had performed 'I Can Only Imagine.' I had to close my eyes the whole time because I would have lost it if I'd seen her in that moment. She's so beautiful when she signs!"

Shani Judd Diehl was also one of the 12 singers on stage that night. "It was such a beautiful, precious time together with my second family. I remember this time especially because it was the first big announcement that I was pregnant with my son Matthew! It was the start of en exciting time for us all—special memories of blessed times together!"

Heritage en Español sang some of their songs for the 35th reunion night. Dénar Almonte, the director of the group for many years, recalled, "I was able to be part of the 30th Reunion and 35th Year Celebration Concert. I never thought that someone coming from such a small country like Chile would have the privilege to sing in those amazing concerts. I'm so blessed that I was part of the Crystal Cathedral Concert, and amazingly, with the people that always sang my favorite music. I can say now, they are my best friends."

"I also feel very blessed to have been a part of the Heritage Singers 35th reunion at the Crystal Cathedral," stated Nino Ocampo, bass guitarist. "It was a concert with great energy. Thank you Max and Lucy for allowing me the honor to be a part of the Heritage Band."

Dave Bell, the bass for Heritage, said, "I was so thankful for the generous sponsors that made it possible to open the doors to the public and not have to charge for tickets. I have had many people tell me that the DVD we were able to make from that concert gets played over and over again in their homes, and that one concert continues to bless. It was impossible to keep tears from flowing while listening to and watching Scott and Holly sing and sign 'I Can Only Imagine.' The video of their gift of worship has been viewed over 275,000 times on YouTube, making it by far the most viewed Heritage Singers video."

"I grew up listening to the Heritage Singers. My family wore out the *Come Along With Me* record as well as the other albums that followed," Art Mapa remembered. "These records were such an inspiration to me. I remember playing along to many of their songs, emulating Pete McLeod's guitar playing and, of course,

Thirty-fifth year celebration concert at the Crystal Cathedral, October, 2005

imagining being a part of the Heritage Singers one day.

"The reunion concerts allowed me to meet the wonderful singers and instrumentalists who made up the sound that I admired for many years! It was such an honor to take one of the torches handed to me, in part, and to carry on the classic and classy sound of the Heritage Singers. Thank you Max and Lucy for giving me this opportunity!"

"When I was a 20-year old, I didn't realize the scope of what I was involved in or what I was really allowed to be part of," said Scott Reed. "But, 15 years later, every time I get to be with the family is very, very special to me. I couldn't even speak my gratitude to all of them on the Czech Republic tour, not for just allowing me to come, but for what they all meant to me. Holly had to say it for me. I've learned leadership from Max and I'll forever be grateful to him and Lucy for the example of Godliness they've always lived out."

"I am so very grateful that it was in God's plan for me to be a part of the Heritage family," Melody Davis said. "I cannot think of any other way I would rather use my gift than singing with this group. Not because they are so well known in some circles, not because they have experienced success, but simply because they are a humble group of people who are believers in the redeeming love of God and the hope of Jesus Christ.

"The fact that I have been given years of opportunity to sing with my friends in order to reach into the hearts and souls of people all over the world and bring glory to God my Savior, is something I will be forever be grateful for."

"Over the years God has given this ministry over 250 singers, and Lucy and I still feel like they are our kids," said Max. "We will cherish this for years to come. We've enjoyed talking and reuniting with everyone. It's just a little taste of what the big reunion will be like when we get to heaven and we once again stand side by side with those we love and sing songs together. What a day to look forward to!"

CHAPTER TWENTY

The Stories Behind the Songs

A S WITH OTHER CREATIVE PROCESSES, SONGWRITING IS AN ART FORM THAT DOESN'T ALWAYS COME EASILY. Sometimes the messages are lessons learned through tough personal experiences. The lyrics to the Heritage Singers' songs often came as messages from God during personal struggles. Other times the music came as a joyful expression -- celebrating victory over struggles, and the happiness and peace God brings to us.

The music of Heritage is the music of a dynamic relationship with God and with life - something that is always changing and always growing, yet is a constant presence. For almost 40 years the lyrics and melodies of the Heritage Singers songs have encouraged and sustained people who are struggling, and have brought comfort and cheer to help people feel God's presence during difficult times in their lives.

Many of the songs the Heritage Singers have been known for through the years were written and initially recorded by other artists. They were not written exclusively by or for Heritage. Max has always appreciated the song writing talents of people like Bill and Gloria Gaither, André Crouch, Dottie Rambo and so many others. Many of their songs have become Heritage mainstays.

Some of the Heritage songs, however, were original. Pete McLeod and Jeff Wood were two Heritage Singers who wrote songs that were performed and recorded in the early years. Jeff Wood's "Side by Side" and Pete McLeod's "Morning Prayer" were especially popular. The two of them also collaborated on Val Mace's solo recordings.

Rick Lange, a talented arranger, also did some original songwriting for Heritage. Especially gifted at composing children's songs, he was an integral part of the Heritage kid's music. He also wrote a song especially for Max to record, "I'm Yours, Lord".

Many of the Heritage Singers through the years have been very talented musically, and helped out with lyrics, harmonies and arrangements. It was always a team effort in Heritage, yet there are some stories that need to be told - stories behind some of the music of the Heritage Singers.

One of the composers Max worked with in the early days of Heritage was Chuck Fulmore. Max and Chuck's wife, Dona, attended grade school together in Idaho. The two families had known each other for years. Chuck and his family had a music ministry of their own, but he also wrote many of the Heritage Singers' songs.

As he contributed more and more material to Heritage, Max began to depend on Chuck to provide songs for the group. On several occasions Max asked him to write something specifically for Heritage. Chuck's contributions included the songs "Never Give Up," "I Got Jesus," We're All God's Children," "Keep Your Hand in the Lord's," "I Know He Loves Me," "Why Tarry Here?" "Thank You for Loving Me," and "Old Time Religion Country Style." He also worked with Max and the singers on the kids' projects. Chuck also wrote, "Heaven is for Kids Volumes I and II."

Chuck Fulmore Trio, Dona, Chuck and their daughter Carla

As Chuck's songs became a more important part of the Heritage ministry, Max invited him and his family to live at the Heritage ranch and work directly for the Heritage Singers. While Chuck's songs encouraged the Heritage Singers and those who heard them in concert, Max, in turn, encouraged Chuck to keep writing and to keep his family ministry going. Their friendship continues to sustain them to this day.

Here are a couple of Chuck's stories behind some of the songs he wrote for the Heritage Singers:

"NEVER GIVE UP"

"I had been struggling with being honest with myself in regard to living a life without sin. I simply could not measure up. I was being a hypocrite. Discouraged and ashamed, I had

quit attending church.

"I moved my family from California to Idaho. A minister there who knew of our situation loved me back into the church. He loved to hold meetings in little towns, and he invited us to sing for the meetings. Our 12-year-old, Dianne, decided she wanted to commit her life to the Lord and be baptized. I was re-baptized with her. That was a high day in our family.

"Shortly after that day Dianne was diagnosed with Leukemia. She was a brave little girl and said she was going to make it to her 13th birthday. Within a few days after her birthday, she passed away in her mother's arms. Her last words were, 'I'll see you in the morning, Mom.' Then she closed her eyes and was gone.

"We moved to another town to get away from the constant reminders, but the heartache went with us. While driving to work one morning, I was unable to see the road for the tears. It was then that the lyrics came to me:

There are days I know when you get so discouraged,
It seems that all hope is gone.
But there's One, only One, who can give you courage
And strength to carry on.
Never give up! Jesus is coming.
It's the darkest just before dawn.
Never give up! Jesus is coming.
Never give up, keep holding on.

It gives us courage when we sing it, and it gives us courage when we hear others sing it."

"THANK YOU FOR LOVING ME"

"To understand why this song is so precious to me, you need to know a little of my personal story. I was born into a family and a church family that believed we might be saved if we were able to live sinless lives. To give us a little slack and keep hope alive, it was decided that it was our characters that had to be perfected if we were going to have a chance at all.

"I was born a redhead with freckles. My saintly grandmother had predicted my doom, saying I was a bad kid all of the time. I can't remember ever being told I was good. I was only five years old when I responded to an alter call and gave my life to Jesus. It didn't seem to help me stay out of trouble, but my grandpa told me that God was real and that He heard us when we talked to Him. I have been praying a lot ever since.

Pete McLeod and Jeff Wood

"So, you can imagine my utter joy when I learned about righteousness by faith. I got into the New Testament and what I call 'the gospel of Jesus Christ.' The more I read, the more hope and courage grew in my heart. Then the song came to me:

> *Many times I think about you, Lord.*
> *How in love you made a blind man see.*
> *And then I know it's no different today, Lord,*
> *When I look at all you've done for me."*

Chuck recently wrote this in a letter to Max and Lucy: "From the first time I heard the Rose City Singers to this day I have been blessed by your ministry. When Dona and I hear you will be giving a concert, if it's within driving distance, we will be there. We want to thank you for recording our songs, for encouraging me to keep writing, and for encouraging our family ministry. And, thank you for your friendship and loyalty through thick and thin. Friendships are priceless."

Pete McLeod was one of the Heritage Singers who wrote some original music for the group to sing. "In the early days of the Heritage Singers, when we weren't singing and I wasn't driving the bus, I would be writing songs. I wrote many by myself and collaborated with Jeff Wood on several others.

"The songs came from ideas in scripture, reflection, and observations on life. I was spending lots of time in prayer and Bible study as well as listening to people's stories every night after our concerts. The songs were born out of those experiences. You might remember 'What More Could He Do?' - 'He gave His life for you! What more could He do?' Or, perhaps the words 'All that I have I gladly give to you, I gladly live my whole life through, Lord living in You!' from the song 'Morning Prayer.' A personal testimony that was put to music in the song 'All About Love' said:

> *Before I met The Lord I thought I only had to be good.*
> *Then I came to understand and realize I never could.*
> *The goodness I had fell short of His wishes for me.*
> *So I gave up trying alone and turned to Calvary.*

"From day one I felt incredibly grateful to be a part of the Heritage Singers. At the time I couldn't imagine a more fulfilling life and so I wrote the song that became the theme song for the Heritage television show *Keep on Singin'!*

> *Well I'll keep on singin til He gets here*
> *I'll keep talking about my Lord*
> *I'll get down on my knees each day*
> *Take time to read His Word.*
> *I'll share the Good News of salvation*
> *With people everyday*
> *And nothin's gonna keep me from goin home*
> *When He calls me on that day!"*

Favorite Songs of the Heritage Singers

The current singers that travel with Heritage have been with the group for more than 10-20 years. A lot of the songs that Heritage sings were not written specifically for the group, but they have come to have a special meaning for many of the current singers. The singers said that it is hard to narrow the list down to just one song. Here are some of their favorites.

"What a Precious Friend is He" and "There is Always a Place"

Max Mace, baritone and director

"If I could write down every song that has blessed my heart over the past 39 years it would fill an entire chapter! One of the older songs that really speaks to my heart is, 'What A Precious Friend Is He.' It says, 'I've a friend who's always near me, I've a friend who always hears me, I've a friend who is so dear to me, What a precious friend is He.' It goes on to say, 'He'll go with me through the valley, and He'll be with me all the way, every day.' We all go through times in our life where we feel discouraged and all alone and the words to this song give me reassurance that we always have a friend in Jesus - someone we can turn to and rely on his promise to never leave us or forsake us.

"One of the newer songs that we recorded recently has such a powerful message for someone that has fallen away from God or just made some bad choices in life. It talks about not knowing where to begin to turn a life around. Then, they get a message from the host, Jesus Christ - an invitation to come back home.

There is always a place at the table
There's a feast that's now waiting all your own
Your place is set each time the family gathers
It will never be the same till you're home
Come home, Come home

My child, come home

"We meet people all the time that feel like they can never be good enough or that they have to clean up their lives before they can come back to the Lord. I pray that when they hear this song it will let them know they can come to Christ just the way they are and He is the one that can change their life. He has set the table and is waiting for them to come."

"When I Turn to You" and "Sinner Saved by Grace"

Lucy Mace

Melody, Tim, Scott, Becki, Shani, Val, Dave and Max

"How do you take nearly 40 years of Heritage music and choose just one song as your favorite? Each time Heritage records a new CD I add another favorite to my ever-increasing list. One of my all time favorites is 'Bryans Hymn,' better known as 'When I Turn to You' that Val recorded on the *Because Of Love* CD. The words give me comfort knowing that He is always there for us even before we ask, with an understanding heart when we don't understand ourselves. Could it be that it's because one of my VERY favorite singers is singing it?

"Another song that I am blessed by every time I hear it is, 'Sinner Saved By Grace.' A line in the song says that we are 'Loved and forgiven, that we are just sinners saved by grace.' It reminds us just how precious the gift of salvation is. God was willing to send his most precious gift, His only son, that we might have eternal life. Where would we be without that wonderful saving grace of Jesus? In Ephesians 2:8 we're told, God saved you by His grace when you believed. You can't take credit for this. It is a gift from God. My prayer is that everyone would believe and accept this free gift."

"He is Our Peace"

Art Mapa, recording studio engineer, producer, and guitarist

"Lyrically and musically, one of my favorite songs from Heritage is 'He Is Our Peace.' I remember this song during the last days of my mother's life. As she lay unconscious in ICU, the portable CD player playing this song, I felt God's peace and reassurance that one day I will see her again, forever restored and perfect. While waiting for that great reunion day, I continue to cast all my cares on Him. He is our Peace - the Peace that passes all understanding."

"What a Day That Will Be"

Val Mace Mapa, first soprano

Kevin Dumitru, first tenor

Dave Bell, bass

Val: "It's amazing to me how you can love a song and sing it night after night, but when you're going through something difficult the song takes on a whole new meaning. The words are now speaking directly to me and giving me hope and peace, with tears running down my face I feel every word I'm singing like it was written just for me. 'What A Day that will Be' held special meaning to me when I was dealing with my son being in the hospital so much of his young life, and also for all the loved ones we've lost. I'm so thankful we have a Hope!"

Kevin: "'What a day that will be' was always one of my favorite songs to sing. It seemed to fit my vocal range just right and when I would sing it and look at the faces of the audience I would almost always connect with someone who had most likely lost a loved one and was imagining that great reunion day. This song took on a whole new meaning for me with the sudden loss of my father on February 10, 2010. At my father's celebration of life service Heritage sang two of my dad's favorite songs, and I was now the one in the audience with tears streaming down my face longing for that day when there will be no more sorrow, no more pain, no more tears, and when we will be reunited with our loved ones. I can't thank Heritage enough for their support, love, and generosity during the years. What a day that will be!"

Dave: "I also love 'What a day that will be.' We sang it at my mother's memorial service, and have also sung it at the services for several family and friends close to the Heritage family. Whenever we sing this song in concert, it brings back memories of my sweet mom, and I get a picture in my mind of that day when we will all be reunited together, where 'There'll be no sorrow there, no more burdens to bear, no more sickness, no pain, no more parting over there,' and we will be forever together with Jesus and our loved ones. What a day, glorious day that will be."

"In the Presence of Jehovah – En Presencia de Jehová"

Marcelo Constanzo, second tenor

Becki Trueblood Craig, alto

Marcelo: "There is one song in particular that has the same effect on me, whether I sing it in Spanish or in English. I believe the song 'In the presence of Jehovah' has a special anointing on its music and lyrics. As I am writing these lines I am having a hard time coming up with words that could describe what this song means to me. It builds up starting with such a worshipful soft melody but, by the time it reaches the big chorus tears are falling down my face and my hands find themselves reaching up in full worship, recognizing that in His presence is where I find the answers to all of my questions and healing to my wounds. It is in His presence where I find peace and rest and where precious lives and hearts are mended with His everlasting love. In the presence of my Savior is where I always want to be."

Becki: "My favorite song is 'In the Presence of Jehovah.' I remember as we recorded this thinking I could literally 'feel' the presence of Jesus . . . His peace . . . this overwhelming sense of calm that I knew could only come from Him. He was with me in that room, and every time I've heard or sung this song since, I've had the same response. The lyrics reflect my heart, making this song very personal for me."

"Holy Spirit Rain Down"

Shani Judd Diehl, alto

"I have a few favorites but one special song for me is 'Holy Spirit Rain Down.' When I was first battling my depression, I would listen to Mel singing that song and just worship with tears running down my face, praying that my Comforter and Friend would rain down on me with His Spirit. What an incredibly healing song this has been for me. Every time I hear it, I am always caught up in the amazing worship and spirit of this song."

"No More Night" and "These are They"

Melody Davis, soprano

"I don't think I could choose a favorite song. There are many I love. Heritage has so many songs that focus on heaven. Many of my favorites are the songs that talk about the hope of life after death. The songs that remind us that this life on earth is not all there is. Whether our life here is good or bad, easy or difficult, filled with abundance or filled with emptiness and despair, we have a hope in Jesus who will come again to take his children home. We are promised a life with no pain, sadness, heartache or trial. We will live in His perfect presence for eternity if we place our trust in Him as Lord and Savior. Songs like 'No More Night' and 'These are They' are powerful testimonies to this promise."

"Champion of Love"

Scott Reed, first tenor

"I love a song that paints a picture like 'Champion of Love.' It makes a clear statement of our powerful and victorious God. We all need to be reminded often that the God we serve is 'otherly.' There is no one beside or above Him. He is the King of all kings!"

"Bowed on My Knees" and "These are They"

Tim Davis, second tenor and vocal arranger

"It is so difficult to pick just a couple of favorite songs from Heritage. I sang 'Bowed on My Knees' at my Mammaw's funeral. I always imagine her when I sing it, and it stirs up a lot of emotion for me. I also love the song 'These Are They,' because it tells the story of being saved by the blood of Christ."

"Hosanna"

Adriane Mace, alto

"Wow, this is a difficult task! There are so many songs that have touched me, and God has spoken to me through different songs at different times in my life. There are songs that will stay with me forever like 'I Bowed on my Knees and Cried Holy.' I remember crying every time we sang that song. Other special songs to me are 'I Can Only Imagine,' 'No More Night,' and I couldn't leave out 'Hosanna.' When we sing 'Hosanna,' I just want to celebrate Jesus. It's all about Him - His power, His love, and His majesty. I'm singing it to my Jesus. That's definitely one of my favorite songs. Lately I find myself really engaged in worship when we sing 'Song of Glory.' That's definitely my favorite one from the latest album. Like I said, it's a difficult task to name only one favorite song!"

"Song of Glory"

Jaclyn Pruehs, alto

"The 'Song of Glory' is my very favorite song to sing in concert, and around my house for that matter. I find myself always saying, 'oh yes' out loud when I'm on stage and the first few notes of the track begin. I love how the guys sing the solos and there is just something about the swell and emotion of this song that never fails to give me goose bumps. 'I will lift up my voice and cry out...from my soul I will send up a shout! Let the words of my life be a song You hear.' These are words to live by! This is just one of those songs that I can sing loud and strong and it gives me the opportunity to open up my heart to God. I love it and I long for the three minutes of that song during every concert!"

Acappella

Cindy Haffner, alto

"I have sung and recorded thousands of songs with Heritage

and each and every song has always given me a peace and the strength to keep going. My favorite project was the album entitled *Acappella.* At that time, there was only five or six of us who were able to record this album. I will never forget working all day in downtown Sacramento, and then driving to Placerville to record until three o'clock in the morning, then drive home, get up the next morning, go to work and do it all over again. We did this for a full week. I remember that we were so exhausted; we would break down and cry. Satan tried hard to cancel this project. But, God is good and He had anointed this project in every way. We would pray, several times each night and become empowered by His strength to keep going.

"I know that only because of God were we able to complete that project. All of the songs on this album were so totally put together by God, and those of us who recorded it. 'Make Me Like You Lord,' 'Jesus The Savior Divine,' 'I Heard the Voice of Jesus Say,' 'Jesus is the Sweetest Name I Know,' 'He's My Lord,' 'Nearer Still Nearer,' 'Give Thanks,' 'How Great Thou Art,' 'Softly and Tenderly,' and 'What Will You do for Jesus' - I love these old songs. To this day, when I listen to the CD, I feel His presence and know that He is there.

"God has totally anointed every song that the Heritage Singers have sung. I believe all those songs have touched many, many lives along with the many singers who were and are able to share His Word in song. I believe with all my heart that God called Max and Lucy, Val and Greg to start this group so many years ago, and to be His messengers of song and to share His light and love to so many around the world."

"I Will Glory in the Cross" and "These are They"

Greg Mace, sound engineer

"My favorite songs are 'I Will Glory in the Cross' and 'These are They.' The power of the words of 'I Will Glory in the Cross' is indescribable - especially on the bridge that says, 'In the cross, in the cross, be my glory ever.' That's the best part. 'These are

They' is describing us, children of God, the chosen ones here on earth going through trials and tribulations, and going into great jubilation. It's another powerful song."

"No One Ever Cared for Me Like Jesus", "Because of Love", "Song of Glory", and "God Will Take Care of You"

Tim Calhoun, first tenor

"Well, to choose one song that means a lot to me is quite a difficult task. I don't have one particular song that wraps up my experiences over the years, but I do have songs that have been monumental with my walk with God and have helped me get through some difficult valleys.

"When I first joined Heritage Singers, I was quite 'green' on how I viewed life and confused about God. It was while I was practicing the song, 'No One Ever Cared for Me Like Jesus' that I fell in love with this song. I believe the writer was sharing his testimony. I was searching and seeking for such a deep connection to Christ as this writer elegantly shared. The message in this song is so beautiful to me.

"Secondly, the song 'Because of Love' has been one of my favorite songs because at that point of my life I was having bouts of depression and was isolated from those who loved me. This song helped me realize how much Jesus loves me and each and every one of us. He died and rose again that I would have life and live abundantly. What a mighty God we serve!

"The 'Song of Glory' has been such a blessing in my life recently because the song has a line that states, 'Let the words of my life be the song that you here.' For many years I found myself trying to please and impress peers with ability and talent that God gave me. This song helped me realize that everything that I do should mirror the ability, talent, and desires that God gave me and should be only to honor and glorify our Heavenly Father.

"Last but not least, the song 'God Will Take Care of You' has been the Heritage Singers theme song recently as well as my family. When I lost my job and became worried and afraid, I emailed Max for some encouragement and he quoted a few lyrics from this song. I have to say this song has gotten me through these tough months. God has definitely blessed us in so many ways I can't even begin to tell you. To God be the Glory.

"I just want to say how grateful and blessed it is to be part of this Heritage Ministry. Max and Lucy have inspired me and so many others. Their continuous walk of faith is something to be revered and learned from. I've heard many people say that there will be many stars on Max and Lucy's crowns in Heaven for all the people and singers they have brought to Jesus over the years. I think there will be a whole galaxy of stars just for Max and Lucy because of all the people they've touched over the years. I love you Max and Lucy and thank you for allowing me to be part of this wonderful ministry."

Dénar, Art, Marcelo and Kevin

"Dios de Paz"— "Peacespeaker"

Dénar Almonte, first tenor – Heritage en Español

"I have always loved the album, *Peacespeaker*. The title song of this album has a special meaning to me. This was the first song that the Heritage Singers Edición en Español learned. The lyrics to this song remind me that no matter what troubles we go through, as long as we know whom our Lord is, and what He can do, we'll find peace in the middle of the storm."

"Fue por Amor" - "Because of Love"

Izzie Moyano Almonte, alto – Heritage en Español

"This song summarizes everything I believe in. I grew up in a Christian home as the daughter of a pastor. From the first moment I heard this song, I felt it was written just for me. Because of the love of God, I have dedicated my life with my husband and children to music ministry."

"High and Exalted"

Keyla Vazquez, soprano – Heritage en Español

"One of my favorite Heritage Singers songs is 'High and Exalted.' Every time we sang this song an image would come to my mind of God sitting on His throne surrounded by worshipping angels who are in complete awe of His glory and majesty. This song always reminds me of how small and insignificant we are and yet how amazing that God would still desire for us to worship Him. What a great honor!"

Favorite Songs of the Heritage Kids

The children of the current Heritage Singers are often seen during concerts clapping their hands and singing along to the songs that they have heard for years. They travel with the group on weekends and have gone on cruise ships and tours to other countries. All of the singers are their "aunties" and "uncles". They are blessed to have such a large family that loves them. Here are some of their favorite songs.

"Because I'm Forgiven"

Austin Mapa, age 15, grandson of Max and Lucy

"My favorite song always changes when a new album comes out. My newest favorite song is 'Because I'm Forgiven' because I really love the arrangement of the song and how it talks about why you have a reason to happy - because Jesus forgives you. We can be free because of what he has done for us."

"I Can Only Imagine"

Amber Mace, age 11, granddaughter of Max and Lucy

"My favorite song is 'I Can Only Imagine' because it tells me that we can only imagine when that day will come and we will see our Jesus again. It will be a glorious day when He comes again.

"HEY" AND "OH HAPPY DAY"

Bella Mace, age 8, granddaughter of Max and Lucy

"My favorite songs are 'Hey' and 'Oh Happy Day.' I like 'Hey' because it's fun to watch the group sing it. I like it when the audience stands up, claps, and raises their hands praising Jesus when Heritage sings 'Oh Happy Day.' I could sing 'Oh Happy Day' over and over again."

"SONG OF GLORY"

Matthew Diehl, age 4, son of Shani and Byron

"Mattie's favorite song is 'Song of Glory,' said Shani. "He walks around the house singing it all the time and tells me that it is his favorite."

"GIVE IT AWAY" AND "OH HAPPY DAY"

Aidan Calhoun, age 2, son of Tim and Diana

"Aidan's favorite Heritage songs are 'Give it Away' and 'Oh Happy Day.' He loves the part of 'Give it Away' when Uncle Dave sings his deep solo part towards the end of the song – 'give it away no,' according to Diana. "His face gets this expression of total surprise and his lips make an 'O' and he says 'ohhhhh.' It's the cutest thing!"

"OH HAPPY DAY"

Emma and Madison Constanzo, ages 4 and 2, daughters of Marcelo and Bettesue

"'Oh Happy Day' is definitely the girls' favorite song," said Bettesue. "They love clapping and dancing along to it and Emma will grab a brush or whatever is near and pretend she is singing into a microphone – especially on the bridge – 'What can wash

Emma and Madison

Amber, Austin, Aidan, Matthew, Bella

away my sins, nothing but the blood of Jesus.' When we are in the car and the song is over, Madison will say 'Appy Day, gain' (translation: Happy Day, again). Marcelo just has to repeat it over and over again. They love it and we're glad that they do!"

"HEY"

Denarcito Almonte, age 3, son of Dénar and Izzie

"My oldest son's favorite song is 'Hey.' When he was just starting to walk, every morning when he got out of bed, he would walk over to the stereo and press play. 'Hey' would be on and he would sing and dance around the living room. It was so cute. We're really glad both of our boys love the Heritage music – both in English and Spanish – as much as we do," said Dénar.

"HOLY SPIRIT RAIN DOWN"

Rowan Dumitru, age 4, son of Kevin and Tori

According to Tori, "Rowan's favorite Heritage song is 'Holy Spirit Rain Down.' We put it on in the car when we all want to 'mellow' out."

"ONE FINE DAY"

Tommy and Brandon Reed, ages 7 and 4, sons of Scott and Holly

The favorite song of Scott and Holly's boys is "One Fine Day." As Scott stated, "They dance around every time they hear it."

"HEY", "GONNA GET UP", AND "GRANDMA'S BIBLE"

Christian and Summer Davis, ages 12 and 5, children of Tim and Melody

Tim and Melody's children have grown up around music and around the Heritage Singers. Although Christian is more of a "sports-nut" than a "Heritage groupie", he still doesn't mind listening to "Hey" during a concert. Summer, on the other hand, has three favorite Heritage songs. According to Melody. "Her top three are 'Hey,' 'Gonna Get Up,' and – believe it or not – 'Grandma's Bible.'"

FAVORITE SONGS OF FORMER HERITAGE SINGERS

There have been greater than 250 Heritage Singers over the past 40 years. Many of the songs that they have sung have remained as their favorite songs throughout the years. Here are just a few of their stories about the songs that have meant the most.

"I WANT JESUS MORE THAN ANYTHING"

Carole Derry-Bretsch, former Heritage Singer

"We are all so blessed with the things that we have in life. We need to remember that earthly things wear out, and have to be replaced. but, the joys that we obtain by making Jesus #1 in our lives will last for a lifetime.

I want Jesus in my life
More than anything this world can offer me
For I know that only He can satisfy!"

"SOMETHING HAPPENED TO DADDY"

Alanna Yost Dunbar, former Heritage Singer

"My favorite Heritage song would, of course, need to be 'Something's Happened to Daddy.' I was very scared but honored to be called off the beach to go to the pool to see what Uncle Max wanted. Was I in trouble? To sing with my dad and to hold his hand (I was very shy) and use a huge microphone and be on stage was big stuff! But I could never figure out why so many people would cry until much later...and the words say it all. Pretty special song and time in my life."

"BECAUSE OF LOVE" ("FUE POR AMOR")

Felipe Vidal, former second tenor - Heritage en Español

"I love the song 'Because of Love' because it is a powerful and magnificent song and I love the way Tim Davis sings it. Its inspiring lyrics tell us about how the Lord gave His life for us without asking for anything in return. Because of His love we have the gift of salvation and eternal life."

"DAYSTAR"

Yvonne Truby, former Heritage Singer

"I have a very special place in my heart for 'Daystar.' One starry moonlit night, God used the words 'lead me Lord I'll follow, anywhere you open up the door' to guide me into a remarkable journey of walking and talking with Him in a way I had never experienced before. I was flooded with knowing that God can speak, even to little 'ole insignificant me. Every time I hear 'Daystar' I feel the Spirit's presence and feel God's love all over again."

"SHELTERED IN THE ARMS OF GOD"

Pete McLeod, former Heritage Singer

"The group currently sings some songs that absolutely thrill me! 'Bowed on My Knees' and 'Sinner Saved by Grace' are two of my recent favorites. They are amazingly powerful songs. Yet, one of my all time favorites is 'Sheltered in the Arms of God.'

"The harmony, lyrics and arrangement have always inspired me! To think that no matter what storm or challenge I might be experiencing in life, I am not alone. I don't have to go through the dark times by myself. God will hold me with a hand that will never let me go. He has assured us that nothing can separate me from His love.

"That assurance eliminates any fear and doubt I might have.
Let the storm rage high,
The dark clouds rise,

They won't worry me,
For I'm sheltered safe within the arms of God!
He walks with me
And not of earth can harm me,
For I'm Sheltered in the Arms of God!
Oh yes! I'm sheltered in The Arms of God."

"HE IS THERE"

One of the songs that Heritage sings has become popular with both the English and Spanish groups. Mark Bond shared the story behind his writing of the song, "He Is There."

"As a frequent leader of worship, I'm always looking for songs that are easy to learn and memorable," said Mark. "This song was a true gift in that it was written in less than ten minutes! It was a Sabbath morning before church, and I was the first one up in my home. I had to lead music at church that morning, and was spending a few moments in quiet contemplation.

Val, Melody, Max, Jaclyn, Dave, Marcelo, Tim, Adriane and Greg

"The verse in Matthew 18 came to mind that says, 'For where two or three are gathered together in My name, I am there in the midst of them.' I realized that was exactly what praise and worship is about, gathering together in His name so that He will be there with us. The simple melody and lyrics just flowed out almost instantly.

"I quickly built the PowerPoint slides for the song, and rushed to the Florida Hospital Church in Orlando to teach the musicians the new song. We sang it that morning, and it has been a favorite there ever since.

"When Heritage started working on a series of praise & worship CDs, I was asked to help with the design of the covers. When they mentioned that they were also looking for original praise songs for the project, I sent them the demo of the song that featured Tim Davis singing lead vocals. The rest is history. It's always a joy to hear Heritage perform that song live. There's a beautiful spirit surrounding their performance of 'He is There.'"

"SIDE BY SIDE"

One of the all-time favorite songs that the Heritage Singers sang was "Side by Side." Jeff Wood was a member of the group and wrote this special song while in college. "In the fall of 1971, I was a sophomore at Pacific Union College toying with the idea of changing my theology major to something that didn't involve Greek. At the time, my good friend Clyde Morgan and I would often lead out in song services. He played an old upright bass and I played guitar. Clyde sang a clear tenor and I sang a husky, sometimes flat baritone. But, we shared a passion for music and the Lord.

"One evening we were asked to help out at a small, student initiated prayer meeting in Dauphinee Chapel. There we found 20 students gathered around the front of the chapel. After leading out in a couple of songs, a short scripture was given by the student leader, Ray Diaz. Then we broke up into small groups for a season of prayer. At the end of prayer, we all stood in a small circle, joined hands and sang 'Shall We Gather At the River.'

"What struck me about the meeting was that it was

completely student run. The next week, there were well over 100 students. Looking around the circle, seeing the hope and commitment in the eyes of my fellow students was inspiring. We all felt we were part of a ground swell of spiritual renewal on campus. It wasn't difficult to imagine this same scene playing out in heaven, with Jesus at the head of the circle.

"I left the Chapel that evening with that image locked in my heart. The next morning, I picked up my guitar and started strumming. The words were easy because the picture was already there: a circle of friends giving the invitation to meet at the Savior's side. I began singing 'Side By Side We Stand.' It was simply putting words to what we all experience and wish to experience. The music fell into place as well - five easy chords and a simple melody. About a half-hour later it was done. I called it 'Meet Me In Heaven,' though later it became known as 'Side By Side.'

"At the beginning of the next prayer meeting, Clyde told the group he wanted to teach them a new song and he sang it for them. By the time he got to the second chorus, the whole group was singing as if they knew it. And at the end of the meeting, instead of 'Shall We Gather At the River' we sang 'Side By Side.'

"A few months later, I was invited to hear a new singing group performing at the Napa church. The Heritage Singers ended their concert with a song that had the whole congregation standing side by side, and raising their joined hands together. Emotion filled my heart as the congregation sang. 'Side by Side' had never sounded so wonderful. I thought back to that little circle of 20 in Dauphinee Chapel, now blossomed into hundreds, who sang that same invitation many months before. "

For at least 15 years, the Heritage Singers ended their concerts with "Side by Side." The audience would stand and join hands, raising them toward Heaven. "Lucy and I are so humbled that the Lord has taken the songs that Heritage sings and used them to bless others," said Max. "Not only have the songs touched those who have heard them, but they have also blessed the singers and their families. The desire of our heart has always been to bring people closer to Christ through our music so that we may all meet together one day in Heaven."

"Meet me in Heaven,

We'll join hands together.

Meet me at the Savior's side.

I'll meet you in Heaven,

We'll sing songs together.

Brothers and sisters I'll be there.

Pray that we all will be there."

Where We Go From Here

CHAPTER TWENTY-ONE

Leaving the Stage

THE HARDEST PART OF BEING A HERITAGE SINGER IS LEAVING. AFTER LIVING TOGETHER AND KNOWING EACH other so well, most of us had to eventually go our separate ways. One by one we had to let go of each other, but each person who left the group was missed and remembered by those who stayed. For those of us who left, we would always have those wonderful memories, deep friendships, and those pictures in our minds of the places we traveled to and the faces of the thousands of people we met all over the world. We would never forget the lessons we learned and the new maturity we found. It all added up to quite a heritage. It was our Heritage experience.

Being on our own after being a Heritage Singer was often very difficult. Upon leaving Heritage Judy Mote Evenson wrote:

Being a Heritage Singer sounded exciting, almost like a dream. I was going to ride around on that big old bus, staying in a different city every night. Literally see the country! Soon it was a reality. Suitcases, strangers, laundromats, new cities nearly every night, and lots of fun.

But being a Heritage Singer has been more than that. It has been crusades and seeing people you've visited accept Christ, smiling at a stranger and through that one smile making a life-long friend,

learning to appreciate people for who they are.

It has also been about finding a terrific husband whose goals are the same as mine: to witness for Jesus Christ through the music talents He's given us. And it has been a wealth of friendships among the other Heritage Singers.

I can hardly believe it! Two-and-a-half years have brought many cherished memories, but soon I won't be a Heritage Singer any more. Oh yes, I'll always be one at heart, but there will be no more big busses, gracious hosts and hostesses taking us in for the night, no more stage lights and crowds of people.

But Steve and I have determined that wherever the Lord leads us, we will, with His help, never stop witnessing for Him. Please pray for us!

Even though some knew when they joined Heritage that it was only going to be for a year or two, it was still very difficult when the time came to decide whether to stay or leave. We weren't the same people we had started out being. We had grown to love these people, and some of us couldn't imagine our lives without them and without Heritage.

Those who left did so for a variety of personal reasons. Some singers were ready to go back to school or begin a new adventure. Whatever the reasons for leaving, it was not an easy thing to do. As part of Heritage, we were part of a family. We were listened to and heard. We were loved and treated like we were special everywhere we went. To choose to leave our friends and the Heritage life was an emotional passage. It was going into a great unknown. It actually took a lot of courage, especially for those who didn't know exactly what awaited them outside of the protective world of Heritage.

Bill Truby said the toughest time for him while he was with Heritage was when he was preparing to leave. "At the time I had been seeking God's guidance," he said. "I prayed for God's will. I felt convicted to leave. At that point, it was the right thing to do, and it was God's guidance given the situation. I never ever wanted to leave Heritage, but I had a deep conviction that I had to go, and I really struggled with that conviction.

Kathleen Ojala, keyboards
Years in Heritage II: 1976-77

John Wohlfeil, bass
Years in Heritage: 1971-73

"Afterwards I knew why my conviction was so strong. God was calling me into the ministry. Very shortly after leaving Heritage, things started happening that showed God's guidance. I believe God guided me in that way because of the need at that time and the choices I made because of my family.

"The hardest part about leaving was telling Max. I saw the look in his eyes. I loved Max. The Maces were my family. This was my life. I remember saying, 'I don't know why or where I'm going, but I feel the need to leave.' Max and Lucy had done so much for me. I was still appreciative. I just had to go, and it hurt so much.

"When I joined Heritage, I had no clue what I was getting into, but I knew it was God's will. I knew it was the place to be. It was the same thing in leaving. Even though I felt devastated, I knew it was time to go, and I had to follow that guidance. So, I did. And yet, Heritage has always been one of the closest things to me."

One thing you learn in Heritage is how to say goodbye and go on without the people you have come to love. It's never easy, but you do get better at it after it keeps happening over and over. You find out that good things don't last forever; that everything changes sooner or later. Whether you're the one who's doing the leaving, or the one who is left to carry on when others leave, you find out how to pull up anchor and catch the wind. You find out that you can do it if you have to.

Lucy said, "Leaving is never easy. Sometimes we had to ask

kids to leave. That was the hardest part for us. Sometimes we cried all the way to the airport. It was like saying goodbye to our own kids."

Val has had to say a lot of goodbyes over the years. "The singers became family to me. It was always so heart wrenching to say good-bye. I would cry for days. We were so close to each other."

"It's extremely sad when we lose a singer, whether we have to ask them to leave or at the end of a touring season and they choose to leave," said Max. "When you spend that much time together day in and day out you become like family—probably closer than some of them are to their own families. Over time you adjust but you still miss them."

Many former Heritage Singers kept in touch over the years and are still friends. No matter how many years go by, the shared history we have of being in Heritage will always be a bond that holds us together like family.

Max and Lucy continually encouraged us to become more accepting of people. By their example, they taught us that what really matters is how we can care about and help others, including our fellow travelers. The more we go through in life, the more compassionate we become toward others.

One morning not too long ago at the ranch, several of us had been sharing stories and getting reacquainted after many years of being away. The weight of the many stories we had shared seemed to diminish him, and a sudden sadness came over him.

Reger Smith, bass and keyboards
Years in Heritage II: 1974-75

Earl Robbins, bus driver
Years in Heritage: 1999-2003

"If only we had known what people were going through; we could have helped each other more," Max said. "I just wish we could have helped each other more."

The more than 250 musicians who have been Heritage Singers are the most blessed people in the world. Max didn't pick us for this priceless experience; God picked us. We were Heritage Singers. And that is the richest Heritage of all!

THE HARDEST GOODBYE

Sadly, at the writing of this book, four former Heritage Singers have passed away. Kathleen Ojala played the keyboards for Heritage II. John Wohlfeil sang bass in Heritage. Reger Smith sang bass and played keyboards in Heritage II. Earl Robbins loved sitting behind the big wheel and driving for Heritage, singing along with every song as they practiced going down the road. He was in the height of his glory when he was behind the wheel of that old bus.

We will always remember them and be grateful for their talents and for the time we had with them. We look forward to the big Heritage reunion in Heaven, when we all will be together again. What a day that will be! What a day that will be!

What a day that will be,
When my Jesus I shall see,
When I look upon His face,
The One who saved me by His grace,
When He takes me by the hand,
And leads me to the promised land,
What a day, glorious day, that will be

CHAPTER TWENTY-TWO

As for Me and My House

Now therefore fear the Lord, and serve Him in sincerity and truth.
—Joshua 24:14

Any Heritage Singer, old or young, will tell you that Lucy is the glue that holds the Heritage ministry together. She complements Max so beautifully, picking up where he leaves off and making sure every detail is taken care of. Max and Lucy are not just life partners; they are a team. And, Val and Greg are very important members of that team, as are Adriane and Art.

Family has always been very important to Max and Lucy. From the beginning, they have involved their children, Greg and Val, their nephews and other family members in the Heritage ministry. Hundreds of people have been involved in Heritage over the years, but the core of Heritage has always been, and continues to be, Max and Lucy and their family.

On a morning in May of 1998, Max sat down at his desk to write his monthly letter to the friends and supporters of the Heritage ministry:

Max and Austin

Greetings from the Heritage Singers. I'm in my office at 6 AM and it's nice and quiet here in the foothills of Placerville. I like to get up early to write to you, my prayer and faith partners, to share what's on my heart.

As you know, I'm a grandpa. I never had any idea how much fun it could be to have Austin throw his arms up to want Grandpa to take him for a ride on the lawn mower! He loves the tractor, so it's hard for Grandpa to get any work done. But you know what? I'm taking the time. The work will always be there, but Austin will be small for only a short time. He just got out of the hospital a couple of weeks ago from his fifth time of having pneumonia. Please keep him in your prayers. He's had a tough start in life. He's the absolute joy of Grandpa's life. His health is getting better. Praise the Lord!

My son, Greg, was married this last June to a beautiful girl he met while on tour in Brazil two years ago. Her name is Adriane. I was beginning to wonder if anyone would get him to the altar, but he finally found the one! We all wish the best for them as they put Jesus first in their marriage.

Almost two years later, in February of 1999, Max wrote:

This was a very special month at the Mace household. Our little Valentine arrived just one day early on February 13th. Our son, Greg, and his wife, Adriane, had a beautiful little girl, Amber Nichole. She has brought a lot of joy into our lives.

Our grandson, Austin, who is now four, thinks Amber was sent just for him. Austin and Grandpa are quite the buddies. He shares my love for popcorn. I have to tell you a story about this little guy. One day, he came into my office with a big bowl of popcorn that he'd made himself. He set the popcorn down on my desk, looked up at me and said, "Grandpa, let's talk!"

I hope I never get too busy to spend time with my kids and grandkids. They are such precious gifts from God.

Who would have thought that an ole' country farm boy from Idaho would be traveling the world like this? I thought I would be a rancher like my dad and granddad, but God had another plan for my life. Can you believe my entire family has stayed together for almost 30 years sharing the good news all over the world? All I can say is, to God be the glory!

Lucy and Max

Austin and Amber

In January of 2003, on the occasion of their 45th wedding anniversary, Max wrote:

Lucy is a wonderful lady – dedicated to the ministry and to our family. She works very hard, never complains, and is always available to help someone with something. I'd be lost without her. I can't believe she has put up with me all these years!

Looking back over our years together, there were times that things took priority over my family. I kept myself way too busy. I would forget to tell my family how important they were to me. Lucy needed to hear me say, "Honey, I love you and appreciate you so much," and Greg and Val needed to hear me say, "I love you and am really proud of you." I thought it, but I didn't always take the time to say it.

Take time to tell your loved ones how important they are to you. I promise you that if you keep God first, family second and your business and all else third, your life will be more content, more peaceful and more fulfilled. God knows your needs and He promises to supply them in His perfect time.

Lucy and I are so proud of our kids and grandkids. And we are so pleased that Greg and Val and their families have dedicated their lives to the Heritage ministry.

Children who desire to serve the Lord are such a blessing to a parent. Greg and Val have played a huge part in keeping this ministry going for all of these years. Lucy and I could not have done this without them.

"Two are better than one because they have a good reward for their labor. For if they fall, one will lift up his companion, but woe to him who is alone when he falls, or he has no one to help him up" Ecclesiastes 4:9-10

GREG AND ADRIANE

The art of being a sound engineer is a special talent. You have to be a really good listener. You have to be able to hear things that other people can't hear. You have to be in tune with your surroundings, be a master at tweaking things and be the most patient person in the world. But the real test of a good soundman is their ability to bring out the best in each singer and instrument and combine all of those elements into the Heritage Sound. It's making the most of whatever the singers put out on any given day and making it sound as good as possible and keeping the consistency from one day to the next.

Greg Mace is the man behind the Heritage Sound. Max hears it in his head and brings it out of the singers. Then, Greg mixes, blends, tweaks and finesses the raw material into that Heritage Sound that is recognizable anywhere. He doesn't say much, but he has the control at his fingertips. All of the singers know that Greg hears every little slip and blunder and somehow smoothes it over. He can make or break the group.

Greg decides how loud a singer is in the mix, and, sometimes, whether they're in the mix at all! It's not about spotlighting certain voices; it's about getting that overall smooth blend without masking the harmonies or blurring the dynamics. It's about mixing the voices and adding the right effects, and adjusting the sound level for the room and the audience. Greg not only controls what the audience hears, but he also controls what the singers hear on stage, which might be an entirely different mix. Last, but certainly not least, he also has to know how to fix the sound system if it breaks down.

Adriane and Greg

Greg at the soundboard

Greg was only 11 years old when he started traveling with Heritage. He actually was a singer! Who knew he could sing? He was never given much of a chance. While Heritage was on tour back in the 70s, they unexpectedly lost their sound engineer during the tour. So, Max asked Greg to fill in for a short time until a replacement could be found. To make a long story short, Greg showed so much natural ability Max wasn't going to let him do anything else! He wanted Greg to be the man behind the controls. He had found his niche. He's been perfecting his craft for most of his life.

With his technical ability, it was a natural progression for Greg to start his own sound and lighting company. GJM Sound and Lighting operates from the Heritage headquarters. Organizations from all over the world call for his sound and lighting advice. He has won numerous awards for his accomplishments with sound manufacturers such as Electro-Voice and JBL.

"Greg started his business on his own and learned his trade at a very young age," Max said, proudly. "He built strong relationships and contacts as we toured over the years. When he puts a system in a church or auditorium, it's always done right."

Adriane's story of God working in her life is summed up by her own words:

Music has always been a big part of my life. My parents said that I was only two years old when I sang on stage for the first time, and I never stopped since then. I, too, grew up listening to the Heritage Singers. Looking back, it's amazing to see what God had in store for me.

I was four years old when my parents took me to my first Heritage Singers concert in Bahia, Brazil. I remember sitting in the audience as the group sang, "Jesus Makes Everything Good." The group was very animated as they used the puppets to make all of the different animal noises. I was so excited that I fell off my chair and started crying. Jim McDonald heard me crying, and stopped singing the song to tell me, "God bless you." Looking back now, I see how God was leading me to become a part of the Heritage Singers' ministry.

My sister Cybelle and I listened to the "Heaven is for Kids" CD, which was our favorite, whenever my dad wasn't listening to his favorite Heritage quartet CD, "Just around the Corner." Little did I know that I would be singing with the Heritage Singers 15 years later!

Amber, baby Isabella and Austin

Through my teenage years, I sang with Grupo Integracao and several other groups. Later we formed a trio that included my sister and a friend who sang tenor. After recording an album in 1992 we toured throughout Brazil, sometimes singing at six different churches in a single weekend. I guess this was preparing me for singing in Heritage on our international tours.

It was in December of 1994, that I saw a flyer in my church announcing the Heritage Singers concert in Vitoria. I was excited about the thought of being able to hear them in person. That is, until I realized that I really couldn't afford to go. Then, to my surprise, a friend of mine, knowing my predicament, handed me four tickets!

It was January 31, 1995, the day Heritage was coming to Vitoria. I could hardly believe that I was actually on my way to the airport with my friends to welcome them! That was a dream come true for me!

That evening after the concert, Max asked my dad, an

interpreter and me to have a talk with him. What happened during that anointed hour has changed my life forever. Max asked me if I would like to come to the Heritage Ranch in California. I could spend some time with the group and learn English. That was way beyond my wildest dreams!

By March 19, 1995, I was in California, amazingly on Greg's birthday. By summer, I was singing with the group. Once again, I saw how God was leading all the way.

God continued to lead as Adriane and Greg's friendship grew into love over the next two years. Greg and Adriane were married on June 1, 1997. They added a princess to their family, Amber Nichole, on February 13, 1999. Greg and Adriane added a second little princess to their family, Isabella Renee, on July 4, 2002.

"These little sweethearts are Lucy's and my pride and joy," said Max, "along with Val and Art's son, Austin Chase. We love our grandkids so much and cherish each moment with them. Lucy has a plaque in her office that says, 'If I'd known grandkids were this much fun, I would have had them first!' I think all you grandparents know what I'm talking about."

VAL AND ART

Val grew up in the Heritage Singers. "It's all I know," she said. She was only nine years old when her parents started the group and went on the road. She began singing solos during the concerts right away. At 10 years of age, she sang her first solo "Sweet Jesus," a song Mrs. Fevec, her second grade teacher had taught her. At age 12, she began singing full time as a soprano with the group and continues to be an important part of the Heritage sound to this day.

"From the very beginning, her smooth, sweet voice has been the foundation of our Heritage Sound," Max said. "She started out singing with singers who were quite a bit older than she was, and she took every opportunity to learn from their experience. Now we rely on her. She sets the pitch of each song and the rest of us just lock into her voice and follow her lead. We count on her consistency."

Val and Greg virtually grew up with their only home being the Heritage bus. They were home schooled over the years and studied by correspondence. And, because Val was a singer in the group, she had to keep up with their schedule in addition to her studies.

Val continued this schedule of singing and studying while on the road until she enrolled as a sophomore at PUC Prep. It was hard for her to be apart from her family.

When Val graduated from high school, she moved to Glendale, California, and took a job as a student teacher at Glendale Academy. She discovered a special love for children and felt blessed to have been given this time to experience a somewhat normal life. About a year passed when Val was asked to tour with the group overseas. She resumed her singing role full time. To this date, she has sung in over 5000 concerts in over 60 countries around the world.

Her role with Heritage goes beyond singing. "She's been taking a lot of pressure off of Lucy and me," Max said. "Val's been my right hand, addressing challenging and sometimes stressful tasks that are essential to keeping this music ministry going."

"What a blessing she is to Lucy and me!" Max continued. "The Lord has given her such a sweet spirit that flows through

Art, Austin and Val

all she does. She genuinely cares about people. Her utmost devotion, dedication and commitment to family and ministry mean more to Lucy and me than words can express."

Growing up in Heritage has given Val a very unique outlook on life. Some might say she has not lived a "normal" life, yet she would say her life has been normal to her, and she would not have wanted it any other way.

Val has no regrets. "My education has been the experience of going all over the world and dealing with all kinds of people."

As a result of her life in Heritage, she has the gift of being able to adapt to any situation easily and comfortably.

Val said her favorite time in Heritage is right now. "The singers are my closest friends. Singing with them is a dream. We share the same passion and connect on so many different levels. I've found a lot of true friends in the group. The live concerts are so enjoyable. I love to see the Lord working through us to meet people's needs and bring them hope. It's an awesome responsibility and honor to be part of this ministry. I also love recording. With the right combination of voices the session is not only rewarding, but fun as well. There's nothing like recording with my best friends!

"Being separated from my parents at such a young age when we stayed in people's homes was really hard on me," she remembered. It never felt right being apart from them but this was part of what we all had to go through being a part of a self-supporting ministry on the road eleven months out of the year.

"Watching my parents struggle was also hard. I wanted so much for them. They are so selfless. If anyone is suffering financially or emotionally they are the first to help. They always forgive and forget and move on and love unconditionally. They are wonderful examples of selflessness, perseverance and of having total faith in God. They taught me to think positively and to believe that everything will turn out fine; that there's light at the end of the tunnel. This is one of the best gifts my parents could have given me, to look at life that way.

"I'm also grateful to be married to someone who is passionate about this ministry. Sometimes your family can suffer if you don't appreciate each other's talents and passions. Art and I are very compatible that way."

Art was born in Manila, Philippines. His father served 20 years in the United States Army with the intent of moving his family to the United States. When Art was only nine years old, his family, including two brothers and three sisters, moved to Fort Leonard Woods, Missouri. A year later, they moved across the country to San Francisco, where Art spent the rest of his growing-up years.

Art said that he's been a fan of the Heritage Singers since the group's first album came out. He was just 15 years old at the time.

"I liked them because the songs weren't typical; there was more excitement, a happy sound," he said. "I had great admiration for the Heritage Singers because they stood out from the rest of what was available in the Christian music scene at that time. I appreciated their unique sound, style of music and arrangements. I always looked forward to their next album."

Early on, Art attributed his interest in Christian music to the Heritage Singers. "They jump-started me. It was exciting to hear such innovative, bold and inspirational music. I wanted to make harmonies like that. It made me appreciate music more."

At age 14, Art's parents bought him an acoustic guitar from Woolworth since he'd shown great interest in playing it. He'd spend hours alone figuring out chords, rhythms and the sounds he liked, quickly gravitating toward jazz.

While in high school Art joined a Top 40 band, playing at clubs and parties. Although he loved the music he was playing, he continued to follow the activities and recordings of Heritage and felt himself drawn to Christian music. He prayed for a way out of the lifestyle he felt himself getting pulled into. On his way to the concert, a block away from the venue, he had a car accident. To this day, Art is convinced that God allowed it to happen—the car accident that kept him from making it to a performance which ultimately led him to quit the band.

One day he saw a small classified ad that was going to change his life. It was a notice that Heritage was looking for a guitar player to replace Pete McLeod.

Here is how Art tells the story:

By that time I'd been playing the guitar for about two years, and decided to make an audition tape. The Heritage Singers were doing a concert in Oakland, and Pete was still playing guitar for them. I went to hear them and remember being thrilled to hear Pete play in person. I mean, Wow! This is the guy who played the guitar on "Sweet Jesus!"

I actually got up the courage to go talk to the band after the concert. I asked Jon Yoshida, the bass player, if they read music. I was worried that I wouldn't be good enough to play with the group because I didn't read music. When Jon said yes, that they did read music, I chickened out and never gave Max my tape. I couldn't imagine myself in a recording studio situation if I had to sight read a track, so I gave up my dream of ever being a part of Heritage.

In 1979, I moved to Los Angeles and worked as an x-ray tech at Cedar-Sinai Medical Center. Although I made a good living, music was still my first love.

In 1983, I heard that Max was looking for another guitar player. I sent that same audition tape to Max. Here it was, several years later, the same exact tape, and I was hired on the spot!

I joined the group in 1984. In those years, Heritage traveled with a live band. I introduced the electronic drums to the live concerts.

In the early1990s, Max put in a recording studio at the Heritage ranch called Turning Point Studio. We not only recorded Heritage albums there, but also took on outside clients with music projects and produced jingles as well. It was a very good fit for me.

Currently Art oversees all Heritage studio productions. This includes writing, producing, engineering, mixing and audio and video editing. He produces and instrumentally arranges and plays on the majority of the Heritage projects.

"Art is an amazing talent," Max said. "He has a natural ear; not one learned out of a book. It's within his spirit. Lucy and I are so happy Art is part of our family. We love him and appreciate all that he does."

Val and Art were married August 11, 1990. They became the proud parents of Austin Chase on June 23, 1995.

Val said that having a child has been one of the greatest joys of her life. However, Austin's life started out kind of rough. The whole experience was traumatic for the whole family, but it did bring them closer to each other and closer to God."

This is how Val tells the story:

The night that Austin arrived, we were so excited because everything seemed to be so perfect. We spent the night in the hospital with him, and throughout the night we noticed that he sounded kind of funny in his throat, kind of gurgley. We tried not to worry about it because we thought that was a normal baby sound. The next morning the doctors came in to give him a routine check-up, and they noticed the same thing.

"We need to take your baby to another room and suction him," they said, *"and we'll be right back."*

A few minutes later they came back, but without the baby.

"We tried to suction him," they said, *"but he has a pouch in his*

![Austin and Val in the hospital]

Austin and Val in the hospital

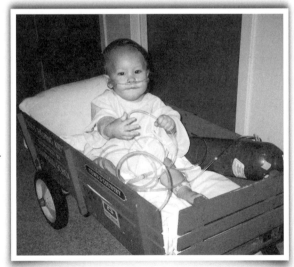

Austin in the hospital

throat which prevented him from swallowing so we're going to have to take him by ambulance to another hospital where they specialize in children."

Art and I looked at each other thinking, "Wow, this is not how it's supposed to be," feeling totally robbed of joy.

Austin ended up having a four-hour surgery for a condition called T-E fistula. Basically his esophagus had detoured and attached itself to the trachea. He was put in intensive care for two weeks after that. I remember the first day he got out of surgery. Art and I spent all day with him there in the hospital, and then we drove an hour back to Placerville, where we lived.

I felt so helpless leaving our baby behind. When we got home and went to the nursery, which of course, we had prepared way in advance for him, I found a praise album and put in on. I turned out the lights and I began to pour my heart out to God. I would pray, then cry, and then pray some more. And I need to tell you it is the hardest thing that I have ever been through. Yet, at the same time, I've never felt God's presence or His peace more real in my life. I knew that no matter what the outcome of that situation, that God would see me through it. And He has.

I would love to tell you that is the end of the story, but it's not. At eight months of age, Austin was hospitalized with pneumonia. By age two he had been hospitalized five different times with pneumonia. I can remember being on tour with Heritage and saying, "Dad, we've got to find a hospital. Austin can't breathe!"

They would take me to the closest hospital and leave me there, and drive on to the next concert. I tried so hard to be strong for Austin, and I would hold him close. I remember singing, "Jesus Loves Me" to him, because I believe, with all my heart, that He does. Yet at the same time, tears were running down my face because it was so hard to see my baby suffering like that again and again.

My last experience was really tough, in that they tried to start an IV on him five times and weren't successful. They had to take him by ambulance to another hospital, put him in a straight jacket, and five hours later, 25 attempts later, they were successful in putting an IV in the top of his head.

Amber, Isabella and Austin

Austin is doing great now. He has no health issues to speak of anymore, and he's not on any medications. I just totally believe that it's a miracle. I feel so blessed that we've come through that whole journey with Austin and to see the way he is today, strong and healthy.

I share this story with people now not because I have all the answers, but because I feel that it is so important when we go through things in life that hurt us deeply—things that don't make sense, that we turn to the one and only Source that can bring true peace and true comfort, and that is Jesus Christ.

"When we were recently in South Africa, a lady came up to me and said that since she heard my story about Austin and his rough start in life, she's prayed for my son every day. I was so humbled to think that someone clear around the world would make my son a matter of her daily prayers! It's just so touching and means so much to me."

At another concert in Portland, Oregon, a man came up to Val and asked if he could pray for Austin. Val said, "Of course." The man prayed that God would heal Austin. Then he proceeded to tell her, "Austin may have pneumonia symptoms, but he will not ever have pneumonia again." Val said she wanted to believe him. Yet, in her mind, she still questioned whether or not the man could be right. She chose to believe him, having faith that Austin would be healed. To this day, Austin has never contracted pneumonia again and we give God the glory!

The Heritage ministry is not just Max and Lucy. It's Val and Greg, Adriane and Art. "The Heritage ministry is my family," Max said, "and it's the singers who are so dedicated to our ministry. It's also the Board of Directors that has been with me through thick and thin. And it's the people who support us and keep us going year after year. But most of all, it's Jesus Christ that deserves all the praise.

"Probably the most important thing I've learned is to trust in the Lord. Without God we can do nothing. Sometimes when we think we've got all the answers, we fall flat. When we take our eyes off of Jesus, we can fail. If you're in this type of ministry, you've got to stay close to the Lord, because if you don't, you're going to fail."

"Whenever my dad walks onto the stage," Greg said, "it's like his very first concert. He stands up there and sings as passionate now as he did 40 years ago! And back home, even though my mom doesn't travel a lot with us anymore, she makes sure that my dad gets his suit on the bus and his shoes are shined. Everyone has a job. My parents are the ones who hold this organization together."

"Just the daily activities, the way they speak," said Adriane, "the way they treat you, one can see how Godly they are."

"All of us here at Heritage strive to be better Christians, because we are communicating the message of Christ," Art said. "I'm amazed at Max and Lucy, at their lives and how far this ministry has come. Your first impression of them is your lasting impression."

"When people have asked me if I knew then what I know now, whether I'd do it all over again," Lucy said, "my answer is, 'Without a doubt.' It has had its good and its bad, but I'll tell you the good far outweighs any bad that ever happened on the road. And to see the lives that have been changed as a result of the music . . . Without a doubt."

Max said, "Sometimes I think I should be in a secure job and relaxing with Lucy, especially since our children are grown.

Christmas with the family

Then I remember back in 1971 after a recurring dream of a full-time music ministry, Lucy and I told the Lord that we'd go where He wanted us to go and be what He wanted us to be. This is the reason I must keep going. This is the motivating factor behind the Heritage ministry."

"My parents have done something with their lives that they are passionate about, and that's what other people wish for and dream about," Val said.

Max thinks he'll know when it's time to quit. "My plans are just to go as long as God gives me health and as long as God continues to provide the means for us to keep a ministry like this on the road. At the moment, though, as for me and my house, we're going to serve the Lord."

"We've chosen together, as a family to serve Him forever,
knowing nothing else will matter in time."
—Tim Shepherd

CHAPTER TWENTY-THREE

A Fireside Chat with Max

My God will meet all your needs according to His glorius riches in Christ Jesus.
—Philippians 4:19

I WAS VISITING WITH MAX IN HIS OFFICE AT THE RANCH. OUTSIDE, A COLD DRIZZLE SENT A DAMP CHILL through your bones. Inside, logs were sizzling in the wood stove and a fire roared in the fireplace, setting a cozy mood for a long leisurely chat. I noticed that Max had a huge collection of CDs and albums from many different artists. He has always enjoyed listening to music of many different artists, for inspiration and for pure enjoyment. Just as he had done when I first came to the ranch as a young Heritage Singer, he reached over and put on a recording for me to hear.

"Listen to this," he said, as he leaned back in his chair amidst the assembled and displayed evidence of his many musical accomplishments. I feel the same awe I felt the first time I sat here many years ago.

In an instant, the lush sound of a recent Heritage recording engulfed us. It was a recording I hadn't yet heard, but there was no mistaking the famous Heritage sound. A familiar mellow baritone voice began singing an old classic hymn, "You may have longed for added strength, your courage to renew." I recognized the opening verse to the song, "It is No Secret."

"Do you know who that is?" he asked.

"Sure I do. It's you, Max." I said as he smiled, sort of humbly, sort of proudly. "Wow, they sure made you sound good!" I teased. "Very Mel Torme!" He laughed and said that he was enjoying singing now more than he ever has; that giving up some of the music direction to Tim Davis has helped him relax more, and it shows in his singing.

I commented on the new Heritage recording he just played

for me. Obviously it was still Heritage, but so much more interesting than it used to be! The sound was more contemporary, rich, and at times, even complex. The harmonies are more intricate. There's more dimension and more contrast. The singers have an edge and an excitement I had never seen. They've come to life!

I told Max I saw a fresh enthusiasm, energy, confidence, and a polished professionalism that is so refreshing. The singers speak and present themselves so much more maturely than I ever could. They sing better. They seem to have mas-

Group rehearsal

tered the art of being perfect Heritage Singers. This group is in an entirely different league.

Not only has the music style become more contemporary, but Max's leadership style has also changed. Now he stays more in the background and Tim Davis seems to be the one pulling it all together creatively in the recording sessions.

"A smart leader puts talented people around him," Max explained, "and gives them more responsibility. I tell Tim what I want, and he takes it from there. Tim was with Heritage for five years under my direction, and has learned the Heritage sound. He knows how to build on that foundation."

"A few years ago I started feeling the anxiety," Max said. "I was in a meeting going over our financial situation, and it suddenly came over me like an attack. My heart was racing and I felt like I couldn't breathe. I just had to get up and leave the meeting. My doctor told me it was a stress attack and he warned me to step back a bit from the day-to-day intensity. At that time I still traveled a lot. After 20 years of being on the road for

11 months out of the year, doing five to six concerts a week, I needed to cut back.

"Tim and Art have taken a lot of pressure off of me. I'm much more behind the scenes now, but I want to be sure we keep that signature Heritage sound. I've produced numerous albums over the years, but I can't do it hour after hour any more."

I marvel at the talent Max has surrounded himself with. God's leading as always, but Max had to know what he wanted and how to get it. All along the way Max had to make decisions about who to hire and who not to hire. He has carefully selected the people around him, and I ask him how he did this, starting with the singers themselves.

"After most every concert we let people know in the audience that we are always looking for singers," Max reminded me. "A lot of my singers were taking a year out of college and would sing for Heritage for a year, then go back to school. The next year we'd need new singers. So I needed to have a pool of singers to pull from whenever I lost a singer.

"What I look for in a singer is expression, pitch, intonation, you know, can they hit intervals? But musical talent is not the only thing we look for," he was quick to add. "We are looking for young people who love Jesus. And that is the first criteria—to find someone who loves the Lord. Once in a while people have said to me, 'Now, Max, I'm a musician, but I'm not into this religious stuff much; but I love music and I love to perform,' and I'd say, 'You know something? You'd be very unhappy in my group, because Jesus is the first thing. If you can sing, that's a bonus.'"

There is more to it than that. There's a certain style of voice that fits into Heritage, and many voices are just not right for Heritage. For one thing, an obvious vibrato or too much stylistic interpretation is not good. Max is able to tell right away if a person has the potential to fit in with the Heritage sound or not.

"It's all about the matching of voices," Max explained. "Vibrato is a part of that. You need to put a little air in your voice. Unison is the key. If you can sound like one voice, you're okay. Throughout the years, when I knew I was going to lose a singer, I'd ask myself, 'Who could come in and not change the overall sound of the group?' That Heritage sound was our signature."

But, if you've heard some of the more recent Heritage recordings, you hear a lot of big gospel vibrato, especially on the big choral songs that build up in emotion. Those new Heritage musicians really belt it out. The sound is all grown up now and quite different from the way we used to sing.

"Tim likes vibrato on some songs when the song calls for it," Max said. "When you use a straight tone, you need a lot of personality and expression. You need to sing with a smile in your voice.

"Now the singers have been in the group long enough to do the studio stuff. The recording group is finely tuned. There is a lot more to do musically in the recording studio than there is on stage. It takes a lot of focus and precision. We've had basically the same sound for the last few recordings," he said. "We have a great combination of singers. We're not the amateurs we used to be. Tim's not afraid to say someone's off. You know he knows what he's doing," he said. "Singers have to have total trust in the director; and the director needs to not be a jerk."

Max has certainly earned the respect of the singers over the

Tim Davis and Max recording

years, and even his ability to turn some of the direction over to someone else is something to be admired.

"Tim knows music," Max said. "He knows what sounds good. That's why people liked the original Heritage Singers. We weren't mechanical. We were pleasant on the ears. I always liked tight harmony," he said. "Remember the Anita Kerr Singers? Ever since I was a little kid I always loved tight harmony, like the Ray Coniff Singers. Some of the early gospel groups had that sound. I'll never forget when Thurlow Spurr and his group came to Portland, Oregon, where Lucy and I were living. They really inspired me. I remember I came home to Lucy and said, 'I have to do that!'

"Actually, quartets have always been my passion," he admitted. "I couldn't just have a quartet, though. It works better if it's a mixed group.

"But you know the Heritage Singers are a lot more than just singing," he pointed out. "I always loved music and performing," he said, "but I also wanted to go out and win people to God. We have grown spiritually. It has gotten stronger and stronger. We found out that if you don't have that spiritual depth, you don't have a group."

There have been many times when his faith has been tested. The insecurity of being a self-supporting ministry requires a lot of faith. "We've had to rely on the Lord," Max said. "God sees the potential for our ministry. We've learned that if we let Him, God will walk us through financial hardships. The whole experience has taught us how to have faith."

God continues to impress people to support the ministry. "Today we got a check for a thousand dollars," he said. "Heritage has always been a self-supporting ministry. That's what I like about it. When we get a donation we're celebrating and rejoicing. It's very different from how a typical corporation operates."

Max and Lucy both have many stories about financial close calls. One such incident happened on payroll day. "We needed a certain amount of money to pay our employees," Max began, "and Lucy told me we couldn't write the checks because the money wasn't there, but she was quick to point out that the mail still hadn't come. That day we got eight to ten letters with donations that, when added together, came to the exact amount we needed for payroll. These letters came from all over the United States, and weren't all mailed on the same day. But how they all arrived on the exact day we needed the money, a person couldn't have planned that if he tried. You don't have to be a genius to realize that God was behind that."

Max told me that this is the way they operated at times. And because the finances were never secure, their faith in God became stronger. There have been times when Max and Lucy haven't taken paychecks. They are in it with the rest of the singers. When the group stayed in peoples' homes, Max and Lucy stayed in peoples' homes, too. Other group leaders tried to tell Max that he didn't need to do that, but since the group survived on free will offerings and record sales, he was compelled to keep expenses down.

"Only 40 percent of an audience gives anything at a love offering," he said, "and the average gift is one dollar. Praise the Lord a few people do think about how much it takes to run the organization. It's not unusual for four or five people in an audience to give what amounts to over half of the offering collected. We are so thankful for them."

"The 70s and early 80s were the best times," he said. "In fact, the demand for our music was so great, we formed Heritage II. But besides all of the problems we had with personnel, our expenses doubled. Then, in the 90s the costs for everything really went up. The stress I felt was mainly over the finances. Our expenses have multiplied, but the offerings have pretty much stayed the same."

"God has chosen a few people to support us. I'll never forget the man who helped us get a loan for the bus. He put his own equipment up as collateral so we could get the loan. If it weren't for people willing to help us, we wouldn't be here. The 29ers Club keeps us going today.

"In our 29th year," Max explained, "we were going behind every month. We decided to ask people to become monthly faith partners by sending in $29 a month, a dollar for every year the singers had been on the road. Today our dear 29ers are what keeps us going along with our CD and DVD sales. The offerings don't begin to cover the expenses.

Art Mapa, producer and arranger for Heritage

In the early years, John Musgrave worked hard with Max to keep things running smoothly from a business perspective. "John was the business manager for Heritage from 1972 through 1978," Max explained. "Even before John, I had a lot of business management help from Les Berreth and Jerry Leiske, the Canadians who were part of the original Heritage Singers. When the Canadians had to leave, John came in and really helped to get us organized. With John's help, we were able to build the lodge and establish our administrative offices."

"Bonnie Ensminger was another person who was instrumental in keeping our ministry going. She was our secretary for 17 years and kept the office organized. She did all of our correspondence and booked two groups. She drove every day from her home in Sacramento to Placerville and was such a cheerful presence in our office," Max said. "In fact, I remember one church pastor stood up in front of his church when we were there giving a concert, and he told his congregation that if they were having a bad day, all you have to do is call the Heritage Singers office and talk to Bonnie. It just gets your day off to the right start!

"We have many unsung heroes who work here at the office and keep this ministry going from day to day," Max said.

Today things are even more organized from a business perspective in that a Board of Directors of Christian businessmen has been formed that advises Max and Lucy on business matters. "We try to have about five or six people on the Board and meet four times a year," Max said. "We recruit Christian people who operate their own businesses and give us sound financial advice.

"Bobbie Brody and Ron Schaafsma did a lot to help us get organized in the early years. Ron later

Bonnie Ensminger, Max's secretary for 17 years

became the president of the Board of Directors. Larry and Paula Smith helped us get our computers and set them up so expenses could be tracked more closely. They helped us establish a professional accounting system. Richard and Colette Barnes have had a great impact on helping us make good decision for Heritage. God has brought people into our lives at the right time to fill a need and give us good direction.

"In addition to our board of directors we have a bookkeeper and an outside CPA. Everything we do is looked at very carefully to be sure we're doing things right. There are checkpoints in the system for accountability.

"It's not possible to predict income," Max said. "A financial plan is pretty hard to do. Selling CDs and whatever we get from love offerings and donations is our income. When it's a ministry, you can't be so exact. If someone calls in and needs prayer, you need to talk longer than three minutes. Business managers didn't

always understand our ministry. When you live by faith, you never know when a donation is coming in. You can't exactly do a five-year plan. It's exciting, but trying. Some people would go crazy. For me, it's exciting to see how God works."

Recently a man called Max and said, "I want to commit $10,000 for this year. I believe in what you're doing."

"We hadn't called him or written a letter to him," Max said. "He called us out of the blue. That's God working. That's the exciting part!

"A few years ago the Worthington Kellogg Company sponsored us for two sizeable concerts. Their donation paid all of our expenses. These are the kinds of sponsors we need in order to keep traveling across the country to do concerts. We are so grateful for their vision and their support. It is enabling us to do so much more with our ministry."

There is a feeling of quiet security in knowing that somehow, God will provide for the financial needs of the ministry. That's the faith that Max and Lucy have. It takes a special kind of person to be on the Heritage Board. You have to understand how to run a business, and you have to believe in the ministry. You have to have a certain level of faith to deal with all of the uncertainty.

"You know, back in 1971 when Lucy and I committed our lives to what looked impossible, we committed one hundred percent," said Max. "And, you know, God has never failed in His promises. Every year, it has seemed more impossible than the last for our ministry to continue. But God has never let us down."

There is so much to keeping a ministry like this going. When you have a love for music and a commitment for ministry like Max does, it has to outweigh the struggles and disappointments. How else could you go on?

Max talked about difficult personnel issues over the years. "Yes, there were difficult years," he acknowledged. "In fact, there were times when the stress was very bad. There were times that whenever the singers voted on anything," Max remembered, "half would go one way; the other half the other way. I was so frustrated. I prayed that the negative people would quit! One year we had an incredibly tight group musically, but we just couldn't get along. That was the year we had the most internal problems. It was like Satan didn't want us out there; so he said, 'If I can't get them from without, I'll get them from within.'

"Team players have always gotten along great in Heritage," he said. "Once in a while we'd get a Prima Donna, and trouble just follows those people. The majority of the people we've had in Heritage have been great. It's just those who were a problem caused problems everywhere.

Richard Barnes, board president, Max and Ron Schaffsma

"I've learned that if someone is unhappy and wants to leave the group, it's best to let them go. If it doesn't fit, don't force it.

"The hardest part about personnel issues was in having to let people go. More than one person stole money from us," he said. "We couldn't believe it ourselves. We had suspicions but no real proof. In one situation, we set a trap by marking some bills. We caught him red-handed. He had been stealing money from us for quite some time, and the amounts were getting larger and larger. He begged us not to tell his mother and promised he'd pay it back even though he had no idea how much he had taken. To his surprise we forgave him and told him we still considered him a part of our family. You don't just kick 'em when they're down. You try to encourage them and help them get through it."

There have been some bits and pieces of stories about some singers over the years that have ended up being disgruntled over financial issues. "Sometimes people expected to get more financial gain out of their time with Heritage and felt that they did not get their fair share, especially if they felt they were more talented. Unfortunately we weren't able to pay the singers what they deserved. It just wasn't there and they all knew coming into the group exactly what they would be paid. I think most of the singers came into the group knowing it was a ministry and were not coming in for financial gain."

There have been several times Max has either been outright stolen from, or cheated out of a large amount of money. Just recently a concert promoter for an international trip guaranteed a certain amount to cover the group's expenses, and they ended up getting only about 20 percent of what they were promised, and we are talking thousands of dollars. Max and Lucy are always taken aback when this happens. And, it has happened more often than they'd like to admit. Even when contracts are signed and sworn by, the money has not been delivered, or checks have been canceled or just outright stolen. One time a conference president swore on a financial agreement saying, "As God is my witness." Well, God was his witness as he failed to deliver on his promise.

"You can steal money from me, but you don't steal God's money," Max said. "That was money people had given us out of the goodness of their hearts to keep our ministry on the road." Although he has never pursued legal action in any of these situations, Max does whatever he can to get the money that is owed to him. Sometimes he has had to simply move on and learn what he can from it and do what he can to avoid having it happen again. It's just not Max's way to fight over these things. International trips are especially risky when it comes to financial details. Max

GRACE NOTES:

"Dear Max,

"I would like to praise God for the song 'Champion of Love.' I feel it is the greatest contemporary 'Hallelujah Chorus' there is on this side of eternity. If our memories will allow, and I believe they will, I will request that song as the coronation of Jesus as the King, Prince and Master of the Universe when all men cast their crowns at the feet of Jesus, the all-time, undefeated Champion of love.

"That song will be sung by the Heritage Singers reunited in heaven, when all those who have been touched and saved by your ministry, like me, will join in the resounding refrain that will echo through the portals of glory for endless decibels of praise. Max, we will be there together. Keep on keeping on the good work, knowing that your labor of love is not in vain.

"Heritage has been a part of my life since before I can remember, through struggles, as well as tragedies I have faced. Heritage has been my form of worship when I didn't want to be in church at all. I don't think I would even be here without your ministry of music. Your words in song have touched my life in countless ways. Through your concerts, I have come to know Jesus in a very personal way. I understand He loves me just as I am."

and Lucy have had to learn the hard way to require cash up front before they leave the country. It's not the way they like to do things, but they've been taken advantage of too many times trusting people, and they have no choice.

Sometimes the financial details with solo artists within Heritage can get a little complicated, especially when the agreements are not clear between parties. There have been times when Max's immediate reaction to someone asking for what they thought was owed them came across as unfair. Max may have paid for the production of an album, and needed to cover his costs before royalties could kick in. Or, even worse, Max may have invested a lot of money to produce an album only to have the artist leave Heritage soon after its release, leaving him with an album he couldn't sell. There is always more than one side to the story.

Max is the first to admit that he may have made some mistakes along the way. "I didn't always do things right," Max admitted. "I made some mistakes. We learn as we go how to work with people. Today I might handle some things differently than how I handled them in the past. But I think most of our experiences with singers were good ones.

"It was interesting to see the personalities develop in these situations," he said. "A good time to tell how a person is going to be in the group situation is to observe them when they get tired. Some people can get nasty. Everything can be going along just fine, but when you get tired, that's when you really see what people are made of. None of us are perfect. We all get tired sometimes."

I looked at Max. He looks great, but he's been through a lot. I asked him how long he plans to keep up this pace and what his future plans are.

"When we first started the Heritage Singers," Max said, "we thought we'd probably go for two years at the most. When that time was up we said, 'Okay, let's go for another year or two,' and when that time was up, we said, 'It doesn't look like God is through with us yet; let's go for another year,' and on and on and on. There's a song the Imperials used to sing that went, 'He didn't bring us this far to leave us.' That's the way I feel about it. 'God, you didn't bring me this far to leave me.' My plans are to do this until God no longer provides for us. I think I'll know when it's time to quit."

"Counting Rose City Singers, I've been directing a music group for over 40 years, and I'm still learning," Max said. "I have people come to me all the time and ask me what to do to be successful, and I don't know what to tell them. These are very talented people! These are young people who have promise and energy. I don't know what the secret is. But, I do know there's a lot more to it than music.

"You learn how to talk to people and how to let the words of a song tell people about Jesus. You learn how to pray with people after a concert, people who are hurting and have never accepted Jesus in their heart. You hear their stories. You encourage them and pray for them. That's the joy. That's the reward. All the bad stuff about being on the road is totally outweighed by the good, especially when you see someone come to Jesus. That is the goal and has always been the goal of the Heritage Singers' ministry—inviting people to come to Jesus."

"I thank God for the mountains
And I thank Him for the valleys
I thank Him for the storms He brought me through
For if I'd never had a problem
I wouldn't know that He could solve them
I'd never know what faith in God could do

Through it all
Through it all
I've learned to trust in Jesus
I've learned to trust in God

Through it all
Through it all
I've learned to depend upon His word"

—Andrae Crouch

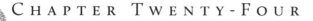

CHAPTER TWENTY-FOUR

Fire at Sea

IN MARCH OF 2006 THE HERITAGE SINGERS PLANNED A 35ᵀᴴ YEAR CELEBRATION CRUISE TO THE WESTERN CA-ribbean aboard the Star Princess. As Lucy stated, "Although the cruise was a fundraiser for the Heritage Singers, the goal of the cruise was to provide our guests with an exceptional Christian vacation experience. Even though the pleasure of this cruise would last only seven days, we prayed the participants would be spiritually renewed and the pleasant memories would last a lifetime!

"Pete McLeod, a Christian comedian and former Heritage Singer, was scheduled to be our Master of Ceremonies. Our cruise was to take us to The Princess Cays, Cozumel, Mexico, George Town, Grand Cayman and Ocho Rios, Jamaica," said Lucy.

On Thursday night, March 16, many of the singers and their families boarded the Heritage bus for the trip from Placerville to Oakland Airport. They took a "red-eye" flight into Ft. Lauderdale, Florida, arriving early Friday morning. As the group congregated at the hotel in Ft. Lauderdale, the excitement mounted as they looked forward to the next week on the Star Princess.

On Saturday, March 18, the singers held a special concert at the Brazilian Seventh-day Adventist Church in Ft. Lauderdale. The church was packed to capacity and the people were very receptive.

Max and Lucy as they board the Star Princess

When Sunday morning arrived, the singers and their families were shuttled to the cruise terminal in Ft. Lauderdale. Excitement was in the air as over 120 people that were with the Heritage group gathered at the terminal and were given permission to board the ship. Tours were given of the ship and many of the singers and guests explored their beautiful home on the water before the required muster station drills. Little did they know that this practice would come in handy a few days later.

The Heritage family celebrated Greg's 47th birthday the first night of the cruise in the formal dining room. The next day was an "at sea" day. The Heritage Singers held a concert for their guests. Pete McLeod was the emcee for the concert. The singers and Pete treated their guests to over an hour of inspiring music. This was to be the first of four concerts while at sea.

Over the next couple of days, the ship traveled to ports of call in Cozumel, Mexico and Georgetown, Grand Cayman. The weather was beautiful and the group with the Heritage Singers was having an amazing time. Early on Thursday morning, all of that changed.

On March 23, 2006, at about 3:00 AM, a fire broke out in the passenger staterooms, on the port side of the ship. Shortly after, the captain sounded the General Emergency Signal—seven short blasts followed by one long blast on the ship's whistle, which woke passengers up all over the ship. Passengers went to muster stations and evacuees were combined into groups, then stationed in cramped rooms for about seven hours. Some passengers who needed regular medication required crewmembers to go into their staterooms and retrieve their medication.

Passengers evacuated their cabins into public areas through smoky hallways, grabbing their life jackets on the way. The evacuation was orderly. Lifeboats were lowered, but proved to be unnecessary as the fire was contained and doused, and the ship headed into Montego Bay under her own power.

A cigarette left burning on a balcony supposedly caused the fire. The fire caused scorching damage in up to 150 cabins, and smoke damage in at least 100 more on passenger decks 9 to 12 (Dolphin, Caribe, Baja and Aloha decks). An elderly passenger from Georgia died from "asphyxia secondary to inhalation of smoke and irrespirable gases" and eleven other passengers suffered significant smoke inhalation.

Here is the account of this incident, from the perspective of the Heritage Singers onboard.

A man shouting outside of their cabin door awoke Max and Lucy. "Get out of your rooms! The ship is on fire!" The next thing they heard was the piercing sound of the fire alarm. Opening their door, they smelled smoke and realized that this was not a drill. Max was so nervous he could not find his clothes or shoes or glasses, but Lucy remained calm and got him put together and out the door heading for their muster station. Everything seemed to be happening in slow motion. Most people were in their pajamas and looked very confused.

Max and Lucy were frantic. The worst nightmare for Lucy was not knowing where her children were. "Where are Greg and Adriane? And Amber and Isabella? Where are Val and Art and Austin? I sure hope they're safe", she prayed, as she scanned

Happy Birthday Greg!

the faces of the passengers surrounding her. "Where are the rest of my kids? My Heritage kids?" She felt so helpless as she desperately searched the room for familiar faces.

Lucy remembered hearing that the fire started on the same floor where some of the singers' cabins were, and she was worried sick about two of the singers' wives, who were both over six months pregnant. There was a tremendous amount of thick black smoke in the hallways. "I just hope they're okay." Not knowing was the worst thing to endure.

Lucy has always been in charge of all of the details of the Heritage tours. It was ingrained in her. She always knew where everyone was. On international trips she totally

Amber, Austin, and Bella are cruizin'

had everything under control. So much could go wrong. She learned over the past 30 plus years of traveling all over the world how to organize things, but there was nothing she could do about this situation.

"My poor little grandbabies," she thought. "They need their Grandma right now, and I can't get to them. Oh, I hope they're safe and not too scared."

As soon as all the people in their muster station had been accounted for, Lucy asked one of the crewmembers if they could check to see if their children were in their muster station. The lady said she would be happy to check for her. Lucy gave the lady their cabin numbers and in just a couple of minutes the best news she had heard all morning came booming over the loud speaker. "The Mapa and Mace families are accounted for." It was a comforting feeling to know that at least they were safe, but what about the rest of her Heritage kids?

Max was worried sick. "Did God bring us this far to have it end like this?" He thought about all of the singers aboard this ship. It's only the third day of the cruise, and most of the planned

Heritage events are yet to come. Max thought about all of the planning that went into putting this 35th anniversary cruise together, and wondered now if it was even going to take place. This was not the celebration that he was hoping for.

Max and Lucy began to pray for God's protection for each and every person on board this ship. They thought of all of the Heritage Singers on board, and all of their friends and supporters. "What about Frank Maas, who was paralyzed and in a wheel chair? Were he and his wife, Barb, able to get out of their rooms in time? Did they need help? What about the sweet older ladies we'd assured would be taken care of on this ship? Did they get out of their rooms?"

Their minds were spinning with questions. "Was that gentleman we heard had a heart attack on the stairway someone from our group? Then there was Neal Warren, a gentleman in our group who we had heard collapsed from smoke inhalation. He was lying on the floor with his sweet wife bending over him. Were they okay? What about Scott's wife, Holly, and Marcelo's wife, Bettesue, who were both pregnant? Were they experiencing anxiety? Were they breathing in too much smoke? So many people had entrusted their lives to our care and now we can't find them. How can we possibly deal with this other than to just turn it over to God?"

Max thought about the concerts planned for this cruise. "Yesterday we had our first concert, the first one of four concerts planned for this cruise. It went well, and felt good. Quite a few people came. In fact, we'd been given permission to open these concerts to the entire ship, which was a great outreach opportunity we were really looking forward to. Now I wonder if we're even going to have the other concerts. Our next one is supposed to be in just a few hours."

He thought about all of the Heritage supporters who were also on board. These people have followed the ministry and supported it through their prayers and financial gifts. He hoped they were okay and that they would get out of this safely.

Max and Lucy wondered how bad the fire was and how long they would be held there in the muster station before they could go back to their cabin. Was their cabin burning at the moment? It had been over 35 years since they started the Heritage Singers. God had opened doors for them to continue the ministry one day at a time, and now look how far we've come. The song, "We've Come This Far by Faith" starts playing in his head, as Max thought back to how he got there. It was all about his dream.

The burned ship

Max settled back and closed his eyes. It was only 4:00 AM. His head was hurting and he was tired. "We could be sitting here awhile," he thought, and tried to find a comfortable position. Maybe he could sleep. Poor Lucy. She was so worried. But what can we do? "God," he prayed, "we don't know what's going to happen here, but we just turn it over to you. Please keep our family and friends safe, and surround us with your love and protection."

Taking a deep breath, Max stretched and nudged Lucy. "I think I'll walk around a bit," he said, as he stood up. He stepped over some sleeping passengers sprawled out on the floor as an announcement came through the ceiling speakers.

"Ladies and gentleman, it appears that the fire has been contained." Applause breaks out among the motley group of exhausted passengers. "The fire is still burning," the voice continues, "but we are winning the battle. In the meantime, we have decided to deploy the lifeboats as a cautionary measure."

People were stirring. Maybe this would be over soon. The sense of relief clears the air in the room like a fresh breeze. At least the fire was under control. Yet, the fact that the lifeboats were being deployed meant that this was still a serious situation. "We might have to actually get into those lifeboats," Max said to himself, realizing that this nightmare was far from over.

"Ladies and gentlemen," the captain's voice boomed over the loud speakers. "Our firefighting crews tell me that the fire is out!" The auditorium broke into applause. "There is a lot of heat. We are cooling down the area to be sure the fire is completely out. Then we will be assessing the damage to the ship." Crewmembers opened the doors to let in the outside air. The sun was starting to come up and light was streaming into the room.

"We have turned the ship around and are headed for the nearest port. We will be arriving in Jamaica some time this morning." The captain continued. "We regret that this cruise will not be continuing. Over 150 cabins have been destroyed. We ask that you wait for further information as we sort this out and make travel arrangements for your journey home."

The pulsating of a helicopter hovering just outside the ship drowned out all other sounds. The people have been sitting there for seven hours. It's over. The whole thing—the whole cruise is over. Three days on board, and it's over. Over 150 cabins destroyed? The fire must have been really bad.

The entrances to the hallways on the burned side of the ship were huge gaping black holes. Yellow tape spanned the doorways like big spider webs. A very tired looking and slightly disheveled crewmember slumped on a folding chair in front of a blocked off hallway. It was a long, hard night. Some hallways were boarded up and totally sealed off. Black soot permeated everything, as if the smoke had solidified.

After they were dismissed from the muster stations, the Heritage family congregated on the Lido Deck. One half of the entire restaurant was roped off because of fire damage. All of the singers and their families were accounted for. Everyone was okay! Some of the Heritage friends who had come along on this cruise were also gathered there. Everyone was in a state of exhausted shock. Many of them were not able to return to their cabins and didn't know if they even had anything left.

Val and Art remembered that early morning. "We got a knock on our door and the room steward told us we needed to report to our muster station. We spent several hours there without knowing what was going on, or where our family and friends were, but we felt very well taken care of by the ship's crew. It wasn't until we were allowed back

Art and Val aboard the ship

to our room where we saw live video of our ship on CNN that we realized how badly it had been damaged. At that point we were so thankful that God once again had protected us. When we arrived back at the Sacramento airport, TV news reporters sought out Art, who had taken video footage of some of the damage on the ship which they used for their reports."

Lucy was busy trying to find people and get them all into one place. She thought everyone was okay. She believed that one of the men in the group was injured or suffered some smoke inhalation. She was trying to find out whatever she could. Lucy didn't show any signs of being tired or upset, and just focused on her mission. Lucy could handle any crisis.

Becki, Scott, and Holly were in their pajamas and looking like they had a very rough night. Val was trying to reassure Holly that things would be okay and that everyone was safe. "I don't know if we have any clothes left, or what state our cabin is in since it was near where the fire started. At least you have some sense of normalcy," Holly said to Val. "At least you know your cabin and all of your things are okay. At least you could go back

to your cabin and get dressed. I just wish I could get out of my pajamas."

As the group sat there looking out at the hills of Jamaica, a somber, eerie mood settled in like a silent fog. A hearse waited on the dock. Two ambulances slowly approached the ship and after a few minutes they drove away. A helicopter landed and took off. Uniformed personnel escorted several small groups of passengers across the dock and into the terminal building. The sadness and weight of what had happened was difficult to grasp. It was obvious that this was a serious fire, and that people may have died.

One by one, the passengers were escorted back to their cabins to retrieve what could be saved of their belongings. The most damaged cabins were left for last.

Becki decided she couldn't just sit around and wait any longer. She took off to see about getting off of the ship. She did not return and it was days before Lucy was able to locate her at a hotel somewhere on the island. Becki had shared a cabin with Art's sister, Elizabeth. Their cabin was not destroyed but had a lot of water damage and soot. Most of their clothing was not wearable, and Becki's cell phone was missing. Elizabeth, along with many other passengers whose clothes were damaged in the fire, were taken to the gift shop where they are invited to select a few new clothing items to get them through a couple of days until they could get home.

Lucy could not rest until she had accounted for all of the Heritage kids on board. Yet, she was amazingly calm and logical. As always, she was the rock. We were told that those who lost their cabins were to be housed in hotels on the island. The rest would stay on the ship until their flights home were arranged. Everyone was being split up and taken in different directions, and Lucy realized that she would have no way of knowing where they were or how they were getting home.

Within an hour of being dismissed from the muster stations, all of the singers were accounted for, but not all of the Heritage friends who were also on board. Lucy felt responsible for them. She was frantic as she confronted the ship personnel. They were doing the best they could under the circumstances, but it was impossible to keep a group of people together. Everyone was pretty much on his or her own.

Marcelo was very excited to be going on his first cruise. Little did he know how "exciting" it was going to be! "This was my first time on a cruise ship," he said. "It was so amazing. Art and I loved eating at all hours of the day on the Lido Deck! My wife, Bettesue, and I were expecting our first child in a few months, and this was our last vacation for a while. That early Thursday morning rattled me. My wife was pretty calm, but I was very worried about her. We grabbed our lifejackets and were guided to our muster station. It was very hot in there and the stewards quickly brought my wife a cup of water and had her sit down. I remember looking out the window and seeing the fire fighters spraying water on the flames, and the lifeboats being lowered. Several other singers were in the same muster station with us. Holly, Scott's wife, who was also pregnant, and Bettesue were guided to an outside door on the opposite side of the fire so they could get some fresh air. We tried to remain calm and comfortable and used our lifejackets as pillows.

"After a few hours, Bettesue and Holly started to get hungry, and Scott and I worried about them not having any food. A very kind cabin steward guided them to the backstage of the theatre and offered them something to eat and drink. We were very impressed with the generosity, courtesy, and professionalism

Holly Reed and Bettesue Constanzo

exhibited by all of the crewmembers.

"Although in many ways the cruise was a disappointment, it also showed us that God was leading, in spite of the turmoil. We were safe and taken care of, as were our friends. God was taking care of all of us."

Dave and Susan Bell's room was on the same side of the boat as the fire. "Everyone that had cabins affected by the fire were called a few at a time to be escorted to their room to see what belongings might be salvaged," recalled Dave Bell. "When it was our turn, we were told not to expect much as we squished down the sloppy wet mucky hallway on Caribe deck. Our door keycard still worked, and as we opened the door, it was pitch dark inside, but a small flashlight and feeling with our hands gave us the astonishing realization that everything was dry. No visible damage whatsoever. The only problem we found was that our baggage and clothing was permeated with the strong smell of smoke and some soot. Susan and I suddenly burst into tears, feeling guilty for what we still had, as we looked directly across the hall into the open door of a blackened room in which nothing was salvageable. Many of our friends had lost nearly everything. Most kept saying that it was "just stuff" and were sadder about the irreplaceable items.

"Many of the crew had just gone off duty at 2:00 AM, but kept doing their assigned emergency jobs for the duration. I didn't see any crew with their own food or water. Even the woman that was our waitress each evening in the dining room was one that was dashing into rooms of more elderly and disabled passengers assisting them to safety, even dragging a frightened person out from under the bed and carrying her to safety. Many other crewmembers braved the unstable, smoke-filled areas to try to retrieve important medications that people had left behind in the evacuation. These were not full-time fire fighters. They were cabin stewards, waiters and waitresses, cruise director staff, etc that performed heroically just as they had been trained to do.

"While collecting our things, I saw cabin stewards bringing people to their more heavily damaged rooms. I witnessed true empathy from these gentlemen. They seemed to feel awful for the people they had been caring for. Ricky, our steward, though he is not the one that escorted us, saw us as we were taking our things to the elevator. 'Mr. & Mrs. Bell, I'm SO sorry,' he said to us, appearing to be on the verge of tears. As we talked with the one that did escort us at about 4:00 PM, we were able to pry out of him that he had been working continuously since 3:00 AM, without any food for himself. We offered some fruit rollups that Susan had in her purse. He at first refused, but we finally convinced him to take it, and he acted so humbly grateful."

Greg and Adriane

Frank John and Carole Lynn Salas were also on the ship during this chaotic event. "While standing out on the promenade deck, looking out, I received a phone call from Sacramento TV station KXTV 10 and was interviewed by phone for the evening news program," said Frank John. We were very impressed with the way the crew handled the emergency. While those of us still on the ship went to dinner, the captain's voice came over the intercom. He took full responsibility for the fire. Even though the fire was caused by the carelessness of a passenger, he took the blame upon himself, reminding me of how our Savior has taken the blame for our sins upon Himself."

As Becki now looks back on the experience, she said, "I didn't realize how much importance I had placed on material possessions until many of my things were lost in the fire. Through this vulnerable and fearful experience, God revealed an area of weakness in me that needed to be turned over to Him. Never

again will 'things' be given such high priority in my life."

Eventually, everyone was either escorted off of the ship, or back to his or her cabin. At dinnertime several members of the Heritage group were at their tables. It was during this meal that they were able to compare stories and reconnect with each other as much as possible.

The waiters and waitresses told them of some heroic rescues and also that they were lucky to be alive since the fire was really bad. Two other cruise ships had heard the captain's calls for help, and were anchored nearby, ready to assist. A cargo ship slowed down, also, in case they needed to abandon ship.

Later that evening, those whose cabins were still intact, got papers for how the cruise line had arranged for them to get home. Greg and Adriane's flights were mixed up and had Bella scheduled to fly alone. Lucy jumped in to take care of the situation, and she and Max were escorted off of the ship soon after that to catch their flight home.

"We were some of the last people to get off of the ship," said Adriane. "Since our room was not damaged, almost everyone got off the ship long before we did. The ship was practically empty. We had the whole ship to ourselves and could have used many of the amenities that were still operational, but that's when we realized that that those things meant nothing without our friends and family to enjoy them with."

Because new flights had to be arranged for Greg's family, they had to stay on the ship. Greg and Adriane and their two daughters ended up staying on the ship until it was ready to leave the harbor four days later. They were stuck on a severely disabled cruise ship with nothing to do. The pools were closed and much of the ship was roped off because it was charred and unsafe. The shops and restaurants were closed. The theatre was closed.

Besides what was left of the crew, they were the only passengers left on the ship. They had food and water, but no air conditioning. Greg was faced with transporting all of the Heritage sound equipment off the ship and had to pay over $400 in porter fees just to get the equipment from the ship to the airport.

Many of the singers boarded a bus to the airport, winding around Montego Bay and up into the hills. As they got farther away from the harbor, they were able to get a good look at the disabled ship. Dwarfing the other vessels surrounding her, she sat proudly, like a stately gleaming white swan—except for the gaping black smudge along her side, like she had lost a wing. They realized just how large an area was destroyed by the fire, and how fortunate they were that none of the Heritage group was physically injured.

It took Lucy several days before she could account for everyone. She took the list of passengers in the Heritage group and called them one by one until all were accounted for. She learned that some of them lost everything in the fire. One couple in the group of Heritage friends had gotten married before the cruise and had booked the cruise as their

Smoke-damaged Heritage Singers brochure

honeymoon. They boarded the ship with five suitcases and left with what little was left of their belongings in a dripping plastic bag. When Max and Lucy heard that they had lost everything they got together with some of their friends that were left on the ship and took up a collection and sent them home with a little over $1000.

When Max and Lucy's flight arrived at the Sacramento airport, they were met by a crew of photographers and reporters from a news crew out of San Francisco. Art had taken video of some of the burned cabins, and these photos were broadcast on CNN. An ABC news crew also came to the ranch to interview Max and Lucy. Little did they know that their 35th Anniversary Cruise would end up being an international news story!

"As you can imagine, every person in our group has their own story to tell," said Lucy. "But all in all, we are so grateful for God's protection. This could have been so much worse. So many more lives could have been lost. Our hearts break for the family who lost their loved one. We praise God for bringing us through this, for His protection, and for the maturity we've gained in Him."

CHAPTER TWENTY-FIVE

Beyond Our Dreams

Heritage Singing at General Conference, 2006

IT IS JUNE 2006. WE ARE SETTING UP THE HERITAGE SINGERS' BOOTH FOR THE GENERAL CONFERENCE, A 10-day event held every five years that draws church leaders from all over the world. It is really hot in the convention hall. Lucy is opening boxes and unpacking lights, speakers, enlarged photos of the group throughout the years, tape and tools, flat screen video monitors, and hundreds of CDs.

Greg Mace and Darrell Marshall are assembling a large black metal framework, which is a grid for supporting all of the photos and lights. Max is talking to people who come by the booth.

Richard Barnes, the president of the Heritage Singers' Board of Directors, has arrived, along with his wife, Colette, who also is a member of the Board. There is excitement in the air as we prepare for what will be the first time appearance of the Heritage Singers at the General Conference. Not only has the group been invited to

Colette and Richard Barnes

exhibit, Heritage has also been invited to perform two songs at a key meeting which is to be televised worldwide. Up to 80,000 people are expected to be at the conference.

This may not seem like such a big deal unless you know the history behind it. For years, the Heritage Singers were told they would have to send in an audition tape to the music committee to see if they would be considered to sing for such a conservative international gathering of church leaders. Of course, this was years ago, and things have changed. They had bypassed the music committee, receiving a personal invitation by the President of the North American Division.

This reversal of attitude is, in part, due to the fact that enough years have passed and the leadership has totally turned over. The new generation of church leaders includes people who grew up listening to and loving the music of the Heritage Singers.

Colette and Richard Barnes have been following the Heritage ministry for years. In fact, their first date was at a Heritage Singer concert, and they've never missed a concert that they could possibly get to. When their oldest son, Jeff, was a baby, Richard would bring the baby out to the lobby and Lucy would watch him so Richard and Colette could enjoy the concert. Then they had Scottie, and brought him to the concerts, too. Every New Year's Eve they come to the ranch. It's a tradition now. Richard cooks breakfast for whoever is there. It's usually Swedish pancakes, an old family recipe from Colette's grandmother.

Judy Boyd, one of the original Heritage Singers

Greg and Val with Giovanni and Monica, friends from Brazil

Colette speaks of their friendship with Max and Lucy, and tells how much they admire and respect Max and Lucy for their ministry. "It's not just the music ministry," she points out, "It's the way they support and encourage people. The Heritage ranch, Max and Lucy's home, is a refuge for people. Anyone who has ever been in the Heritage organization knows that they are always welcome at the ranch. Over the years Max and Lucy have welcomed hundreds of singers and musicians into their home, for as long as they needed to stay. They have helped so many people," she said.

Richard, an enthusiastic and inspirational guy, speaks of his absolute joy to be involved with the Heritage ministry. "I could just shout from the mountaintops!" he said. "What a group!"

Throughout the week, the most surprising thing to Max and Lucy and the rest of the singers has been the overwhelming response we've had from international visitors. People from all over the world have come into the booth sharing stories, many times in very broken English or no English at all. It is clear that these people are very emotionally attached to the Heritage Singers, and that the Heritage ministry has been very meaningful to them.

People from New Guinea, Australia, Brazil, England, Russia, Korea, South Africa, Ghana, Zimbabwe, Peru, and more places came into the booth telling stories of how Heritage has influenced their lives. Heritage has never even traveled to some of these countries.

Russia is another country where Heritage has had a tremendous impact, totally unknown to Max and Lucy. Before it was even legal to have Christian music in the country, people managed to smuggle in some Heritage music. We heard stories of how the Russian people listened to Heritage albums for years in their secret in-home worship services. And now, some of these same people were actually in the Heritage booth, telling these stories to Max and Lucy in person. It truly was overwhelming.

Many of these people talked to Max about the logistics of bringing Heritage to their country; others were interested in setting up distribution channels for the sales of Heritage

CDs and DVDs. Max collected business cards from many of these international visitors, but whether anything comes of any of these contacts is yet to be seen. The whole experience was quite affirming to Max and Lucy, and just so unanticipated. Although Heritage has traveled to over 60 countries around the world, nobody had any idea of the scope of the ministry and the worldwide influence of Heritage in countries where they've never even been.

Four years later:

Since the Heritage Singers went to the General Conference in 2006 new doors have opened for even more international travel. Their travels have taken them to several countries, including their first trip to Romania and the Czech Republic. They also recently returned to the Philippines, where they sang to huge crowds of up to 70,000 people.

Lucy shared her memories of their first trip to Romania. "International travel at it's best always has surprises in store for the group. When we boarded our plane headed to Romania, little did we know what this adventure would bring.

"We had just buckled our seat belts, sat back in our seats and were heading down the runway when we came to a screeching stop. Then over the speakers the captain made the announcement that we had to return to the terminal due to a sick passenger that needed to get off the plane. After a lengthy delay we finally took off and were thankful to make it to Chicago in time to make our connecting flight. We meet up with Shani, her parents, Jan & Warren Judd, Matthew, Dénar, Izzie and little

Dragos Penca with Max and Lucy

Max with sponsor, Daniel Piturlea

Dénar to go on to Munich, Germany. Once we arrived in Munich we were told that part of our group would have to catch the next flight since there weren't enough seats on our flight. We pleaded and begged but they said they couldn't retrieve their baggage and it was already tagged for the later flight. It was hard leaving them behind in a foreign country but knowing they are seasoned travelers, I left my cell phone with them and said we would make sure someone would meet them later that evening in Timisoara.

"When we arrived in Timisoara, we were met by some of our sponsors. They were waiting in a beautiful bus that they had rented for our tour. Unfortunately, Shani's suitcase didn't arrive, and it happened to be the one with her performing clothes and the diapers for little Matthew. A quick stop at the market and Matthew was all fixed up but Shani was left to wonder what she would wear for the concert should her suitcase not show up. After making arrangements to have a car at the airport to pick up the boys, we were headed off on what was to be an incredible journey.

"As we headed off to Arad where we would have our concert the next day, Shani was praying that her suitcase would come on the flight with the boys or with Dave Bell the following day. Great News! Shani's suitcase arrived the next day with Dave. Unfortunately his suitcase was nowhere to be found and the concert started in two hours! Dragos, our tour manager, came to Dave's rescue and brought him a suit, shirt and a pair of shoes.

"As we headed to the concert, we were wondering how the Romanian people would respond. Well, it didn't take long for us to find out. They were so responsive and enthusiastic, singing along with every song. Looking into their smiling faces gave us the energy for our three-hour concert.

"After a 45-minute flight to Transylvania, we were once again met at the airport with another beautiful bus. We stopped at the wonderful old theater where we would have our concert that evening. All the hand-painted ceilings and beautiful tapestry reminded us of the Royal Albert Hall in London where we had sung several years back.

Mihai and Kundri Gadea with Max

"Our accommodations for the next several days were at the Apollo Wellness Club Hotel owned by Mr. & Mrs. Benta. They were waiting to greet us with a gorgeous bouquet of flowers and immediately took us to the dining room for a fantastic lunch. The homemade bread—well we all ate too much. It was just like going to grandma's house.

"It was time to leave for the concert and it was borrowed clothes again for Dave, still no suitcase! Since we were traveling by bus we got to see a lot of the beautiful countryside.

Emanuel Suciu, Remus Benta Jr., Remus Benta, Maria Benta, Mihai Gadea, Violeta Piturela in Targu Mures in front of the Hotel Apolo

"The following day we drove through the mountains and stopped at a little church that was built in 1464. It had survived a fire that had destroyed most of the city. We were amazed to find that they still have services in that little church. We asked our guide if we could sing a song and she said that would be great. As the singers sang 'Jesus Is The Lighthouse' I saw the guide wipe a tear from her eye and as we were leaving she told me that

was the highlight of her day and that she had never heard such beautiful music in that little church.

"Another highlight of our trip was going to an organ concert at the Black Church, a huge Gothic church in Brasov. It got its name because of a fire that had blackened the entire outside of the church and it was just left that way. The church has the largest pipe organ in all of Eastern Europe.

"As we continued our tour to Bucharest, we stopped at a fortress and walked a quarter of a mile up a cobblestone street to a spectacular view of the village below. After climbing more steps that I can count, Isabella my little granddaughter said, 'Too many steps.' I had to agree!

"Our next stop was at the Peles Castle, probably the most beautiful castle we have ever seen. King Carol had it built for their summer home and if you ever get the chance to go to Romania you must make time to see it!

"Finally, we arrived in Bucharest, the capitol of Romania. It was much bigger than I expected and the architecture was so amazing! One of our sponsors was the owner of one of the largest hotels in Europe and he put us up in his hotel and provided all our meals. We aren't used to being spoiled like that, but very much appreciated his generosity.

"Mihai Gedea, who would be the master of ceremonies and interpreter for our concert, has a very high position at the most popular television station in Romania. His program is similar to *Meet The Press* here in the US. He took one of our CDs to the station and was playing it for the producer of a popular variety show on their network. When she heard it she said, 'Oh, do you think you could get them to come on my show?' He told her he was sure the group would be glad to come sing on her program. She quickly canceled the guests that were scheduled to appear that day and arrangements were made for Heritage to be there. She had the

Rene Stoica, Constantin Todici, Max and Lucy and Liviu Barbu, friends from Romania

group on for over an hour and kept asking questions about our ministry. This gave us a perfect opportunity to witness for Jesus. They opened up the phone lines to take calls giving away tickets for the concert to the first ten callers. The phone lines were immediately jammed and calls even came from Toronto, Canada and the US. We found out that people get this program all over the world using the Internet.

"Now here is the real miracle! This was the first time in the history of Ro-

Heritage in Romania at the Arenele Romane where they sang

mania television that a Christian group was allowed to come on any secular TV show! We had the opportunity to share Jesus for over an hour! Not only in Romania but also all over the world. This would not have been the case if we were a pastor of a church, but since it was music, it opened the door for us to

witness. After the TV program, they took us to the mall to have lunch. People at the mall recognized the singers from the TV program and stopped to talk to them, giving us one more chance to witness.

"Friday evening the singers were invited to a special dinner. The sponsors had invited some people whose lives had been touched by the Heritage Singers music during the time they were under Communist rule," said Lucy.

"When we sang some of the older Heritage songs and looked at their smiling faces, they were singing every word along with us!" Max said.

After dinner, Mihai introduced several well-known Romanian musicians: Rene Stoica, founder of the children's choir "Flowers and Stars"; Constantin Todici, one of the most acclaimed conductors in Romania; and Liviu Barbu, a very famous piano player, arranger and conductor. These men translated much of the Heritage Singers music into Romanian to teach their choirs. This was a risk for them since under Communist rule they were not allowed to have any religious music.

"It was a very touching experience for us to hear what these people had gone through," Max said. "We praise God that our music was a source of comfort and peace to these dear people during the Communist rule."

"Saturday evening in Bucharest was to be our biggest concert," said Lucy. "We woke up to dark rain clouds just hoping and praying they would pass. The outdoor venue was the Arenele Romane, a Roman style arena with beautiful pillars all around. When the band went to set up, it started to sprinkle and then it poured and poured. Things weren't looking too promising. The singers arrived just after a big down pour and the workers were busy wiping off all the chairs for the 3rd time. The singers got together and prayed that if God wanted them to do the concert he would hold back the rain. God honored our prayers!

"The arena started to fill up and about 2,500 people attended the concert, singing and clapping with each song. Just as soon as they would hear the intro for some of the old songs they had learned from the old cassettes, they started to applaud. It was bringing back sweet memories for them. One of their favorite new songs was 'Hey' off our latest CD. To our astonishment they already knew all the words. We tried to bring them a message of hope through music and testimony. Sharing with them that even

though they are now free from Communist rule, total freedom comes through asking Jesus to be their personal Savior.

"We went to Romania in hopes of blessing the Romanian people, but I think we came home with a much bigger blessing. The people of Romania treated us like kings and queens and we made some wonderful new friends for life," said Lucy.

The following year, during the summer of 2009, Heritage was invited to come to the Czech Republic. With great enthusiasm, the answer was "yes, we will come!" Dave Bell shared his account of the trip.

"Our alarm clocks blared at 3:00 AM Wednesday morning. Somewhat blurry-eyed, we gathered our luggage together, stumbled into the bus, and set out from Placerville, CA for the Sacramento airport for our 6:00 AM flight. With long layovers, it was 20 hours later that we arrived in Prague, Czech Republic. The sponsors met us at the airport and whisked us off to the hotel.

"Since there is a nine hour time difference from California to Prague, we were well into Thursday by the time we reached our hotel. While sleep was of utmost importance in most of our

Heritage at Radim Passer's picnic in Stetkovice, Czech Republic

minds, we were asked to be ready in a couple hours to go out for a tour of the city. It turns out that this was really a blessing, as forcing ourselves to stay awake until later in the evening helped to reset our body clocks.

"Our guide had spent hours planning our route, pointing out landmarks and giving us interesting facts of history. We toured through the magnificent St. Vitus Cathedral inside of Prague Castle, which dominates the downtown Prague skyline. We walked across the 700 year old ornately decorated Charles bridge and strolled through Old Town Square's cobblestone streets with its intriguing 15th century Astronomical Clock and breathtaking views of the gothic architecture of the Tyn Cathedral and baroque St. Nicolas Church. All of this was just setting the stage to what would be one of the most memorable tours we had ever experienced.

"Our first concert was on Saturday night at the Congress Centre—the same venue where President Obama met with the European Union representatives in April of that year. Nearly 3,000 people filled the seats in the beautiful auditorium, many traveling from other countries such as Germany, Poland, Romania and Austria. Knowing that most of the people had never seen us in live concert before, we wanted to give them our all. Three hours later they were still clapping for more.

"Sunday afternoon we were treated to a drive through the gorgeous countryside to the little town of Stetkovice where Mr. Passer had arranged to have a picnic for his entire town with the Heritage Singers providing a mini concert on the soccer field.

More filming at the Tyn Cathedral in the Czech Republic

Many of those attending were not Christians, and it was wonderful to see them enjoying the music. We learned later that many were asking to learn more about what we were singing about.

"In the evening we got another chance to browse through old town Prague. Art Mapa was also anxious to take advantage of the beautiful setting to get some footage to make a music video for the song 'Oh Happy Day'. While Scott Reed held the boom box playing the track of the song, Tim Davis unabashedly began singing in full voice as curious tourists strolled by. Then something incredible happened. A group of teenagers from Belgium were relaxing nearby and they spontaneously jumped up behind Tim and began clapping and echoing the chorus lyrics of 'Oh Happy Day'! With the beautiful Tyn Cathedral as a backdrop, these exuberant teens helped bring the song to life. We could not have done it better if we had planned it. I think God placed those precious souls right there when we needed them. We filmed segments of the song in many different locations throughout the trip, with many Czech and Slovakian people participating in the chorus. I can't wait to see the finished product.

"Monday took us cross-country to Ostravice where we would have our second concert. On the way we stopped at the Punkva caves in the Moravian Karst protected nature reserve. We were mesmerized by the beautiful formations of stalagmites, stalactites, columns, and draperies found in the underground wonderland. This walking tour led us to a river 600 feet underground where we boarded small boats and were guided through dimly lit windy passageways where the narrow tunnel opened up

Touring Prague with our wonderful new friends

into a cathedral-like room. We got out of our boats and sang an acappella chorus of 'Gentle Shepherd' with the natural reverberation supplied by our Creator!

"We marveled at the beauty around us as we arrived at our hotel nestled in the mountains of eastern Czech Republic where we would be celebrating Val's birthday. It was a welcome site knowing we were to have a relaxing day here to rest and rejuvenate before our next concert.

"Our next stop was in Ostravice where our concert was to be held in a hockey arena. Again, many people traveled from far away, some even came from Prague for a second helping. We felt the Spirit's presence as we saw tears in the eyes of many people as we sang about our wonderful Lord.

"These gracious people put such an amazing amount of work into making sure that every aspect of the trip went smoothly. Over the span of only two weekends we became very attached to our new friends and we all had tears in our eyes as we said goodbye at the airport.

"Just a few days after we returned from the trip, I received an email from one of the trip organizers telling me the following story. A friend's 16-year-old daughter brought her cousin to one of the concerts just to "please dad". They weren't expecting to like it but the next day the DVDs with Bible lessons disappeared from his bookshelf. When he asked his daughter if she knew where they were, she told him that her cousin wanted to borrow them. So, God used our concert to promote a teenager to study the Bible on DVD! Isn't that amazing?

"We'll never know until we get to heaven all the lives that were touched by our concerts over there, but without the generous sponsors that stepped out in faith to bring us there none of it would have been possible.

"We were blessed to have met new, wonderful friends who traveled with us throughout our whole tour, being our tour guides, translators and making sure we were well taken care of. We miss you all!"

It has been a long journey from where Max and Lucy started

to where the Heritage ministry is today. There are so many wonderful memories and so many stories of lives that were forever changed. And, the story continues. God is the author and will finish His work. He alone knows the beginning and the end.

As the Heritage Singers look down the road and wonder what's around the next turn, Max said he is looking forward to the future with anticipation of what God has in store for the ministry.

"What a wonderful journey this has been!" he said. "Even though the struggles have been great and the Devil has tried his hardest to discourage us, I would not trade one day of this. What an honor it is to invite people to know Jesus. There's such a joy and peace of mind when we serve Him with our whole heart. I want the entire world to know what I have found in Jesus, and the Heritage Singers share that with everyone in our concerts.

"On a trip to Jamaica, we were visiting a little church in the country. Before the service began, Heritage Singer recordings played over the speakers and the congregation sang along with every song. As I sat there listening to the entire church full of people singing the songs of the Heritage Singers, I thought about the journey of my life," said Max. "I remembered the difficult times and the struggles, and I remembered the miracles and the many ways God had blessed the Heritage ministry. And now I was sitting in a little church in Jamaica, listening to the very music that had become the underscore for my entire life. The emotion of the moment was just overwhelming.

Lucy and Max

"Not long ago, we had a concert in Southern California. The church was packed to the rafters with people even in the choir loft, and chairs were being set up in the foyer. It reminded me of the crowds we had 40 years ago when we started this ministry. My faith was restored. It was as if the Lord was telling me, 'I'm not through with the Heritage Singers yet. There's still work to be done.'

"Never in my wildest dreams would I have thought I'd be on the road at my age, still dreaming and still planning. My life has been a continual journey with lots of unexpected twists and turns, all of which have made me who I am, and for which I am truly thankful.

"God didn't bring me this far to leave me. God can see way down the road even if we can't. Sometimes what looks like an ending is really a new beginning. We don't know what the future holds. But what I do know for sure is that we're getting closer to the return of our precious Savior, and I can only imagine what that day will be like!

"Who would ever have thought that God would give me the desire of my heart in such a mighty way? By all rights, Heritage should never have been a success, yet God had a plan for me. He gave me a vision and a desire to serve Him through music. Friends, never be afraid to dream. God rejoices when we dream!

"I praise God for His amazing grace and goodness and for every decision that was made for Christ through the Heritage ministry. And I praise Him for this journey—this journey that has been *Beyond Our Dreams!*"

*The God who started this great work in you will keep at it and bring it
to a flourishing finish on the very day Christ Jesus appears.*
—Philippians 1:6